"Well done good and faithful servant! Ron Sider's steadfast voice is welcome during this trying time. He continues to be a beacon for followers of Jesus who care about justice and morality and being told the truth. I commend this book to anyone struggling to align their faith with their choices at the ballot box. I am grateful for his ongoing witness to God who loves us all with a passion for justice and a heart full of mercy."

—**Tony Hall**
Ambassador and former U.S. Representative (1979–2002);
author of *Changing the Face of Hunger*

"The dominant narrative in the public square is that the evangelical Protestant church provides unwavering support for Donald J. Trump. While this may be true, I am thankful for the witness of the editors and contributors of *The Spiritual Danger of Donald Trump* that this claim is far from universally true of all evangelicals and also for their crucial warning that continued support will lead to the deepening erosion of the church's witness to the world. My hope and prayer is that all Christians, whatever their present political leanings, will be open to the case made in this book."

—**Tremper Longman III**
Author of *The Bible and the Ballot: Using Scripture in Political Decisions*

"People who care about this country (and the whole world) need to use every medium to urge the public to restore sanity in the highest echelon of our government. Yes, including a full-length book. A sharp contrast to curt, snarky remarks through social media, *The Spiritual Danger of Donald Trump* is a thoughtful, interdisciplinary multi-voiced, Christ-centered, prophetic exposé of danger—social, political, and spiritual—that every person of faith must read."

—**Al Tizon**
Executive Minister of Serve Globally, Evangelical Covenant Church

"*The Spiritual Danger of Donald Trump* is a compilation of timely essays that document the perilous seismic and public shift from evangelicals endorsing the policies of a presidential candidate to evangelicals ordaining that same candidate. Today may be a great day for evangelicals politically but this day may ultimately lead to believers having less and less real spiritual influence on their neighbors around them. Judged by our own actions, good news will be seen as fake news and Jesus will soon be relegated to the alternative way, the alternative truth, and the alternative life. That's the spiritual danger of Donald Trump."

—**Eric Swanson**

Director, Leadership Network; co-author of *The Externally Focused Church*

"Ron Sider is one of the most faithful followers of the person and teachings of Jesus Christ that I have ever known. I wholeheartedly believe that in this Trump era or any other, the silence of many white evangelicals to outright evil who seek to occupy the quiet political center is instead an insidious form of complicity that affirms the morally indefensible status quo. I pray that *The Spiritual Danger of Donald Trump* will help spark conversations across the country that will finally end that silence for good. It's time to move from caution to courage in the most important election of our lifetimes."

—**Jim Wallis**

Founder and President, Sojourners

"This book is an appropriate lament that faithfully records a dark chapter in American evangelicalism. Its warning notes to the blind guides who have anointed Donald Trump as God's instrument are firm, urgent, and offered out of loving concern for the integrity of Christian witness. The contributors consistently plead for the embrace of the foundational Christian virtues of humility, truth-telling, and justice. They remind us that Jesus *alone* is King, that his politics were decidedly not based on fear and hate, and that he is the only person to whom unqualified allegiance is due."

—**Amy L. Sherman**

Author of *Kingdom Calling: Vocational Stewardship for the Common Good*

"The support of American evangelicals for the presidency of Donald Trump will likely be recorded as one of the most consequential acts of any religious group in world history. It cannot be overrated. That is why this carefully compiled collection of essays is so timely and important. Whether you agree with their opinions or not, Ron Sider, his fellow editors, and their contributors treat this subject with the seriousness it deserves. If Trump supporters believe it is worth risking the very reputation of the gospel to re-elect their candidate, they should at least explore what these dissenting voices have to say. If Trump detractors believe evangelical support for his presidency is, indeed, dangerous, this book will equip them to defend their positions and persuade others to join them in opposition. Regardless of where one stands on Christians and Donald Trump, this compilation explains significant political differences within evangelicalism and sets out reasons why evangelicals across the theological and social spectrums will continue to play a critically important role in the political life of our nation, for good or for bad. Evangelicals and those who want to understand them better cannot afford to ignore this book!"

—Rob Schenck

President, The Dietrich Bonhoeffer Institute; author of *Costly Grace: An Evangelical Minister's Rediscovery of Faith, Hope and Love*

"Whether you agree or disagree with these voices, I believe their perspectives and arguments are urgently in need of being heard. Listening should always be the first act of a leader, and even more, for a leader seeking to live as a follower of Jesus. What I so appreciate about this collection of essays is the careful way these authors have tried to listen carefully— to Donald Trump, to his supporters and detractors, and to the national and international climate of our day. Beyond that, however, they are all people trying to listen as deeply and wisely to God in Jesus Christ as they can. This is what I believe leads them to conclude that the United States, including especially the church in this nation, faces in Donald Trump not just a political leader with a political vision that some like and some don't, but a personal and spiritual force-field of a far more dangerous and destructive kind. Whether or not you accept these voices, I hear in their perspectives and arguments many things that are urgently in need of being heard. What is at stake is far too important to do otherwise and risks multi-generational damage. Lord, may it not be so."

—Mark Labberton

President, Fuller Theological Seminary

"This timely and careful critique of the evangelical movement's surprisingly fervent embrace of Donald Trump draws on biblical, theological, sociological, and historical sources to argue persuasively against his leadership and re-election to a second term of office. Humble and sacrificial loyalty to Jesus Christ should reign above all other loyalties including seeking political, personal, or cultural power. In light of Trump's documented 'badly damaged soul,' the authors warn of the spiritual damage to the soul and witness of evangelicalism in America. Issues of character, speech, and behavior as well as policy choices on racial justice, immigration, treatment of women, and the needs of the poor and marginalized should be shaped by the teaching and example of Jesus and the Scriptures. Christian witness and faithfulness to the gospel are all at stake. I recommend this book."

—**Roberta Hestenes**

Presbyterian minister; former President, Eastern University; theology faculty member, Fuller Seminary; International Minister-at-Large, World Vision

"If you are looking for deep religious wisdom about the 2020 presidential election, here it is. For those wanting their faith to inform their vote, there is no more important book to read before November 3. Ron Sider has always helped the evangelical community see truth—carefully, biblically, fairly, and courageously. In bringing forth *The Spiritual Danger of Donald Trump*, he has done so again. The title says it all. These thirty outstanding evangelical voices are not talking mere politics. They explore the roots and reasons underlying the spiritual crisis created by Donald Trump's presidency. Their well-reasoned, well-researched, theologically grounded voices, from the US and the world, are compelling. Listen. Share. And then you'll be better equipped to answer: how does being a disciple of Jesus Christ shape the choice I am asked to make about the next president of the United States?"

—**Wesley Granberg-Michaelson**

General Secretary Emeritus, Reformed Church in America; author of *Without Oars: Casting Off into a Life of Pilgrimage*

"Ron Sider curated essays that integrate biblical insights, with deep reflection to challenge Christians to think about what their faith should look like, lived out in the public sphere. The voices from the global evangelical community provide helpful nuance to short-hand versions of evangelicalism. A thoughtful collection of essays, grounded in biblical reflection, that helps Christians ground their conclusions on the heart of Jesus' teachings. A timely, thought-provoking book!"

—Nikki Toyama-Szeto
Executive Director, Evangelicals for Social Action

THE SPIRITUAL DANGER OF DONALD TRUMP

The
SPIRITUAL DANGER
of DONALD TRUMP

30 Evangelical Christians
on Justice, Truth, and Moral Integrity

EDITED BY
Ronald J. Sider

CASCADE *Books* • Eugene, Oregon

THE SPIRITUAL DANGER OF DONALD TRUMP
30 Evangelical Christians on Justice, Truth, and Moral Integrity

Cascade Books
An Imprint of Wipf and Stock Publishers
199 W. 8th Ave., Suite 3
Eugene, OR 97401

www.wipfandstock.com

PAPERBACK ISBN: 978-1-7252-7178-4
HARDCOVER ISBN: 978-1-7252-7179-1
EBOOK ISBN: 978-1-7252-7180-7

Cataloguing-in-Publication data:

Names: Sider, Ronald J., editor.
Title: The spiritual danger of Donald Trump : 30 evangelical Christians on justice, truth, and moral integrity / edited by Ronald J. Sider.
Description: Eugene, OR: Cascade Books, 2020 | Includes bibliographical references.
Identifiers: ISBN 978-1-7252-7178-4 (paperback) | ISBN 978-1-7252-7179-1 (hardcover) | ISBN 978-1-7252-7180-7 (ebook)
Subjects: LCSH: Trump, Donald, 1946-—Influence. | Rhetoric—Political aspects—History—United States—21st century. | Evangelicalism—United States—History—21st century.
Classification: E913.3 .S35 2020 (print) | E913.3 (ebook)

Manufactured in the U.S.A.   MAY 13, 2020

"Come now, and let us reason together," says the LORD.
Isaiah 1:18

Contents

PART III: ON THEOLOGICAL, HISTORICAL, AND CONSTITUTIONAL ISSUES REGARDING TRUMP

Contributors

Michael W. Austin, PhD, is professor of philosophy at Eastern Kentucky University. He has a BA in Political Science from Kansas State University, a MA in Philosophy from Biola University, and a PhD in Philosophy from the University of Colorado. He has authored numerous articles in ethics and philosophy of religion. He has published twelve books, most recently *God and Guns in America*. He is also the current president of the Evangelical Philosophical Society.

Randall Balmer, PhD, holds the John Phillips Chair in Religion at Dartmouth, the oldest endowed professorship at Dartmouth College. He earned a PhD from Princeton University in 1985 and taught as Professor of American Religious History at Columbia University for twenty-seven years before going to Dartmouth in 2012. He has written more than a dozen books, including *Redeemer: The Life of Jimmy Carter*; *God in the White House: How Faith Shaped the Presidency from John F. Kennedy to George W. Bush*; and *The Making of Evangelicalism: From Revivalism to Politics and Beyond*.

Vicki Courtney is a national speaker to women of all ages and a bestselling author of dozens of books and Bible studies, including *5 Conversations You Must Have With Your Daughter* and *5 Conversations You Must Have With Your Son*. She is a two-time ECPA Christian Book Award winner and has appeared on CNN and Fox News as a youth culture commentator. Vicki graduated from the University of Texas in Austin with a degree in economics.

Daniel Deitrich is a singer-songwriter, worship curator, and pastor. You can listen to *Hymn for the 81%* at DanielDeitrich.com or wherever digital music is streamed or sold.

Samuel Escobar, PhD, is professor emeritus at Palmer Seminary. He graduated in Arts and Education from San Marcos University in Lima, Peru, and obtained a PhD at the Complutense University, Madrid. Presently he keeps a preaching and lecturing ministry in Spain.

John Fea, PhD, is Professor of History at Messiah College. He holds a PhD in American History from Stony Brook University, a MA in Church History from Trinity Evangelical Divinity School, and a MDiv from Trinity Evangelical Divinity School. He is the author of numerous books, including *Believe Me: The Evangelical Road to Donald Trump.*

Irene Fowler is a Nigerian lawyer (LLM, Harvard) based in Lagos, Nigeria. Her career background spans the United Nations in Geneva, Switzerland (World Health Organization and High Commissioner for refugees), the Nigerian educational and energy sectors (Shell Petroleum and Conoco), human rights advocacy, and gender issues. Currently, she is a director at Vivian Fowler Memorial College for Girls, Lagos, Nigeria and an ordained Christian evangelist.

Mark Galli is a public theologian, former editor-in-chief of *Christianity Today*, and author of *When Did We Start Forgetting God?: The Root of the Evangelical Crisis and Hope for the Future.* His op-ed in *Christianity Today*, "Trump Should Be Removed from Office," gained the attention of national media, including CNN, MSNBC, *The Washington Post*, and *The New York Times.*

J. Colin Harris, PhD, is Professor Emeritus of Religious Studies, Mercer University. He has a BA in psychology from Mercer University, a MDiv from Southeastern Baptist Theological Seminary, and a PhD in systematic theology from Duke University.

Stephen R. Haynes is the A. B. Curry Professor of Religious Studies and Director of the Liberal Arts in Prison Program at Rhodes College, where he has taught since 1989. He holds a PhD in Religion and Literature from Emory University, a MDiv from Columbia Theological Seminary, a MA from Florida State University, and a BA from Vanderbilt University. He is the author of several books on Dietrich Bonhoeffer, including *The Bonhoeffer Phenomenon; The Bonhoeffer Legacy; Bonhoeffer for Armchair Theologians* (with Lori Brandt Hale); and *The Battle for Bonhoeffer: Debating Discipleship in the Age of Trump.*

Matt Henderson, PhD, is assistant professor in the Department of Sociology at Union University, where he specializes in religion, family, and health.

He has a BA from the University of Houston and a MA and PhD in sociology from Baylor University.

Christopher A. Hutchinson, MDiv, is a senior pastor and graduate of Duke University and Gordon-Conwell Theological Seminary. Prior to entering the ministry, Chris served in the US Army, including a combat tour during Operation Desert Storm. He is the author of *Rediscovering Humility: Why the Way Up Is Down*.

Bandy X. Lee, MD, MDiv, is a forensic psychiatrist at Yale School of Medicine and a graduate of Yale Divinity School. She is the author of more than 100 peer-reviewed articles and chapters, the editor of sixteen academic books, the author of *Violence: An Interdisciplinary Approach to Causes, Consequences, and Cures*, and the editor of *The New York Times* best seller *The Dangerous Case of Donald Trump: 37 Psychiatrists and Mental Health Experts Assess a President*.

David S. Lim, PhD, is President of the Asian School for Development and Cross-Cultural Studies. He is also President of China Ministries International-Philippines and serves as the Board chairman of Lausanne Philippines. He earned his ThM in New Testament from Asian Centre for Theological Studies and his PhD in New Testament from Fuller Theological Seminary.

David C. Ludden, PhD, is Professor of Psychology at Georgia Gwinnett College and the author of *The Psychology of Language: An Integrated Approach*. He has a BA in modern languages, a MA in linguistics from Ohio University, and a PhD in cognitive psychology from the University of Iowa.

Ryan McAnnally-Linz is Associate Director of the Yale Center for Faith & Culture. Ryan received a MDiv and PhD from Yale. He is co-author of *Public Faith in Action* and co-editor of *The Joy of Humility* and *Envisioning the Good Life*.

Steven Meyer, PhD, is the Dean of Graduate Studies at the Daniel Morgan Graduate School of National Security (Washington, DC). He received bachelor's degrees in mathematics and political science from the University of Wisconsin, a MS in political science from Fordham University, and a PhD in political science from Georgetown University. He worked for many years at the Central Intelligence Agency as an analyst and upper-level manager and at the Department of Defense (DOD) teaching national security policy, American foreign policy, and European and Russian politics at the DOD's National Defense University.

Napp Nazworth, PhD, is a freelance writer and editor. He previously worked for more than eight years as a politics editor, political analyst, and journalist for *The Christian Post*. He left that position in December, 2019, over a pro-Trump editorial, a decision that gained the attention of national news media, including CNN, *The Washington Post,* and *The New York Times*. His doctorate in political science from the University of Florida specialized in religion and politics and his dissertation was about the Christian Right.

D Zac Niringiye, PhD, is a theologian and social justice activist. He previously served as the Assistant Bishop of Kampala Diocese in the Church of Uganda and team leader of International Fellowship of Evangelical Students in English and Portuguese speaking countries in Africa. He has a PhD in Theology and Mission History from Edinburgh University and is the author of *The Church: God's Pilgrim People*.

Christopher Pieper, PhD, is senior lecturer in the Department of Sociology at Baylor University and the author of *Sociology as a Spiritual Practice: How Studying People Can Make You a Better Person*. He has a BA from Southwestern University and a MA and PhD in sociology from the University of Texas at Austin.

Reid Ribble is the son of an ordained minister, the brother of three pastors, and the father of one ordained son. He served in the US House of Representatives as a Republican member of Congress from Wisconsin's 8th congressional district from 2011 to 2016. He was the first Republican member of Congress to warn others of the potential risk of electing Donald Trump as President.

Ronald J. Sider, PhD, is Distinguished Professor emeritus of Theology, Holistic Ministry and Public Policy at Palmer Theological Seminary at Eastern University and President Emeritus of Evangelicals for Social Action. In 1982, *The Christian Century* named him one of the twelve "most influential persons in the field of religion in the U.S." His *Rich Christians in an Age of Hunger* (6th ed., 2015) was recognized by *Christianity Today* as one of the one hundred most influential religious books of the twentieth century and named the seventh most influential book in the evangelical world in the last fifty years. He has published more than forty books and has a blog at ronsiderblog.substack.com.

Edward G. Simmons, PhD, worked for thirty-four years for the State of Georgia. In retirement he teaches history at Georgia Gwinnett College. He has a BA from Mercer University in history and a MA and PhD in history from Vanderbilt University.

James R. Skillen is an Associate Professor of Environmental Studies, and Director of the Ecosystem Preserve and Native Gardens at Calvin University. He earned a BS at Wheaton College, a MA at Gordon-Conwell Theological Seminary, and a PhD at Cornell University. His forthcoming book, *This Land Is My Land*, explores the growing partisan divide over federal land management in the American West and the prominent role of American civil religion in land and environmental politics.

James W. Skillen is founder and the first director/president (retired) of the Center for Public Justice (1981–2009) in Washington, DC, and former professor of political science at three Christian colleges. He earned a BA at Wheaton College, a BD at Westminster Theological Seminary, and a PhD at Duke University. His most recent books are *God's Sabbath with Creation* and *The Good of Politics: A Biblical, Historical, and Contemporary Introduction*.

Julia K. Stronks, JD, has practiced law and has a PhD in American government. She is a professor of political science at Whitworth University. Her publications focus on Constitutional law, First Amendment religious freedom, and the intersection of gender, faith, and policy.

Chris Thurman, PhD, is a psychologist and author of numerous books, including the best seller *The Lies We Believe*. He has a BA in psychology from the University of Texas at Austin, a MS in counseling from East Texas State University, and a PhD in counseling psychology from the University of Texas at Austin.

Miroslav Volf is Henry B. Wright Professor of Theology at Yale Divinity School and Director of the Yale Center for Faith & Culture. After receiving the BA from the Evangelical-Theological Faculty in Osijek, Croatia, Miroslav received his MA from Fuller Theological Seminary and both his Dr. theol. and Dr. theol. habil. from the University of Tübingen. He is the author of several books, including *For the Life of the World: Theology that Makes a Difference; Public Faith in Action; A Public Faith;* and *Exclusion and Embrace*.

Peter Wehner is a contributing writer at *The Atlantic*, a senior fellow at the Ethics and Public Policy Center, and Egan visiting professor at Duke University. He had major positions in the administrations of Presidents Ronald Reagan, George H. W. Bush, and George W. Bush, and writes widely on political, cultural, religious, and national security issues. He is the author of *The Death of Politics: How to Heal Our Frayed Republic After Trump*.

George Yancey is a Professor in the Institute for Studies of Religion and Sociology at Baylor University. He has a BS in economics from West Texas State University, a MA in economics from the University of Texas at Austin, and a PhD in Sociology from the University of Texas at Austin. He has published several research articles and books on the topics of institutional racial diversity, racial identity, atheists, cultural progressives, academic bias, and anti-Christian hostility. He is currently working on research contrasting conservative and progressive Christians.

When We Respond to God's Calling

BANDY X. LEE

Sacrifice and offering you did not desire—but my ears you have opened—
burnt offerings and sin offerings you did not require. Then I said, "Here I am,
I have come—it is written about me in the scroll. I desire to do your will, my
God; your law is within my heart."

(Psalm 40:6–8)

THIS BOOK IS THE PRODUCT OF A SERIES OF RESPONSES TO A CALLING—
that still, small voice that beckons and, when we drop everything to answer,
reveals a larger plan.

Three of us were involved. Dr. Chris Thurman started it with great
boldness and no hesitation. As a psychologist, he knew of the book I edited, *The Dangerous Case of Donald Trump*, a collection of essays by mental health professionals who felt a duty to warn the public about the new
president's psychological dangers. Despite being a multi-authored book of
specialized knowledge, it became a runaway best seller that even one of the
biggest publishers in the country had not prepared for (it took five weeks for
them to replenish the stocks in a way that would not deplete within hours).
Chris noticed "MDiv" at the end of my name and saw the possibility of doing something similar for Christians.

I did not know Chris at the time, but he recognized something important: while I made use of my training and knowledge, the book I edited was
not mine. There was divine work behind the timing, the preparation, and
the way the circumstances came together. I simply happened to be available.
With the passing of my mother, a devout Christian, I had nothing more of
true value to lose in this world. I had rid myself of most of my possessions,
and all that I was seeking in my remaining days was to gaze on the beauty
of the Lord and to seek him in his temple (Psalm 27). Thus, when the Lord
called, I had but one response: Here I am— "I am the Lord's servant" (Luke
1:38). This is when he plunged me straight into the center of the political
world, and all my credentials, university affiliation, medical degree, background in violence prevention, and work with prisoners were put to use.

I witnessed something similar happening with Chris: he answered a
call and was obedient all the way, regardless of the personal or professional
cost. Early in the quest, however, Chris encountered a difficult challenge: he
came to the painful realization that because of his lack of formal theological
training he was to do all the work but not be listed as an editor. The editor
of any book knows of all the work that goes into selecting and recruiting
authors, bringing them together, and getting them to contribute on time.
With a sensitive topic like this one and the tight timeline we were proposing,
it was a monumental task. Yet Chris took it all on without a complaint, and
now without the prospect even of recognition. I gave no small protest, but
Chris would not waver and remained steadfast. Gracious and generous in
all his dealings, he emulates Christ like few I have seen. His attitude is what
has become the backbone of this book and will be its nourishment when the
work is ready to take flight. Christians know the power of the humility he
exemplifies: The Lord calls, we respond, and things happen.

Third among us is Dr. Ron Sider. He is the theologian we recruited
when it was clear that neither of us could speak authoritatively from a
Christian point of view. Ron was gracious and bold in responding, coming
fully on board with two strangers who had no standing in the Christian
world but our personal faith. I was overjoyed to have a fellow Yale Divinity
School graduate on board, with his theological and intellectual rigor, not to
mention the clear Christian values he brought, having dedicated a lifetime
to compassion, generosity, and work for justice. We agreed on most things,
and, because of Ron's willingness to come on to the project and to give it the
weight of a respected theologian, it seemed for a while we had all that we
could hope for—until I came to the reluctant recognition in prayer that I
was not to be listed as editor, either. It should have been quite the shake-up,
little more than a week before the manuscript was due, but Ron gracefully

and magnanimously accepted the situation as God's will, and for this I will be eternally grateful.

My reasons for wishing to be on the project were personal. Reaching out to Christians was dear to my heart, as I consider it one step closer to reaching out to Christ, whom my mother has recently joined. I also considered spiritual healing for the land to be the next stage of progression from psychological healing. I wished to reach out to as much of the nation as I was able to with my earlier, secular one. Finally, I felt compassion for all the Christian Trump supporters I connected with, who are among the most good-hearted people I have met, making great sacrifices to do the right thing. They were strangers reaching out to me, defending their president, exasperated that I would dare criticize him—then, each time I responded, they were amazed that I would even bother to do so.

In truth, I feel humbled before them, for the greatness of their humility and often childlike faith, which I cannot claim to have. We know that, in the Lord's eyes, many who are first in the world will be last, and many who are last will be first (Matthew 19:30); people look at outward appearances, but the Lord looks at the heart (1 Samuel 16:7). I count myself as being beneath them. I do not presume to be better because I happen to have the education and know how to navigate the complex informational systems to have access to the facts. Rather, it is the meek who will inherit God's land (Psalm 37:11). I tried nothing more than to demonstrate to them that my goals, too, were humanitarian, that I cared for the president as a human being, and merely wished for him to get the right care and for the nation to be safe. The more convincing I was, the harder it seemed for them to continue engaging with me, as I shook their firmly held, cherished beliefs. Yet it would be enough if I planted a seed—if, in their moment of disappointment, they would remember there was another place where Christians could be, and that, if they chose to abandon their president, we would welcome them as brothers and sisters.

It is for these people that I initially agreed to this project, knowing that their simplicity has made them vulnerable to exploitation and oppression, now by a Christian establishment that has chosen to ally with worldly power. Chris and Ron were impassioned to do something about it, and we would be partners in this mission—as were all the authors of this book. Hence, it was sad for me to leave it, but the Lord has called me elsewhere, and the readiness and powerful examples that these two have set helped me to accept this situation. Our work will still be complementary—and I know that, with Chris and Ron, both men of God, the book is in excellent hands.

This is an extraordinarily important work. While I embarked on *The Dangerous Case of Donald Trump* because I found our nation and humankind at existential risk, in truth, the spiritual danger is greater. We can lose our lives, but we should not lose our souls. And this book deals with just that matter. With all the disagreements it is sure to raise, in the end, as Christians, we know that we will have passed from death to life because we love one another (1 John 3:14).

Christians are selfless and ready for sacrifice. With all our hearts we seek the Lord and delight in the Lord's commandments (Psalm 119:10). But the Lord did not desire sacrifice and offering—only that we open our ears (Psalm 40:6). Burnt offerings and sin offerings, and all the twisting of what we hear and think to prop up a false prophet who demands idolatry, he did not condone. Rather, we know that the Lord's yoke is easy and his burden is light (Matthew 11:30). The true God awaits us as a father who calls on his sons and daughters (2 Corinthians 6:18). We need only reply, "Here I am, I have come"—and, because he has made us for himself, our hearts will no longer be restless when they find rest in him (Augustine, *Confessions*, 1.1.1).

Introduction

Our Common Commitment to Christ

RONALD J. SIDER

WE PUBLISH THIS BOOK WITH DEEP SADNESS AND PERSISTENT HOPE. Sadness, indeed grief, that current politics is so divisive and dysfunctional. And hope that biblical values and constitutional standards will prevail.

We write frankly about current politics and presidential leadership, but we do not do that as people committed to one political party. We are Republicans, Democrats, and Independents. We do not all agree on how faithful Christians should vote on November 3, 2020.

We do, however, share a common commitment to Jesus Christ our Lord. We all want to let Christ be Lord of every part of our lives, including our politics. We all want to live out our conviction that unity in the body of Christ is far more important than any political disagreement, however deep. We all seek to speak the truth in love, even when we sharply disagree with other Christians. We are evangelical Christians, pleading with other Christians, especially evangelicals, to allow biblical principles to shape all our political activity.

We are deeply worried: first about the good name of Christianity and second about the future of our beloved nation.

Growing evidence shows that more and more Americans are rejecting Christian faith. That is especially true of young people, including youth who grew up in evangelical churches. And many attribute their turning away from Christianity to what they consider immoral, fundamentally wrong, political engagement by Christians, especially evangelical Christians.

Everyone knows that our national politics is so fundamentally dysfunctional that our future as a thriving democracy is in danger. A commitment to truth, respect for opponents, and willingness to negotiate reasonable bipartisan compromise is in dreadfully short supply. Serious observers wonder whether the great American experiment in freedom and democracy can survive.

We believe it can!

We believe that Christians can make a huge contribution to preserving a good future for our children and grandchildren by praying for God's guidance, submitting unconditionally to biblical principles about truth, justice, and moral integrity, and faithfully applying these biblical principles in all our political decisions in this election year.

In that faith and hope, we share these essays with all Americans, especially our sisters and brothers in Christ.

PART I

ON TRUMP

Chapter 1

Why "Mere" Words Matter

The President's Words—and Our Words
about the President

M ARK G ALLI

A S I WATCHED A RECORDING OF THE E VANGELICALS FOR T RUMP RALLY ON January 3, 2020 in Miami, I couldn't help but admire one speaker who has worked tirelessly for pro-life concerns at California State University at Fresno. And I was grieved that the school's administration tried to block her student group's efforts at making their views known—and that it took a lawsuit for them to enjoy that right.[1]

Examples like this energize Mr. Trump's evangelical supporters, so much so that they wonder why many pro-life Christians are so furious with the president's public moral bearing, especially how in his tweets and comments he insults and mocks his opponents and Matthew Croasmun. "When the lives of hundreds of thousands of babies in the womb are at stake," they say, "why make such a big deal about the president's bad manners?" They go on: "So he has a few rough edges; we need a leader who will stand up to the liberal bullies and rough them up a bit if we're going to defend life in the womb and freedom of speech."

---

1. January 3, 2020, https://www.c-span.org/video/?467813–1/president-trump
-speaks-evangelical-rally-miami.

I grasp the logic here, but I wonder if these Christians have thought deeply enough about the nature and power of speech—and how destructive is the culture of contempt the president is fostering. They seem to subscribe to the aphorism, "Sticks and stones may break my bones, but words will never hurt me"—that is, actions count, but words are ephemeral and, in the end, don't matter all that much.

That is not how the biblical writers viewed words, and it fails to appreciate that Mr. Trump's caustic speech will in fact hurt America more than do sticks and stones. Deafness to this serious moral failing, hurts not only America, but the gospel Christians proclaim.

The Trouble with Trump's Tweets

I recognize that contempt for one's political enemies did not start with Mr. Trump. I'm not sure when exactly it ascended as it has, but all of us now are tempted by this manner of speaking. Certainly Mr. Trump's opponents are not guiltless, with the most notable example being Hillary Clinton's dismissal of many Americans as "a basket of deplorables."[2] And if we are honest with ourselves, we each have to confess that we've succumbed to the temptation to disparage those with whom we disagree. In many ways, we live in a society that breathes the polluted air of contempt.

And yet there is this: our nation is led by a man who, instead of working to clean up this caustic environment, only adds more poisonous fumes to the mix. This only makes our society's battle with contempt that much harder.

In his tweets and comments, Mr. Trump habitually ridicules, describing his opponents as "unhinged," "crazy," "lying," "disgraced," "losers," "crooked," "phony," "fake," and people "of low I.Q." He mocks political enemies with demeaning nick names, like calling Elizabeth Warren "Pocahontas." His comments, which rage every day of the year, are the epitome of contempt for other human beings.[3]

At that January 3 rally, Mr. Trump spoke of the need to love one's neighbor. He clearly means only some neighbors. Other neighbors he delights in despising. This is not, as many of my evangelical friends like to say, a man with "some rough edges," but someone who is threatening to unravel the last threads of decency in our culture. This will only have disastrous consequences for America and for many evangelical concerns.

2. https://time.com/4486502/hillary-clinton-basket-of-deplorables-transcript/.

3. https://www.nytimes.com/interactive/2016/01/28/upshot/donald-trump-twitter-insults.html.

What Does the Bible Say About All This?

My evangelical friends seem to have forgotten the many sobering biblical sayings about the great power of the tongue. Like:

> There is one whose rash words are like sword thrusts, but the tongue of the wise brings healing.
>
> —Proverbs 12:18 (ESV, as are the quotes below)

> The good person out of the good treasure of his heart produces good, and the evil person out of his evil treasure produces evil, for out of the abundance of the heart his mouth speaks.
>
> —Luke 6:45

> I tell you, on the day of judgment people will give account for every careless word they speak.
>
> —Matthew 12:36

> If anyone thinks he is religious and does not bridle his tongue but deceives his heart, this person's religion is worthless.
>
> —James 1:26

In the book of James, in fact, we find the most sobering passage on this theme:

> A word out of your mouth may seem of no account, but it can accomplish nearly anything—or destroy it! It only takes a spark, remember, to set off a forest fire. A careless or wrongly placed word out of your mouth can do that. By our speech we can ruin the world, turn harmony to chaos, throw mud on a reputation, send the whole world up in smoke and go up in smoke with it, smoke right from the pit of hell. (James 3:4–6, The Message)

Is this not a near perfect description of what is happening in American culture today? Donald Trump may not be the cause, but he certainly throws gasoline on the fires that rage across our land.

An atmosphere of sanctity hung over much of that January 3 event, with many pious words coming out of the president's mouth about matters of faith. But as James put it long ago:

> The tongue runs wild, a wanton killer. With our tongues we bless God our Father; with the same tongues we curse the very men and women he made in his image. Curses and blessings out of the same mouth! (3:7–10)

Again, this sounds like it was written yesterday, just for us.

It is not an accident that the Bible calls Jesus "the Word of God," a Word that became flesh and dwelt among us. It is through the Word that redemption comes to our world, the Word that was, as John put it, "full of grace and truth" (John 1:14). Such phrases have overtones and nuances about which books have been written.

And yet at the simplest level, in describing Jesus as the Word, John is implying that all our words have the potential to participate in grace and truth, that is, in the very life of God. This is why the Bible, from cover to cover, is so concerned with how we use words. How we speak can drive us and our communities toward life in God, or drive us far from it, as far as hades itself.

This has specific import for Christians, of course. But it also speaks about the nature of language itself, no matter who is using it. From a Christian point of view, the degree to which a culture's public conversation traffics in muck, the more godless it becomes. No, we're not to expect any president to be our pastor in chief—of course not. But we can rightly expect that our leaders use language that treats others with respect, and even honors them when they do good things for our land—even if we disagree with their politics. Language that tries to bridge our differences, that fosters some level of unity in the midst of our diversity. Language that harkens to our nation's greatest ideals and thus inspires us to let our better selves shine forth.

Who Should Disciple Us Here?

My conservative Christian friends deeply worry about the degradation and even possible death of American culture. That's what "Make America Great Again" is all about. What they don't recognize, in my view, is that when our nation's leader speaks with disdain and contempt about those with whom he disagrees, he's making America worse. And even more troublesome: he's discipling all of us to do the same. He's teaching us by example how to treat our political and cultural enemies—and his example has nothing to do with love of enemies or turning the other cheek. He is modeling speech that not only puts his soul in danger, he's putting the soul of the nation in peril.

Let me note one specific consequence of this. If we ignore or even cheer on this culture of contempt, what do we think will happen to us and the life of the unborn when Mr. Trump's opponents end up in power, as they inevitably will? Will they not treat the unborn and those who champion their cause with a revengeful contempt that we can now only imagine, and will not the whirlwind of their disdain demolish any judicial gains that Mr. Trump has made? I fear it will be so if we don't change our ways.

I'm not questioning the politics of my friends, for I can still imagine an argument that justifies a vote for Mr. Trump, especially given alternatives. But it is mighty difficult to fathom how so many ardent Christians can suggest that his caustic public speech is a mere quirk of personality, and—according to the Scriptures we claim is our final authority—not something profoundly dangerous for the life of the nation.

This is one reason I argued in my December 19, 2019 *Christianity Today* editorial[4] that Mr. Trump is morally unfit for office. I certainly am in no position to judge his relationship with God—though I admit that some of my language seemed to suggest that. Who of us does not have a great deal to confess to God when it comes to personal failings? To be sure, we are getting a peek into the troubling state of Mr. Trump's soul, for as Jesus notes, "for out of the abundance of the heart his mouth speaks." But I'm mainly interested in Mr. Trump's *public* character, in his habitual public actions and, in this case, his caustic public words *when he acts as president.*

And I'm especially concerned about the unwillingness or inability of his evangelical supporters to speak openly and truthfully about all this. This is not only a sad indictment of our faith, but a missed opportunity to be a witness for Jesus Christ in the public square.

The Editorial's Big Surprise

There have been many surprises in that editorial, but no surprise has been greater than the cheering of atheists, agnostics, Jews, and former evangelicals. They responded with grateful emails, subscriptions, and donations to the magazine.

The episode has opened my eyes to one crucial role that evangelical religion must play in the nation's life: To speak and act in the public square in ways that are consistent with the theology and ethics of evangelical faith.

As I've argued, it is deeply troubling that Mr. Trump's evangelical supporters refuse to condemn the president's unethical behavior in office. That failure stands in sharp contrast to their reaction to Bill Clinton's moral failings, boldly summed up in a 1998 Southern Baptist resolution. "We implore our government leaders to live by the highest standards of morality both in

---

4. https://www.christianitytoday.com/ct/2019/december-web-only/trump-should -be-removed-from-office.html.

their private actions and in their public duties," it read, "and thereby serve as models of moral excellence and character."[5]

This sentiment appears all but forgotten when it comes to measuring the current president.

Evangelicals are latecomers to partisan politics, of course. Mainline Christianity was at center stage in the 1960s and '70s, when Congregationalists, Presbyterians, Episcopalians, and Methodists, among others, used their national gatherings to weigh in on every hot-button political issue, taking stands that often merely mirrored the platform of the Democratic Party. Their early moral support of the civil rights movement is to be praised; their conclusion that politics was the way to stay relevant is today recognized as a mistake, a leading cause of both a decline in membership and, ironically, in loss of relevance.

It's not that Christians should avoid the give and take of political life. As citizens in a democracy, participation in political arm wrestling is not only a right, but a duty. The duty, however, is mostly an individual one, with religious bodies weighing in with moral judgments only at crucial moments. It is a sure sign of a church's internal decay when the sum and substance of its religious activity becomes entwined with political partisanship, especially when loyalty to a political figure is equated with loyalty to God.

At that January Evangelicals for Trump rally, the opening prayer included these words: "We declare that no weapon formed against him will be able to prosper and every demonic altar erected against him will be torn down" and that "he will rise high, and he is seated in the heavenly places."[6]

Christians have traditionally denounced such talk as idolatry.

In this light, it is no wonder that Trump-supporting evangelicals don't comprehend the moral gravity of the lies and contempt that characterize Mr. Trump's words, and that they excuse the manifold corruptions of his office. He's a political messiah, after all; by definition, he can't do wrong.

And yet, the most serious problem we Christians face today is not idolatrous politics. That's a mere symptom of a deeper disorder, one that transcends left and right, mainline and evangelical, Catholic and Protestant. As I've written elsewhere,[7] and argue in my recent book,[8] I believe that what Alexander Solzhenitsyn said about America in his 1983 Templeton Prize

5. http://www.sbc.net/resolutions/773/resolution-on-moral-character-of-public-officials.

6. January 3, 2020, https://www.c-span.org/video/?467813-1/president-trump-speaks-evangelical-rally-miami.

7. https://www.christianitytoday.com/ct/opinion/columnists/elusive-presence/.

8. https://www.amazon.com/When-Did-Start-Forgetting-God/dp/1414373619/ref=sr_1_1?keywords=mark+galli&qid=1580485611&s=books&sr=1-1.

address applies specifically to Christians in America today: We have forgotten God.[9]

Some assume I champion a retreat into a life of private devotion, and thus a withdrawal from engagement. Far from it. But we too often step into the public square clumsily and trip over our own moral ideals because we have forgotten our First Love. We fail to recall that the one gift we have to offer the nation is not a partisan vote, but a consistent moral voice grounded in the perfect love and perfect righteousness of God.

Christianity Today's nonreligious supporters certainly do not agree with everything the magazine stands for. An evangelical such as me hopes, of course, that they will now study and consider the more spiritual claims we make. But even if that's never the case, their support was an affirmation that they rightly expect the religious to be consistent with their faith's teaching—and to have the courage to speak up about serious moral issues, even if our words have to be directed at a party or leader we otherwise sympathize with.

To be sure, Christianity has much more to offer than this—for one, a life redeemed and shaped by Christ's self-sacrificing love. But striving for integrity in word and deed in the public square—that's the least we can do for the nation. And by itself, is an unparalleled witness to the gospel we claim to live by.

Author Note: The latter part of this essay was adapted in minor ways from an article that first appeared in *The Los Angeles Times*, January 24, 2020.[10]

---

9. https://www.nationalreview.com/2018/12/aleksandr-solzhenitsyn-men-have-forgotten-god-speech/.

10. https://www.latimes.com/opinion/story/2020-01-24/i-questioned-trumps-moral-fitness-for-office-in-christianity-today.

Chapter 2

God Hates A Lying Tongue

CHRIS THURMAN

ALL PRESIDENTS LIE. SOME OF THE LIES THEY TELL ARE "LITTLE WHITE lies" and others go all the way to big and reprehensible. While every president lies, not every president is a pathological liar. Donald Trump is a pathological liar.

Trump isn't someone who "sometimes misspeaks like all of us do" as Franklin Graham, one of the president's most enthusiastic evangelical supporters, falsely put it.[1]

Trump lies so often even those who know him say he is a pathological liar. Trump's former lawyer, John Dowd, said to him "You can't tell the truth. You just make things up."[2]

Dowd warned Trump he would end up going to jail and be fitted for an "orange jumpsuit" if he testified to the Mueller investigation because his inability to tell the truth would inevitably lead to perjuring himself. George Conway, one of Trump's harshest critics and husband of senior presidential advisor Kellyanne Conway, rhetorically asked on his Twitter page, "Have we ever seen this degree of brazen, pathological mendacity in public life?"[3] and

---

1. https://www.huffpost.com/entry/franklin-graham-trump-lies_n_5c529489e4b0 93663f5b2335.

2. Bob Woodward, *Fear* (New York: Simon & Schuster, 2018), 357.

3. George Conway, Twitter, March 13, 2019.

added, "But one lie on any subject is never enough for Donald Trump. So, he next tells a different lie."[4]

Anthony Scaramucci, who was fired after eleven days as Trump's Communications Chief, said in an interview on CNN, "So if you want me to say he's a liar, I'm happy to say he's a liar."[5]

When those who know Trump say he's a pathological liar, we need to take that seriously and with great alarm.

Not only does Trump pathologically lie, he frequently sends his enablers out to lie for him. One of the first lies out of Trump's mouth after becoming president was to send Press Secretary Sean Spicer out for the initial press conference and have him lie about the size of the inauguration crowd. Saying exactly what the president told him to say so he could stay in Trump's good graces and keep his job, Spicer claimed the inauguration crowd was the biggest ever and watched by the largest number of people in history. Both are lies.[6]

Kellyanne Conway is one of Trump's most frequent truth-spinners. Television news journalist Chuck Todd, interviewing her on *Meet the Press*, asked Conway why Spicer used the first press conference to lie about the size of the inauguration crowd. Todd got a response that immediately went viral. Conway said the White House was providing "alternative facts" to counter the mainstream media's inaccurate description of the inauguration. Todd responded, "Look, alternative facts aren't facts, they're falsehoods," at which point Conway proceeded to lecture Todd about the fact that his job was "not to call things ridiculous that are said by our press secretary and our president."[7]

I'm sure Todd greatly appreciated being told by a chronic truth-bender like Conway how to do his job.

Rudy Giuliani, Trump's personal lawyer who is known for playing fast and lose with the truth himself, stated on *Meet the Press* while defending the president's legal strategy regarding the Mueller investigation, "Truth isn't truth." That comment also went viral and was widely derided. Chuck Todd was the interviewer that day as well. With his head in his hands, Todd replied, "Truth isn't truth? This is going to become a bad meme."[8]

4. Conway, Twitter, March 13, 2019.

5. www.cnn.com/2018/10/24/politics/anthony-scaramucci-donald-trum-liar-cnntv/index.html.

6. https://www.nydailynews.com/news/politics/trump-press-secretary-claims-inauguration-grew-largest-crowd-article-1.2952666.

7. https://www.cnn.com/2017/01/22/politics/kellyanne-conway-alternative-facts/index.html.

8. https://www.nytimes.com/2018/08/19/us/giuliani-meet-the-press-truth-is-not

Todd was right, it did become a bad meme and Giuliani was widely derided for saying it.

Finally, Trump's lawyer, Jay Sekulow, admitted the president lied to him about the Trump Tower meeting. Taking a bullet for the president while throwing his personal integrity out the window, Sekulow said, "I had bad information at that time and made a mistake in my statement . . . Over time facts develop."[9]

In the Trump White House, it seems that "over time facts develop." Most of us were raised to believe that if something is a fact it remains a fact over time.

Anyone trying to be the least bit objective about Trump has to admit he is a pathological liar. How bad is his lying? Pretty bad.

Breaking the Lie Barrier at the Speed of Sound

After just three years in office, Trump had made over 16,000 false or misleading statements, a number previously unimaginable when it comes to the most powerful person in the world. And, tragically, the frequency of his lying is accelerating. In 2017, Trump told 1,999 lies, an average of six a day. In 2018, he told 5,689 lies, an average of sixteen a day. In 2019, Trump told 8,155 lies, an average of twenty-two a day. There is no telling what record for lying he might set this year. Trump is off to a very fast start given how much pressure he is under and how many people are deeply dissatisfied with his performance as president.[10]

We have become so immune to Trump's lies that we no longer seem shocked by them. Nevertheless, take a minute to think about the fact that just last year Trump, on average, lied *twenty-two times a day*. And, those are just the lies he told in public. Can you imagine how often Trump lies when he is having private conversations with staff, friends, or loved ones? Thirty a day? Sixty a day? We can't know for sure, but it is likely to be a much higher number than the lies he tells in public. As a country, we have grown increasingly numb and unresponsive to the numerous lies Trump tells us from day to day.

Why does Trump lie? If you examine his lies, it seems that two primary things are motivating Trump. First, he lies to prop himself up, to make

-truth.html.

9. https://www.huffpost.com/entry/jay-sekulow-bad-information_n_5b67229ee4b0fd5c73dabfa8.

10. https://www.washingtonpost.com/politics/2020/01/20/president-trump-made-16241-false-or-misleading-claims-his-first-three-years/.

himself look better in other people's eyes than he is in reality. Second, Trump lies to be mean, to sadistically tear other people down and make them feel small. There are many other reasons Trump lies, but his narcissistic desire to make himself look good and sadistic desire to demean others are the two most powerful motivations behind his tenuous relationship with the truth.

What is the effect of Trump's lies? Psychologist Daniel Gilbert proposed a theory over two decades ago about how lies impact the human brain. Gilbert argued that we initially hold a lie to be true because we first have to accept something to be able to understand or evaluate it. If Trump says three million people voted illegally in the 2016 election, we initially accept that to be true, even if only for a moment, so that we can then assess its validity. Gilbert argues that after initially accepting a lie as true we must then do the hard work of assessing its validity. Given the limitations of time, energy, or conclusive evidence, many of us fail to "unaccept" some of the lies we are told. Consequently, we sometimes continue to believe something as true even though there is ample evidence to disprove it.[11]

Trump, of course, takes all of this to an even more nefarious extreme by repeating his favorite lies over and over so that people will unwisely assume he's telling the truth. *The Washington Post* has been fact-checking Trump since he has been in office, and they report that Trump has told certain lies *hundreds of times*.[12]

Trump is sociopathic enough to know that statements repeated frequently are far more likely to be accepted as true, regardless of their factual validity. Sadly, some people are so pro-Trump that all the president has to do is say something *once* for them to believe it and accept it as fact.

In light of Trump's narcissistic need for ego-stroking and sadistic desire to denigrate those he dislikes, we can expect a further escalation of his lying while he remains in office. Even if he only ends up serving as president for four years, our country will have never seen a leader as shameless and remorseless as Trump when it comes to lying. Trump is the greatest Liar in Chief our country has ever elected, and we'd better hope and pray that we never see another president who comes anywhere close to his "pathological mendacity."

11. www.politico.com/magazine/story/2017/01/donald-trump-lies-liar-effect-brain-214658.

12. https://www.washingtonpost.com/politics/2020/01/20/president-trump-made-16241-false-or-misleading-claims-his-first-three-years/.

Some of Trump's Biggest Whoppers

Given that Trump has told over 16,000 lies during his time in office, it is difficult to know where to start in discussing the wide variety of lies he tells. How do you do it? Do you focus on the lies he tells the most frequently? Do you focus on the ones that are the most damaging in terms of the negative impact they have on our country and the world at large? Or, do you simply select the most laughable and mockable lies Trump has told, falsehoods that make you want to hold your head in disbelief?

I'm going to scatter shoot across these categories to review just a small sample of the lies Trump has told. One could literally fill volumes with all of Trump's lies given how many he has shamelessly told. But with no further ado, here are some of Trump's most notable lies.

"I went from VERY successful businessman to top TV Star to the President of the United States (on my first try). I think that would qualify as not smart, but genius . . . and a very stable genius at that!"[13]

This is false and misleading on three counts. We have no idea if Trump is a successful businessman because he refuses to release his taxes. We know he has borrowed hundreds of millions of dollars over the years, not paid contractors, inherited hundreds of millions of dollars from his father (something he lied about), filed for bankruptcy numerous times, and lost over a billion dollars in a ten-year period.[14] [15]

None of that suggests Trump is a "VERY successful businessman." In fact, it suggests Trump is a *very* unsuccessful businessman and con artist. On the issue of being a "stable genius," Trump is neither stable nor a genius.

"The rain should have scared them away. But God looked down and he said, 'We're not going to let it rain on your speech.' In fact, when I first started, I said, 'Oh no.' First line, I got hit by a couple of drops. And I said, 'Oh, this is, this is too bad, but we'll go right through it.' But the truth is that it stopped immediately. It was amazing. And then it became really sunny, and then I walked off and it poured right after I left."[16]

13. https://www.cnn.com/2018/01/06/politics/donald-trump-white-house-fitness-very-stable-genius/index.html.

14. https://www.washingtonpost.com/politics/2016/live-updates/general-election/real-time-fact-checking-and-analysis-of-the-first-presidential-debate/fact-check-has-trump-declared-bankruptcy-four-or-six-times/.

15. https://www.vox.com/policy-and-politics/2019/5/8/18536708/trump-lost-1-billion-taxes-nyt.

16. https://www.independent.co.uk/news/world/americas/donald-trump-us-president-false-claims-inauguration-white-house-sean-spicer-kellyanen-conway-press-a7541171.html.

The truth of the matter is it rained throughout Trump's inauguration speech, the sun never broke through, and it didn't "pour" after he left.

"I know more about _____ than anybody."[17]

There is a painfully humorous video on YouTube in which Trump says he knows more about taxes, income, construction, campaign finance, drones, technology, infrastructure, ISIS, environmental impact statements, renewables, the power of Facebook, polls, the courts, steelworkers, banks, trade, golf, nuclear weapons, tax laws, devaluation, "the system," debt, contributions, politicians, and "the other side" than all the experts.[18]

Given that he has filed for bankruptcy six times, Trump may very well know more about tax laws *than most people*, but he certainly doesn't know more about tax law than the experts. And, all the other things he says he's an expert in? Not a chance.

"This is the greatest economy in the HISTORY of America."[19]

Trump has told this lie over 250 times. Our economy was better under a number of other presidents, including Eisenhower, Johnson, and Clinton.

"We have the biggest tax cut in history."[20]

Nope, Reagan passed one that was three times larger. Trump has told this lie over 180 times.[21]

"One thing that I do have to say is: Tremendous amounts of wall have already been built, and a lot of—a lot of wall."[22]

Not true. The truth is the government has been repairing and replacing fencing that has been there all along and very little new wall has been built. Trump has told this lie over 240 times.

"Terrible! Just found out Obama had my 'wires tapped' in Trump Tower just before the victory."[23]

There is no evidence from *any* investigative branch of the US government that President Obama wiretapped Trump Tower.

"The United States is respected again."[24]

17. https://www.axios.com/everything-trump-says-he-knows-more-about-than-anybody-b278b592-cff0-47dc-a75f-5767f42bcf1e.html.

18. https://www.youtube.com/watch?v=o7xU4JYPNKI.

19. https://fortune.com/2018/06/07/trump-eisenhower-greatest-economy-history-america/.

20. https://www.bbc.com/news/world-43790895.

21. https://www.washingtonpost.com/politics/2020/01/20/president-trump-made-16241-false-or-misleading-claims-his-first-three-years/.

22. https://www.npr.org/2018/12/11/675892744/fact-check-trump-says-a-lot-of-wall-has-been-built-as-he-demands-we-build-more.

23. https://www.factcheck.org/2017/09/revisiting-trumps-wiretap-tweets/.

24. https://www.economist.com/graphic-detail/2017/11/15/republicans-believe

Actually, worldwide views of the US have become more negative since Trump took office.

"I don't mind releasing [my tax returns]. I'm under a routine audit. And it'll be released. As soon as the audit's finished, it will be released."[25]

Trump clearly doesn't want to release his tax returns because they are likely to show he is a horrible businessman and has been cheating the government out of money for decades. Also, we don't actually know if Trump's tax returns are under audit, so that could be another lie. Finally, even if Trump's tax returns are under audit, the IRS has made it clear he can still release them. Trump gets three Pinocchios on this one.

"No Collusion, No Obstruction, Complete and Total EXONERATION. KEEP AMERICA GREAT."[26]

Robert Mueller was unable to prove Trump and his cronies *criminally conspired* with the Russians to win the election, but he laid out a damning case that Trump's minions *colluded* with Russia to win the election and that Trump obstructed justice by covering it up. "KEEP AMERICA GREAT"! Trump's motto should be "KEEP AMERICA IN THE DARK!" given all the unethical and immoral things he has done to make sure the truth never comes out.

"The rest of the 20-block area, all the way back to the Washington monument was packed!"[27]

Trump is obsessed with the crowd size at his inauguration, claiming a million-and-a-half people attended. The crowd was nowhere near that large and wasn't watched by the largest television audience in history. And, much to his chagrin, Trump's inauguration crowd was noticeably smaller than President Obama's.

"I haven't had an empty seat at a rally."[28]

Trump certainly can "pack 'em in" at his self-glorifying rallies, but more than a few of them have had empty seats. Again, we are back at Trump's obsession with the size of the things associated with him, an obsession that leads him to frequently exaggerate.

-that-america-is-now-more-respected-under-donald-trump.

25. https://www.huffpost.com/entry/trump-tax-returns_n_5884e7cfe4b070d8cad32f89.

26. https://www.cnbc.com/2019/03/24/trump-responds-to-mueller-findings-no-collusion-no-obstruction-complete-and-total-exoneration-keep-america-great.html.

27. https://www.vox.com/policy-and-politics/2017/1/21/14347298/trump-inauguration-crowd-size.

28. https://thehill.com/homenews/campaign/453645-trump-falsely-claims-his-events-have-never-had-an-empty-seat.

". . . and we are considered far and away the hottest economy anywhere in the world, not even close."[29]

No, China, India, and numerous other countries had a higher economic growth rate at the time he said that than we do.

"I watched in Jersey City, N.J., where thousands and thousands of people were cheering as that building came down."[30]

Trump was attacking Muslims with this statement, and there is no evidence that anything like this took place.

"I was the best baseball player in New York when I was young."[31]

Trump may very well be a good athlete, but there is no evidence he was the best high school baseball player in New York City. If he was, Trump would have been pursued by colleges and even the pros, and there is no evidence of that taking place. His lying often takes the form of exaggerating his talents, abilities, and accomplishments, making them far greater than they are in reality.

"[I had] the biggest electoral college win since Ronald Regan."[32]

Trump trailed five of the previous seven electoral totals.

"In addition to winning the electoral college in a landslide, I won the popular vote if you deduct the millions of people who voted illegally."[33]

Bipartisan study after bipartisan study showed that only a few thousand illegal votes were cast in 2016.

"It's all happening much faster than anybody can believe. Even one of them recently said that President Trump made promises but he's kept many more promises, I mean far more than I made."[34]

First of all, that doesn't make any sense. A person can't keep more promises than he or she made. Trump was probably trying to say he had kept more promises than he had broken, but, as he often does, got in his own way in an effort to glorify himself. Even if that is what he was trying to say, it isn't true. At the time Trump said this, he had kept 23 percent of his

29. https://www.cbsnews.com/news/us-economy-is-less-hot-than-president-trump-claimed-in-his-state-of-the-union-address/.

30. https://www.politifact.com/factchecks/2015/nov/22/donald-trump/fact-checking-trumps-claim-thousands-new-jersey-ch/.

31. https://www.sportsgrid.com/as-seen-on-tv/media/donald-trump-i-was-the-best-baseball-player-in-new-york/.

32. https://www.independent.co.uk/news/world/americas/donald-trump-news-electoral-college-ronald-reagan-biggest-win-claim-a7584481.html.

33. https://nypost.com/2016/11/27/trump-says-he-lost-popular-vote-because-millions-voted-illegally/.

34. https://www.newsweek.com/trump-tells-rally-hes-kept-more-promises-hes-made-1198181.

sixty key promises, broken 23 percent of them, and many of them remain unfulfilled.

These are only the tip of the iceberg when it comes to the sheer number of shameless and head-scratching lies Trump has told. And, Trump is lying at a more rapid clip than ever given he was impeached for shaking down a foreign country in an effort to get dirt on a potential political opponent. Given the negative impact being impeached had on him and the frequent criticism he receives for so incompetently and immorally leading our country, the number and outrageousness of Trump's lies is likely only going to get worse.

Trust in a president depends on many things. One of the most important elements related to trust is that a president will tell the truth. You simply can't trust a leader who pathologically lies. Couple Trump's relentless lying with his utter remorselessness about it, and you have a dangerous mix of defects in the president that will continue to cause great harm to our country and countries around the world.

You can't trust a pathological liar. Trump is a pathological liar. You can't trust Trump.

Does It Really Matter When a President Chronically Lies?

When a holy God tells us there are things he *hates*, we would be wise to listen. According to the Bible, "There are six things the Lord hates, seven that are detestable to him: haughty eyes, a lying tongue, hands that shed innocent blood, a heart that devises wicked schemes, feet that are quick to rush into evil, a false witness who pours out lies, and a person who stirs up conflict in the community" (Proverbs 6:16–19). This passage of Scripture paints a disturbingly accurate picture of Donald Trump. Whatever good has come out of the Trump presidency, the majority of his time in office has been spent lying, devising wicked schemes, rushing into immoral actions, bearing false witness against his perceived enemies, and stirring up conflict in our country and around the world.

Great power often brings to the surface the worst flaws and defects in people. This is what happened with Donald Trump. Being elected president only emboldened his proclivity for cutting moral corners, being lazy when it comes to doing his job, using others to gratify his ego, attacking those who oppose him, obstructing justice, and lying at every turn. Every time Trump's feet aren't held to the fire for the immoral and unethical things he does, he becomes even more arrogant, empowered, and out of control.

If we give Trump four more years, we are inevitably going to experience the further erosion of every institution we cherish as Americans and our status in the world as a force for good. If, as Christians, we continue to enable a pathological liar to remain president, we are going to see greater damage inflicted on the cause of Christ and our God-given authority as Christians to speak out against immorality and injustice.

We proudly proclaim in the Pledge of Allegiance that we are "one Nation, under God." If we truly are, we have to start acting like it. We must return to loving what God loves and hating what God hates. God hates a lying tongue. Whoever we cast our vote for in the next presidential election or in the elections to come, we must vote for someone who is committed to both believing the truth and telling the truth no matter what the cost might be to them personally or to their administration. To do otherwise is to waste our vote on someone who is not worthy of the office of president of the United States.

Chapter 3

Donald Trump's Low View of Women

Silence Is Not an Option

Vicki Courtney

ONE OF THE KEY QUESTIONS AN AUTHOR MUST CONSIDER WHEN EMBARK-
ing on a writing project, is "who is the audience?" As I have written this essay, I have wrestled to answer that question. I have written dozens of books
and Bible studies over the past two decades and my audience has always
been clearly defined. My primary readership can best be described as conservative, Christian mothers in the Bible Belt. Most would consider themselves "evangelicals," and truth be told, I would describe myself in a similar
fashion. That said, writing a chapter about Donald Trump's misogyny will
not likely appeal to my traditional audience base. However, as someone who
has written extensively about the culture's objectification of girls and women
and the devastating fallout it has produced, I feel compelled to speak up.

In my writing and speaking ministry, I have encouraged parents to
raise their children to be critical thinkers and more importantly, biblical
thinkers. In the first decade of my ministry, I held mother/daughter events
throughout the country. A core tenet of my ministry has been the mission
of helping girls and women of all ages define their worth and value by God's
standards, rather than the shallow standards of the culture. In the early
2000's, I publicly challenged the hypocrisy of the fashion magazine industry
for pedaling a "girl power" message of empowerment on front covers next
to subtitles such as, "22 Jeans that Scream 'Nice Butt,'" "Swimsuit Tops that

Tease and Please," and "How to Be a Guy Magnet." For two decades, I have pointed to the good news of the gospel and heralded the message that true empowerment comes from knowing and following Jesus Christ.

Regardless of whether you are a Democrat, Republican, Independent, never-Trumper, or apolitical, surely we can unite on that front and agree that the objectification and sexualization of girls and women is never acceptable on any level. It is not my goal in writing to influence your vote. Truth be told, most minds are made up at this point. Many, if not most of my friends voted for Donald Trump in 2016 and some later confessed they did so as "the lesser of two evils." While I came to a different conclusion and voted instead for a third-party write-in candidate to soothe my conscience, I can certainly respect the difficult position many Christians found themselves facing in 2016, and find themselves again facing in 2020.

My sincerest goal in writing this essay is to assess Donald Trump's troublesome view of women through a spiritual lens for a higher purpose: Examining how we, as believers should respond in the aftermath. Much damage has already been done to the name of Christianity. Remaining silent will only further damage the witness of the church, as onlookers struggle to understand how Christians who claim to value human life can essentially turn a blind eye to the brazen and unapologetic devaluation of women by our nation's leader. While we do not have control over Trump's words and actions, we do have control over how we respond. Silence is simply not an option. Too much is at stake.

Words Matter

In Matthew 12:34, Jesus reminds us, "For the mouth speaks what the heart is full of." One Bible commentary notes, "The heart is the fountain, the words are the streams."[1]

In other words, if you want to know what is contained in the fountain, look no further than the stream of words flowing from it. Words spoken over time can offer a window into the soul. Likewise, when it comes to Trump's own words regarding women, they offer us a clue about his value system related to women.

Consider a sampling of statements below that Donald Trump has made over the years related to women. As you read them, see if you can detect a common theme.

---

1. Matthew Henry, *Matthew Henry's Commentary on the Whole Bible,* Matthew 12:22–37 (Peabody, MA: Hendrickson, 1996).

"Look at that face. Would anybody vote for that? Can you imagine that, the face of our next president? I mean, she's a woman, and I'm not supposed to say bad things, but really, folks, come on. Are we serious?" (Referring to Carly Fiorina.)[2]

"She's certainly not hot." (Referring to Jessica Chastain)[3]

"You know, you're in such good shape. Beautiful." (Referring to France's first lady, Brigitte Macron)[4]

"You never get to the face because the body's so good." (Referring to Steffi Graf)[5]

"I'm not saying she's an unattractive woman, but she's not beauty, by any stretch of the imagination." (Referring to Angelina Jolie)[6]

"I do own Miss Universe. I do own Miss USA. I mean I own a lot of different things. I do understand beauty, and she's not." (Referring again to Angelina Jolie)[7]

"Does she have a good body? No. Does she have a fat ass? Absolutely." (Referring to Kim Kardashian)[8]

2. Paul Solotaroff, "Trump Seriously: On the Trail With the GOP's Tough Guy," https://www.rollingstone.com/politics/politics-news/trump-seriously-on-the-trail-with-the-gops-tough-guy-41447/.

3. Marlow Stern, "Donald Trump's Gross History of Misogyny: From Rosie O'Donnell to Megyn Kelly," https://www.thedailybeast.com/donald-trumps-gross-history-of-misogyny-from-rosie-odonnell-to-megyn-kelly.

4. Angela Moon, "President Trump says French first lady is in 'such good shape,'" https://www.reuters.com/article/us-france-usa-trump-brigitte-macron/president-trump-says-french-first-lady-is-in-such-good-shape-idUSKBN19Y2XT.

5. Jeva Lange, "61 things Donald Trump has said about women," https://theweek.com/articles/655770/61-things-donald-trump-said-about-women.

6. "Donald Trump On Angelina Jolie: 'She's Not Beauty,'" October 18, 2007; https://www.accessonline.com/articles/donald-trump-on-angelina-jolie-shes-not-beauty-61181#Ad42aQ17oGprOAmi.99

7. "Donald Trump On Angelina Jolie."

8. David A. Fahrenthold, "New clips show Trump talking about sex, rating women's bodies, reminiscing about infidelity on Howard Stern's show," https://www.washingtonpost.com/news/post-politics/wp/2016/10/14/new-clips-show-trump-talking-about-sex-rating-womens-bodies-reminiscing-about-infidelity-on-howard-stern-show/.

When asked if Kim Kardashian's butt is big: *"Well, absolutely. It's record-setting. In the old days, they'd say she has a bad body."*[9]

"Sadly, she's no longer a 10." (Referring to Heidi Klum)[10]

To a contestant on Trump's show, *The Apprentice*: *"It must be a pretty picture, you dropping to your knees."*[11]

"But you have to like freckles, I've seen a close-up of her chest. And a lot of freckles. Are you into freckles? . . . She's probably deeply troubled, and therefore great in bed. How come the deeply troubled women—deeply, deeply troubled—they're always the best in bed?" (Referring to Lindsey Lohan—she was eighteen years old at the time)[12]

"Now, somebody who a lot of people don't give credit to but in actuality is really beautiful is Paris Hilton. I've known Paris Hilton from the time she's twelve, her parents are friends of mine, and the first time I saw her she walked into the room and I said, 'Who the hell is that?'"[13]

When asked in a Howard Stern interview in 2005, if he'd stay with Melania if she was in a disfiguring car accident: *"How do the breasts look?"*[14]

9. Antoinette Bueno, "Donald Trump: Kim K. and J. Lo's Butts Are 'Absolutely' Too Big," https://www.etonline.com/news/147555_donald_trump_thinks_jennifer_lopez_and_kim_kardashian_butts_are_too_big

10. Antoinette Bueno, "Donald Trump Says Heidi Klum 'Is No Longer a 10'—See Her Amazing Response!," https://www.etonline.com/news/170120_donald_trump_disses_heidi_klum.

11. Associated Press, "Some of Donald Trump's most insulting comments about women," https://apnews.com/2eea389b1e5b49f8afb28c4a6d079b09/some-donald-trumps-most-insulting-comments-about-women

12. David A. Farenthold, "New clips show Trump talking about sex, rating women's bodies, reminiscing about infidelity on Howard Stern's show," https://www.washingtonpost.com/news/post-politics/wp/2016/10/14/new-clips-show-trump-talking-about-sex-rating-womens-bodies-reminiscing-about-infidelity-on-howard-stern-show/.

13. Marlow Stern, "Donald Trump's Craziest Interview Ever: 'Any Girl You Have, I Can Take From You,'" https://www.thedailybeast.com/donald-trumps-craziest-interview-ever-any-girl-you-have-i-can-take-from-you.

14. Marc Fisher, "More Trump tapes surface with crude sex remarks," https://www.washingtonpost.com/politics/more-trump-tapes-surface-with-crude-sex-remarks/2016/10/08/7129cea2-8d92-11e6-bff0-d53f592f176e_story.html.

When asked in 2006 by the ladies of *The View* how he would react if his then twenty-four-year-old daughter Ivanka posed for *Playboy*: *"I don't think Ivanka would do that, although she does have a very nice figure. I've said if Ivanka weren't my daughter, perhaps I'd be dating her."*[15]

"You know who's one of the great beauties of the world—according to everybody—and I helped create her? Ivanka. My daughter, Ivanka. She's six feet tall, she's got the best body." (Ivanka was twenty-one at the time.)[16]

"Yeah, she's really something, and what a beauty, that one. If I weren't happily married and, ya know, her father..." (Referring again to his daughter, Ivanka.)[17]

Referring to his then-infant daughter, Tiffany: *"Well, I think that she's got a lot of Marla,"* Trump said. *"She's a really beautiful baby, and she's got Marla's legs."* Trump then proceeded to motion to his chest and added, *"We don't know whether she's got this part yet, but time will tell."*[18]

After reading the sampling above of Trump's own words made in reference to various women, including his own daughters, even the most objective of people would have to admit to a disturbing trend of chronic objectification and sexualization of women (and girls). His comments indicate that he views himself as the self-appointed arbiter of beauty (as defined by his own personal standards). Women (and girls) are nothing more than the sum of their parts, created for the visual and physical consumption of men.

In the twelfth chapter of Matthew, Jesus warned that everyone will give account on the day of judgment for every word spoken. "For by your words you will be acquitted, and by your words you will be condemned" (Matthew 12:36–37). These are sobering verses that for most Christians, produce conviction followed by introspection and hopefully, repentance. While Trump has stated he has no sins he is aware of that require repentance, he will not escape judgment day. No amount of money will atone for his demeaning

15. Associated Press, "Trump jokes that he'd date daughter," https://www.today.com/popculture/trump-jokes-he-d-date-daughter-wbna11714379.

16. Stern, "Donald Trump's Craziest Interview Ever."

17. Paul Solotaroff, "Trump Seriously."

18. Ashley Collman, "The weird way Donald Trump talked about then-infant daughter Tiffany's future breasts is uncovered interview from 1994," https://www.dailymail.co.uk/news/article-3528887/Donald-Trump-talks-infant-daughter-Tiffany-s-breasts-uncovered-interview-1994.html.

words toward women (and others). On that day, he will be powerless. I pray for the president, but I pray for an awareness of his sin that illuminates his need for a merciful Savior. Only then will he experience true godly sorrow that leads to repentance and in turn, a changed heart. Unless that happens, we can expect the stream of vitriol from the fountain of Trump's heart to continue.

The Impact of Objectification

Objectification occurs when someone is treated as an object to be valued for its use by others.[19]

In a ground-breaking study in 2007, the American Psychological Association linked objectification to common mental health problems in women such as disordered eating, self-esteem, body image issues, and depression.[20]

Another study related to the effects of female objectification found that "women who are objectified are viewed as less than fully human, perceived to have less of a mind for thoughts or decisions and viewed as less deserving of moral treatment by others."[21]

Additional studies have found the denial of mental capacity can also be linked to other negative repercussions for objectified women, including increasing men's willingness to commit sexually aggressive actions towards them,[22] and decreasing perceived suffering in cases of sexual assault.[23] [24] [25]

19. Dawn M. Szymanski, Lauren B. Moffitt, and Erika R. Carr, "Sexual Objectification of Women: Advances to Theory and Research," *The Counseling Psychologist* 39 (1) 6–38, http://tcp.sagepub.com; https://www.apa.org/education/ce/sexual-objectification.pdf).

20. "Sexualization of Girls is Linked to Common Mental Health Problems in Girls and Women—Eating Disorders, Low Self-Esteem, and Depression; An APA Task Force Reports," https://www.apa.org/news/press/releases/2007/02/sexualization.

21. N. A. Heflick, J. L. Goldenberg, D. P. Cooper, and E. Puvia, "From women to objects: Appearance focus, target gender, and perceptions of warmth, morality and competence," *Journal of Experimental Social Psychology* 47 (3) (2011), 572–81.

22. K. R. Blake, B. Bastian, and T. F. Denson, "Perceptions of low agency and high sexual openness mediate the relationship between sexualization and sexual aggression," *Aggressive Behavior* 42 (5) (2016), 483–97.

23. S. Loughnan, N. Haslam, T. Murnane, J. Vaes, C. Reynolds, and C. Suitner, "Objectification leads to depersonalization: The denial of mind and moral concern to objectified others," *European Journal of Social Psychology* 40 (2010) 709–17.

24. S. Loughnan, A. Pina, E. A. Vasquez, and E. Puvia, "Sexual Objectification Increases Rape Victim Blame and Decreases Perceived Suffering," *Psychology of Women Quarterly* 37 (4) (2013), 455–61. 10.1177/0361684313485718.

25. C. Cogoni, A. Carnaghi, and G. Silani, "Reduced empathic responses for sexually objectified women: An fMRI investigation," *Cortex* 99 (2018), 258–72.

Objectification is a serious matter. Sexual assault, sexual abuse, rape, pornography, sex trafficking, and many other heinous crimes begin with objectification. When a person is denied personhood and viewed instead as an object, they are at risk of becoming someone's victim.

To date, Donald Trump has been accused of rape (including by his first wife, Ivana, who later dropped the charges), sexual assault, and sexual harassment by more than two dozen women.[26]

At some point, even the most objective of supporters would have to stop and consider, "Can *all* the women be lying?" I remember the moment news aired of Trump's 2005 *Access Hollywood* hot mic moment with host, Billy Bush. Standing in my living room, I was speechless as I listened to the Republican nominee for the highest office in the land describe a previous attempt to seduce a married woman.

Bragging to Bush, Trump says in the audio, *"I moved on her, and I failed. I'll admit it." "I did try and f*** her. She was married." "And I moved on her very heavily."*[27]

As I listened, my jaw literally dropped, "Wait, did he just describe a sexual assault?" If there was any doubt in my mind, his remarks that followed would answer my question. He and Bush were on their way to meet a woman who was part of the segment they were taping. *"I better use some Tic Tacs just in case I start kissing her. You know I'm automatically attracted to beautiful—I just start kissing them. It's like a magnet. Just kiss. I don't even wait. And when you're a star, they let you do it. You can do anything. Grab 'em by the pussy. You can do anything."*[28]

At the time the *Access Hollywood* audio tape released, it was about one month shy of the 2016 election. I naively assumed this would be the nail in the coffin and Trump's evangelical base would abandon him with this revelation. News that Melania was pregnant with their first child during the time Trump made the remarks certainly wouldn't help his case. I was obviously mistaken.

While Trump did issue a tepid apology for his comments on the *Access Hollywood* audio tape and chalked it up to "locker room talk,"[29] accusations

26. Eliza Relman, "The 25 women who have accused Trump of sexual misconduct," https://www.businessinsider.com/women-accused-trump-sexual-misconduct-list-2017-12.

27. David A. Fahrenthold, "Trump recorded having extremely lewd conversation about women in 2005," https://www.washingtonpost.com/politics/trump-recorded-having-extremely-lewd-conversation-about-women-in-2005/2016/10/07/3b9ce776-8cb4-11e6-bf8a-3d26847eeed4_story.html.

28. Fahrenthold, "Trump recorded."

29. Meghan Keneally, "What Trump previously said about the 2005 'Access

of his misogyny continued to swell in the months prior to the election. Over and over again, Trump defended himself by proclaiming his "respect" for women, including at a rally in Eugene, Oregon where he told the crowd, *"First of all, nobody respects women more than Donald Trump, I'll tell you. Nobody respects women more."*[30]

"Respect" can be defined as: "esteem for or a sense of the worth or excellence of a person."[31]

Does Donald Trump respect women? I'll let you be the judge.

Since being elected, more allegations and scandals have emerged, including a former *Playboy* model and an adult-film actress, both alleging affairs with Trump shortly after the *Access Hollywood* incident (during the time Melania was pregnant and a brand-new mother). He has denied the affairs, but Trump's personal lawyer Michael Cohen is serving a three-year sentence for crimes including tax evasion and campaign finance violations related to hush-money payments to keep the women quiet.[32]

As we consider the mounting evidence related to Trump's view of women, the words of the great poet Maya Angelou come to mind. "When someone shows you who they are, believe them the first time."[33]

Trump has left us with little doubt about who he is, and how he views women.

Excusing the Inexcusable

As I mentioned in the introduction of this essay, it is not my intent to sway your vote. Regardless of whether or not you support Trump, it is my sincerest desire to implore Christians to speak up about the dangers of objectifying women, even if the perpetrator is the president of the United States. To remain silent, or even worse, make excuses for his words and behavior, will send a dangerous message that objectification, allegations of sexual assault, and allegations of sexual abuse are not to be taken seriously. We cannot

---

Hollywood' tape that he's now questioning," https://abcnews.go.com/US/trump-previously-2005-access-hollywood-tape-now-questioning/story?id=51406745.

30. Gregory Krieg, "12 times Donald Trump declared his 'respect' for women," https://www.cnn.com/2016/10/07/politics/donald-trump-respect-women/index.html.

31. https://www.dictionary.com/browse/respect?s=t.

32. Joe Palazzolo, Nicole Hong, Michael Rothfeld, Rebecca Davis O'Brien, and Rebecca Ballhaus, "Donald Trump Played Central Role in Hush Payoffs to Stormy Daniels and Karen McDougal," https://www.wsj.com/articles/donald-trump-played-central-role-in-hush-payoffs-to-stormy-daniels-and-karen-mcdougal-1541786601.

33. "Maya Angelou Quotes," https://www.brainyquote.com/quotes/maya_angelou_383371.

shrug it off with a trite, "Boys will be boys," or in its graduated form, "Men will be men." (Sadly, the latter was uttered by Melania in defense of Trump's misogynistic remarks about her.)[34] Women have come too far to accept this mind-set as the norm any longer.

How can we with a straight face encourage the next generation of young men to value women based on their personhood, if we make excuses for a man with a rap sheet of offenses a mile long? Is it not confusing to young men to be taught in their churches and homes to honor, protect, and cherish women, but hear a deafening silence in response to Trump's low view of women by many of those same chivalry-promoting Christians? Just as we should stand against the objectification of women, we too, should stand against dangerous stereotypes that liken men to animals on the prowl, ruled primarily by raging hormones and uncontrollable impulses. This is an insult to principled men who exhibit great respect for women and value them for their personhood, rather than their collective parts.

It is imperative that Christians unite and begin the hard work of repairing the damage to the good name of Christianity. One way to do this is to simply be honest about the horrible dilemma Christians faced in 2016 and will face again, in 2020. If your personal convictions lead you to vote for Trump (or rather, the platform of the party), you can do so without supporting Trump, the person. You do not have to join the throngs of proud Trump supporters who are more concerned with showing allegiance to a political party than allegiance to the Christian faith. As Christians, we are called to a higher standard. A party or a platform cannot save us, so let us point to the only One who can.

Further, it is a damaging witness to the name of Christianity to defend Trump's anti-Christian words and actions. It is counter-productive to argue that you are not voting for "a pastor-in-chief, but a commander-in-chief,"[35] claim Trump is merely a "baby Christian,"[36] compare him to "a modern-day King Cyrus,"[37] or post the latest defense on social media to downplay Trump's misogyny (or other unbiblical actions). Just last week, a new defense

34. Caitlin Yilek, "'You're on your own with this one': Melania was livid with Trump over Access Hollywood tape," https://www.washingtonexaminer.com/news/youre-on-your-own-with-this-one-melania-was-livid-over-release-of-access-hollywood-tape.

35. "CNN's Anderson Cooper speaks with Jerry Falwell Jr., president of Liberty University about his endorsement of Donald Trump," https://www.youtube.com/watch?v=G42VEGGmliQ.

36. "Dr. James Dobson on Donald Trump's Christian Faith," http://drjamesdobson.org/news/dr-james-dobson-on-trumps-christian-faith.

37. Tara Isabella Burton, "Why evangelicals are calling Trump a 'modern-day Cyrus," https://www.vox.com/identities/2018/3/5/16796892/trump-cyrus-christian-right-bible-cbn-evangelical-propaganda.

showed up in my Facebook newsfeed that was written by a mother of a Navy Seal who is rallying women to vote for Trump. In her article, she attempted to downplay Trump's misogyny by comparing him to nothing more than "a salty sailor."[38]

I'm not making this up.

You cannot stand for moral decency and express outrage over the objectification of women if you are willing to give Trump a free pass. No one will respect your opinion. I recently watched an example of this play out on Twitter in the aftermath of the 2020 Super Bowl halftime show. Franklin Graham tweeted concern that Shakira and J. Lo's performance was "showing young girls that sexual exploitation of women is okay."[39]

I share much of Graham's sentiment, but many of his Twitter followers were quick to call him out on a double standard. One follower tweeted back: "It's worse than you think, sir. This exploitation of women reaches to the highest levels of government" and attached a full list of women who have accused Donald Trump of sexual assault.[40]

Another commenter tweeted, "Stay out of this conversation, kind sir. . . .You've said ZERO about this president's immorality so you don't get to talk about being disappointed in ANYTHING."[41]

Many others tweeted back to Graham with direct pull quotes of Trump's exploitive comments about women. A Christian pastor posted a blog about the blatant hypocrisy and called out not just Graham, but all Christians who expressed concerns about the Super Bowl halftime show, but have turned a blind eye to Trump's objectification of women. "Suddenly, in the span of ten minutes on Sunday they became concerned with the welfare of women and girls."[42]

The Franklin Graham Twitter exchange perfectly illustrates the larger-scale problem Christians face if they choose to ignore, minimize, or make excuses for Trump's misogyny (and other immoral offenses). No one will take Christianity seriously if we shout about the moral injustices of past presidents, but are struck dumb when it comes to the moral injustices of the current one. No one will respect Christian leaders who call on men to respect, honor, and cherish women if they fail to hold the president to the same standard. No one will hear our pleas for the unborn if, at the same

38. Karen Vaughn, "Letter: The salty sailor and the fireman," https://www.inforum.com/opinion/letters/4619057-Letter-The-salty-sailor-and-the-fireman.

39. twitter.com, https://twitter.com/Franklin_Graham/status/1224168046367072257.

40. twitter.com, https://twitter.com/TylerHuckabee/status/1224200535236075520.

41. twitter.com, https://twitter.com/RevMLTillerJr/status/1224342721961365511.

42. John Pavlovitz, "The Super Bowl of MAGA Hypocrisy," https://johnpavlovitz.com/2020/02/03/the-super-bowl-of-maga-hypocrisy/.

time, we ignore the devaluation of other marginalized populations outside of the womb. No one will respect our stand for traditional marriage if we are silent about the thrice-married adulterer in the White House. No one will see our Jesus if they can't see past our blind allegiance to a man who is nothing like him. I dare say we already find ourselves facing this situation. For the sake of the gospel and those we hope to convert, I beg you to consider the bigger picture in play.

Waking Up

As painful as it has been for women to witness and attempt to process Trump's misogyny, there has been a silver lining. A long and overdue conversation has begun. Something triggered in women in the aftermath of the election. Trump's brash and unashamed objectification of women, coupled with his lack of sorrow and repentance, thrust the issue of objectification into the spotlight, warts and all. The underbelly has been exposed for all to see and it cannot be unseen.

Objectification is not the real issue, but rather, a by-product of a much bigger problem. Trace it back to its origins and at the foundation you'll find a power structure that for centuries, has remained largely unchallenged. A structure where men make the rules and women are expected to follow along, without question. A structure where men are the consumers and women are the product. A structure where men are entitled to women and women are expected to comply. A structure where women are blamed for the lust of men. A structure that tells women to "go home" if they fail to adhere to their assigned roles.[43] A structure, that if challenged, will silence, shame, and blame anyone who dares to speak up.

For the first time, many women are beginning to connect the dots and see the damage that results when we excuse objectification as the norm. The cracks in the foundation have been exposed. Women are reading the fine print of this unspoken agreement that has been in place for centuries. And one by one, many are choosing to opt out. Unlike the generations of women that came before us, we have a choice. We don't have to remain silent any longer. The younger generation might refer to this as being "woke," but I think a more accurate term might be "waking up." Waking up can take a bit

---

43. "John MacArthur Told Beth Moore to 'Go Home' for Having the Audacity to Preach the Gospel and Help People," https://relevantmagazine.com/current16/john -macarthur-told-beth-moore-to-go-home-for-having-the-audacity-to-preach-the -gospel-and-help-people/.

longer for some than others, but let us rejoice that the long slumber is over and the great awakening has begun.

A manifestation of that "waking up" helped generate the #MeToo movement, and the #ChurchToo movement that followed in its wake. Though painful to watch, it has forced Christians to reexamine many of the patriarchal structures and attitudes in the church that have put Christian women at an increased risk of abuse. It has exposed churches and Christian leaders who silenced victims of sexual assault and/or sexual abuse in order to protect the men. Victims are slowly but surely emerging from the shadows of silence and shame to tell their stories. Because of their courage, many of us are learning what it means to be better listeners and certainly better responders. Many Christian men are recognizing their own misogynistic tendencies and repenting of their sins. They too, are waking up and reevaluating what it means to see women as fellow "image-bearers," made in the likeness of God (Genesis 1:27). George Bernard Shaw once said, "Progress is impossible without change, and those who cannot change their minds, cannot change anything."[44]

Rest assured, God is up to something. He is purging hearts and minds of dangerous attitudes that have no place in his kingdom. I know this because he is in the process of doing so in my own life. I too, am waking up. I am not the same person I was prior to the 2016 election. I have spoken with countless other Christian women and men, including many of my own family members, who like me, are also waking up.

And therein lies the hope. For where there is Christ and his life-changing gospel, there is always hope.

---

44. "George Bernard Shaw Quotes," https://www.brainyquote.com/quotes/george _bernard_shaw_386923.

Chapter 4

Race-Baiter, Misogynist, and Fool

Napp Nazworth

Most white evangelicals backed President Donald Trump in the 2016 election and their support has been rewarded. Evangelical leaders have access to the White House and Trump's court picks have been a solid victory. Politics is transactional. Trump made promises to evangelicals in exchange for their support and he has kept some of those promises.

There is nothing inherently wrong with this type of horse trading. Democracy would be impossible without the deal making and compromises necessary to reach a majority consensus. The problem with making a deal with Trump wasn't that evangelicals shouldn't engage in politics. The problem was who they made a deal with, and the way in which they justified that deal.

Trump's low moral character and inexperience isn't the main issue. We've had presidents who were unqualified or of low moral character before. What makes Trump particularly dangerous for evangelicals was the manner in which he campaigned for our vote. He promised to be our protector and to make us successful by filling our pews. Trump's promises to evangelicals were similar to Satan's offer to Jesus. While tempting Jesus in the desert, the Bible tells us, "the devil took him to a very high mountain and showed him all the kingdoms of the world and their splendor; and he said to him, 'All these I will give you, if you will fall down and worship me.'" I'm not saying Trump is the antichrist. It is Trump's and Satan's use of similar methods that should concern us.

Christians already have a protector and his name isn't Trump. Even as president, Trump has no power to protect us from our enemies because our enemies are not of this world. Ephesians 6:12 tells us, "For our struggle is not against enemies of blood and flesh, but against the rulers, against the authorities, against the cosmic powers of this present darkness, against the spiritual forces of evil in the heavenly places." So, when Trump promised evangelicals protection if they voted for him, it was a ruse and many evangelicals fell for it.

The knowledge and views contained here come from four of my life experiences: faith, politics, education, and family. I'm a theologically conservative evangelical Christian. This is written from the viewpoint of one evangelical speaking to his fellow evangelicals. I'm also a political conservative and a pre-Trump Republican. I've never voted for a Democrat. I've spent most of my life studying the intersection of religion and politics in the field of political science. My maternal grandfather was a farmer and my paternal grandfather was a police detective. I come from working-class stock, which is to say, Trump supporters are my family, people I know and love.

The Bible doesn't provide specific guidance on who to vote for or what policies to support. Instead, it provides foundational principles. How to apply those principles is debatable, and those debates should happen, but in a loving manner that honors Christ. Christian growth happens in community. We should debate political issues through our communities, and if we're doing that well, the way we contribute to public life through our democratic processes will improve. Consider this essay a contribution to those discussions.

The main problem with evangelical support for Trump isn't what happened on Election Day, it's the defenses of Trump. In deciding to vote for Trump, many evangelical Trump supporters didn't just pull the lever for him to prevent a Hillary Clinton presidency, they helped elect him by defending his unscrupulous behaviors, and that pattern has only worsened ahead of the 2020 election. I will focus on two examples—his race-baiting and misogyny. Then I argue we should avoid associating with Trump based upon what the Bible teaches about associating with fools.

"I have a great relationship with the blacks"

Trump's evangelical supporters should confront these three disturbing facts: 1) Only white evangelicals voted for Trump in high numbers; 2) Racists, like the alt-right movement, supported Trump and have been energized by his presidency; 3) Trump mobilized racist sentiments in his campaign.

Trump has denounced racism and racist groups, but only when pushed to do so. In other ways, Trump sends messages that racists like to hear. Before he ever became a candidate for president, his most well-known political act was to promote the "birther" conspiracy, the notion that President Barack Obama wasn't really born in the United States. Being a birther doesn't necessarily mean you're a racist, but racists were more attuned to the birther conspiracy because it reinforced the notion, in their minds, that the first black president wasn't "one of us."

Trump's central campaign features—building a wall on the southern border and "America first"—is appealing to racists. Trump's campaign slogan, "Make America Great Again," was designed to appeal to white people. When was America previously great? I'm sure the 1950s seem like a pleasant period to return to if you're white. If you're black, that would be a return to lynchings and Jim Crow. This doesn't mean that everyone who liked those platforms is racist, but racists did find them appealing. It's the reason racists endorsed him.

Trump purposely used the tribalism of white people and the fear of nonwhite people to mobilize voters. A January 2019 study[1] found a spike (from the end of 2016 through 2017) in hate crimes in the counties that strongly supported Trump. By aggravating the racist impulses of many voters, Trump brought out the worst of our natures. He bred divisiveness and hatred. Racist groups have been emboldened by the election of Trump.

In mid-March, 2017, white supremacist groups gathered in Charlottesville, Virginia, to protest the removal of a Confederate statue. The protests turned violent. One person was killed and several more were injured when one of the protesters drove his car into a crowd of counter-protesters.

The day of the protest, Trump made a public statement. Presidents often make speeches in times of unrest, to try to ease the tension. Trump, however, didn't at the time denounce the protesters by name, instead declaring there was violence on "many sides."

Trump is correct, of course, in noting that there had been violence from the left as well. Recall, for instance, riots in Ferguson and Baltimore, or campus protests at Berkeley and Middlebury. In July, 2016, Micah Johnson, a Black Lives Matter sympathizer, shot and killed five police officers in Houston. On the day of Trump's inauguration, rioters injured police and destroyed property in downtown DC.

The problem with the "many sides" comment wasn't that it wasn't true, it was the context in which he said it. That Trump failed to explicitly call out

1. Griffin Sims and Stephen Rushin, "The Effect of President Trump's Election on Hate Crimes," https://ssrn.com/abstract=3102652.

the racists by name—white supremacists, neo-Nazis, and the alt-right— was a failure of moral leadership.

Trump's evangelical supporters, meanwhile, were mostly supportive or silent. "Finally a leader in WH. Jobs returning, N Korea backing down, bold truthful stmt about #charlottesville tragedy. So proud of @realdonaldtrump," Jerry Falwell Jr. tweeted.

Trump doesn't normally have a problem condemning people or groups he doesn't like. He often lashes out, for instance, at the media and Democrats. He called his Republican opponents "human scum."[2]

Why then, does he find it so difficult to strongly condemn racists?

Contrast Trump's statements on Charlottesville with his response to NFL player protests during the national anthem. "Wouldn't you love to see one of these NFL owners, when somebody disrespects our flag, to say 'get that son of a bitch off the field right now. Out! He's fired! He's fired!'" Trump said at a September 22, 2017 rally in Alabama.

During the Charlottesville protests, Trump saw nuance—there was violence on "many sides," there was "blame on both sides," and there were "many fine people" among the neo-Nazis. Trump could've handled the Anthem protests with nuance by saying, for instance, that the protesters have some legitimate concerns but they're going about it the wrong way. Instead, Trump saw the issue in black and white—the "son of a bitch" should be fired, fans should boycott if owners don't comply. Trump's clear, decisive rejection of disrespecting the National Anthem as a form of protest was the type of response he should've given to the Charlottesville racists. In that context, he would have united the vast majority of the country. In the NFL context, he divided the country.

Racial and ethnic divisions break down at the foot of the cross. After Jesus said the second greatest commandment is to love your neighbor as yourself, he was asked, "Who is my neighbor?" To answer the question, Jesus told the parable of the Good Samaritan, one of the most familiar passages in the Bible.

A priest and a Levite both passed by a robbed and beaten man on the side of a road. Instead of a Jew, Jesus makes a Samaritan, a hated enemy of the Jews, the hero of his story. In taking care of the man, the Samaritan behaved as a neighbor.

---

2. @realDonaldTrump, "The Never Trumper Republicans, though on respirators with not many left, are in certain ways worse and more dangerous for our Country than the Do-Nothing Democrats. Watch out for them, they are human scum!," https://twitter.com/realdonaldtrump/status/1187063301731209220.

"Which of these three, do you think, was a neighbor to the man who fell into the hands of the robbers?" Jesus asked the questioner. "The one who showed him mercy," was the questioner's reply.

Jesus then responded with the lesson of the parable, the lesson for all of us—be like the Samaritan, who didn't think in tribal terms but just saw a fellow human in need—"Go and do likewise."

When there were divisions in the churches in Galatia over ethnic, class, and gender differences, Paul delivered a similar message. "There is no longer Jew or Greek, there is no longer slave or free, there is no longer male and female; for all of you are one in Christ Jesus," he wrote (Galatians 3:28).

The election of Trump illustrates the need for white evangelicals to seek to understand our nonwhite brothers and sisters. Too often, attempts at racial reconciliation carry a tone of "let's bring nonwhites into the white churches," as if white churches should be considered the norm. That tone can be seen in reactions to the election race gap as well, as if the solution is for nonwhite Christians to become Republican. Instead, evangelicals need to build a church that is "neither Jew nor Greek," and challenge racial and ethnic bigotries wherever they exist, regardless of electoral consequences.

During the height of the civil rights movement in the 1950s and '60s, most white evangelical churches were either silent or on the wrong side. Six decades later, evangelicals are still struggling with the consequences of those choices. Most would say they regret what happened.

Without a significant shift in approach to Trump, our evangelical descendants will look back on this period with the same feelings of regret. White evangelicals will be known as the people who defended the guy who defended the neo-Nazis.

"Grab 'em by the pussy"

The *Access Hollywood* tape showing Trump brag about assaulting women sent a shock wave through the evangelical community. It shouldn't have shocked anyone, however, given the way Trump had demeaned women in other widely available interviews, especially with "shock jock" Howard Stern. In his own books even, he bragged about his sexual conquests.

After the tape was released, ten women came forward and accused Trump of doing what he bragged about doing—groping or kissing them without their consent. Another said he offered her $10,000 to have sex with him. (Since then, the list has grown to at least twenty-three accusers.)[3]

3. Meghan Keneally, "List of Trump's accusers and their allegations of sexual misconduct," https://abcnews.go.com/Politics/list-trumps-accusers-allegations-sexual

I'll grant the possibility that during a presidential campaign some may falsely accuse candidates to score a political hit. But are we to distrust all of them after Trump was heard bragging about doing the very thing he's accused of doing?

"Women, you have to treat them like shit," Trump said in a 1992 *New York* magazine interview. Evidence suggests he has maintained that philosophy.

In *TrumpNation: The Art of Being the Donald* (2005), Trump wrote, "My favorite part [of the film *Pulp Fiction*] is when Sam has his gun out in the diner and he tells the guy to tell his girlfriend to shut up. 'Tell that bitch to be cool. Say: Bitch be cool.' I love those lines."

To Trump, a woman's worth is in direct proportion to her physical beauty. "You know, it really doesn't matter what they write as long as you've got a young and beautiful piece of ass. But she's got to be young and beautiful," he said in a 1991 *Esquire* interview.

In the days following release of the *Access Hollywood* tape, evangelical leaders supporting Trump were asked to respond. The rest of the nation wondered, what will the evangelicals say now? Evangelical leaders were given a platform and an opportunity to speak to an important moral issue of the day—a situation they usually crave. It was also a test. Does morality matter for politicians, as evangelicals' leaders have long argued, or does raw partisan politics trump the dignity of women? Most of Trump's evangelical supporters failed the test.

Taking their cue from Trump himself, the Trump evangelicals repeated the talking point that Trump's abusive language was "just locker room banter," it happened a long time ago, and it had no bearing on the election. For other evangelicals, especially women, the unwillingness of these evangelical leaders to denounce misogyny in furtherance of a political goal revealed old wounds.

"I honestly don't know what makes me more sick. Listening to Trump brag about groping women or listening to my fellow evangelicals defend him," wrote evangelical journalist and radio talk show host Julie Roys.[4]

Popular evangelist Beth Moore similarly responded via Twitter, "Try to absorb how acceptable the disesteem and objectifying of women has been when some Christian leaders don't think it's a big deal . . . Wake up, Sleepers,

---

-misconduct/story?id=51956410.

4. Julie Roys, "Defeating Hillary is Not Worth Sacrificing Our Witness," https://julieroys.com/defeating-hillary-not-worth-sacrificing-witness/.

to what women have dealt with all along in environments of gross entitle-
ment & power. Are we sickened? Yes. Are we surprised? NO."[5]

Trump treats women the way Roman culture treated them at the time
of Jesus—as property, objectified and ridiculed. We see in Gospel stories
Jesus' radical approach to treating women with honor and respect.

When Jesus encounters a Samaritan woman at a well, he asks her for
a drink (John 4). Just speaking to her was considered inappropriate for his
day, the Gospel account tells us in verse 9. "The Samaritan woman said to
him, 'How is it that you, a Jew, ask a drink of me, a woman of Samaria?'
(Jews do not share things in common with Samaritans.)" And verse 27 says
the disciples "were astonished that he was speaking with a woman."

But it wasn't just the act of speaking to a woman, it was what Jesus told
her that was also counter-cultural. Jesus shared the truth of the gospel, his
truth, the same truth that his disciples had, at this point, difficulty grasping.

"Everyone who drinks of this water will be thirsty again, but those who
drink of the water that I will give them will never be thirsty. The water that
I will give will become in them a spring of water gushing up to eternal life.
. . . ," Jesus told her.

"I know that Messiah is coming," the woman responded. "When he
comes, he will proclaim all things to us."

Jesus replied, "I am he, the one who is speaking to you."

In that short conversation, the woman embraced Jesus' message and
became an evangelist. "Then the woman left her water jar and went back to
the city. She said to the people, 'Come and see a man who told me everything I have ever done! He cannot be the Messiah, can he?' They left the city
and were on their way to him" (vv. 28–30).

Christians should apply the same shock treatment to Trump that Jesus
did to Roman culture. If Christians are to be counter-cultural, and show
that the way of Christ is better than the way of prevailing culture, they must
stand up for the dignity of women, regardless of the worldly, short-term
electoral consequences that may come. Honoring women trumps electing
Trump.

---

5. @BethMooreLPM, "Try to absorb how acceptable the disesteem and objectifying
of women has been when some Christian leaders don't think it's a big deal . . . Wake
up, Sleepers, to what women have dealt with all along in environments of gross en-
titlement & power. Are we sickened? Yes. Are we surprised? NO," https://twitter.com/
BethMooreLPM/status/785126388776873985.

"Sorry losers and haters, but my I.Q. is one of the highest —and you all know it! Please don't feel so stupid or insecure, it's not your fault"

Trump is a fool. That sounds like a slur, but in the Bible, "fool" has a specific meaning that applies to how we should relate to Trump. Two things we know about Trump is that he boasts about himself often and he doesn't seek the counsel of others. Trump is the very biblical definition of a fool.

Translated from the Hebrew *ewil*, a fool is the opposite of one who is wise. "Wisdom is at home in the mind of one who has understanding, but it is not known in the heart of fools" (Proverbs 14:33). Those who think of themselves as wise are even worse off than a fool. "Do you see persons wise in their own eyes? There is more hope for fools than for them" (Proverbs 26:12).

Trump often lashes out in anger when insulted. A fool "show(s) their anger at once, but the prudent ignore an insult" (Proverbs 12:16). A fool is "quick to quarrel" (Proverbs 20:3) and "gives full vent to anger, but the wise quietly holds it back" (Proverbs 29:11).

Trump doesn't read.[6]

His foreign policy knowledge comes from watching "the shows."[7]

The counsel he seeks is to talk to himself.[8]

Fools don't listen to advice. "Fools think their own way is right, but the wise listen to advice" (Proverbs 12:15). "A rebuke strikes deeper into a discerning person than a hundred blows into a fool" (Proverbs 17:10).

Trump does delight, however, in sharing his opinions on Twitter. A fool "takes no pleasure in understanding, but only in expressing personal opinion" (Proverbs 18:2). Fools show that they are fools by what comes out of their mouths. "The mind of one who has understanding seeks knowledge, but the mouths of fools feed on folly" (Proverbs 15:14). "The mouths of fools are their ruin, and their lips a snare to themselves" (Proverbs 18:7). "For fools speak folly, and their minds plot iniquity: to practice ungodliness, to utter error concerning the Lord, to leave the craving of the hungry unsatisfied, and to deprive the thirsty of drink" (Isaiah 32:6). "The words of their mouths begin in foolishness, and their talk ends in wicked madness; yet fools talk on and on" (Ecclesiastes 10:13–14).

6. David A. Graham, "The President Who Doesn't Read: Trump's allergy to the written word and his reliance on oral communication have proven liabilities in office," *The Atlantic*, January 5, 2018, https://www.theatlantic.com/politics/archive/2018/01/-americas-first-post-text-president/549794/.

7. Interview, NBC, "Meet the Press," August 16, 2015.

8. Interview, MSNBC, "Morning Joe," March 16, 2016.

The Bible shows particular concern about fools who are wealthy or in positions of authority. Trump is both. "Better is a poor but wise youth than an old but foolish king, who will no longer take advice" (Ecclesiastes 4:13). "It is not fitting for a fool to live in luxury . . ." (Proverbs 19:10). And in Luke 12, Jesus shares a parable about a rich fool. It doesn't end well.

Given that Trump is a fool, in the biblical sense, how should we relate to him?

Regarding fools, the Bible says: 1) Don't speak to them. "Do not speak in the hearing of a fool, who will only despise the wisdom of your words" (Proverbs 23:9); 2) Don't hang out with them. "Leave the presence of a fool, for there you do not find words of knowledge" (Proverbs 14:7); 3) Don't deliver their messages. "It is like cutting off one's foot and drinking down violence, to send a message by a fool" (Proverbs 26:6). And don't honor them. "It is like binding a stone in a sling to give honor to a fool" (Proverbs 26:8). Trump's evangelical supporters have done all four of those.

The Bible also uses the word *fool* in another way. This second type of fool can be one who upends the wisdom of this world, who turns weakness into strength, who makes the lowly powerful, who flips the script on all we thought we knew. In this sense of the word, God is the greatest fool of all.

In his first letter to the church in Corinth, the Apostle Paul wrote about being a fool in this second sense.

"For Christ did not send me to baptize, but to preach the gospel—not with wisdom and eloquence, lest the cross of Christ be emptied of its power. For the message of the cross is foolishness to those who are perishing, but to us who are being saved it is the power of God. For it is written: 'I will destroy the wisdom of the wise; the intelligence of the intelligent I will frustrate'" (17–19).

Later in the letter, Paul refers to himself and the other apostles as "fools for the sake of Christ" (4:10). He's not saying that he's an actual fool, in the first sense of the word, but that he's willing to appear to be a fool to the world for the sake of Christ. To the "wise" of this world, Paul is saying, the message of the cross—that Jesus paid the price of our sin through his death so that we might enjoy eternal life with our creator—is foolish. Indeed, Paul continues, the cross demonstrates the "foolishness of God."

> Where is the wise person? Where is the teacher of the law? Where is the philosopher of this age? Has not God made foolish the wisdom of the world? For since in the wisdom of God the world through its wisdom did not know him, God was pleased through the foolishness of what was preached to save those who believe. Jews demand signs and Greeks look for wisdom, but we

preach Christ crucified: a stumbling block to Jews and foolishness to Gentiles, but to those whom God has called, both Jews and Greeks, Christ the power of God and the wisdom of God. For the foolishness of God is wiser than human wisdom, and the weakness of God is stronger than human strength. (20–25)

Among the mistakes of evangelical Trump supporters was a failure of imagination. Obedience to God often means taking actions that don't make sense to the wisdom of this world, but human ways won't achieve God's goals. Electioneering methods can win political contests but work against advancing the kingdom of God here on earth when those methods lead Christians to abandon biblical principles.

Instead of electing a fool in the first sense, Christians should be a fool in the second sense. "Fools for Christ" turn worldly wisdom on its head and proclaim the gospel to the world.

Chapter 5

Humility, Pride, and the Presidency
of Donald Trump

Michael Austin

There are many topics about which Donald Trump is a self-proclaimed expert. In fact, according to Donald Trump, there are many things that Donald Trump knows more about than *anyone*:[1]

"I know more about courts than any human being on earth."

"I know more about drones than anybody."

"I think nobody knows more about campaign finance than I do."

"Who knows more about lawsuits than I do? I'm the king."

"I understand politicians better than anybody."

"Nobody knows more about trade than me."

"I know more about renewables than any human being on Earth."

"I think nobody knows more about taxes than I do, maybe in the history of the world."

"I'm the king of debt. I'm great with debt. Nobody knows debt better than me."

"I understand money better than anybody."

1. https://www.axios.com/everything-trump-says-he-knows-more-about-than -anybody-b278b592-cff0-47dc-a75f-5767f42bcf1e.html.

42

"Nobody knows more about construction than I do."

"Technology—nobody knows more about technology than me."

And this is just a partial list. According to him, President Trump is also an expert on television ratings, ISIS, social media, the US infrastructure, the visa system in America, Democrats, Senator Cory Booker, and the economy. It's a remarkably wide-ranging list of self-proclaimed expertise, and it is, of course, false. More troubling is the lack of humility it reveals.

Certainly, all of us, including all forty-five presidents, have our shortcomings related to humility. Yet it appears that President Trump has a serious character defect here. Given the power and influence he has as the president of the United States, this is a serious problem. Humility is a central virtue for leaders, because it restrains the ego, undermines the vice of pride, and sets the stage for many other virtues. A lack of humility in any person, especially a person of power, should never be taken lightly. This is especially true for those of us who follow Jesus, the paradigm example of humility.

Soon after the election, I had a conversation with a fellow evangelical Christian who believed that Trump would change. He thought that as Trump felt the weight of responsibility that goes along with the presidency, he would rise to the expectations of the office. Unfortunately, there is little to no evidence that this has happened. In fact, there is much evidence to the contrary. For his sake, and for the sake of our country, I hoped at the beginning of his presidency that whatever better angels are present in his character would begin to have more say. But over the past four years, the strength of that hope has greatly diminished. Honestly, it has almost been extinguished. This is in great part due to the apparent lack of humility that Trump possesses, in conjunction to the influence of pride in his life.

As Christians, we look to Jesus to understand humility. We also look to him to help us be humble. A study of the Scriptures, with a focus on Jesus, tells us much about the nature of this virtue.[2] For example, consider Paul's words about the humility of Christ in his letter to the Philippians:

> Do nothing from selfish ambition or conceit, but in humility regard others as better than yourselves. Let each of you look not to your own interests, but to the interests of others. Let the same mind be in you that was in Christ Jesus, who, though he was in the form of God, did not regard equality with God as something to be exploited, but emptied himself, taking the form of a slave, being born in human likeness. And being found in human

---

2. Michael W. Austin, *Humility and Human Flourishing* (New York: Oxford University Press, 2018), chapter 2.

form, he humbled himself and became obedient to the point of
death—even death on a cross. (Philippians 2:3–8)

From this and other passages of Scripture, we can see several things about
the humble person. Such a person takes the interests and needs of others to
be more important than his own. He also understands and appreciates his
own limitations and flaws. This includes the limits we all possess as human
beings, as well as his own unique flaws as an individual. The humble person
is not concerned with honor or status. He also is willing to make sacrifices,
even at great personal cost, for the good of others. We see such humility in
the life of Jesus. As Christians, we long to exemplify it in our own lives as
well.

Plainly put, Donald Trump does not exemplify much, if any, of the
virtue of humility. He seems captive in many ways to the vice of pride. Much
of what he says and does shows a severe lack of humility, as well as the consistent and powerful influence of pride. He said early in his campaign that
he sees no need to ask for forgiveness from God. In the years since, I'm not
aware of Trump undergoing a change of mind on this, expressing a godly
sorrow that leads to repentance.

It can be dangerous to criticize the character of anyone, especially as a
follower of Jesus. As Christians, we are aware that we all fall short of God's
perfect and loving moral character. We all do things that we shouldn't do,
and we fail to do things that we ought to do. The more we grow in our faith,
the more aware we become of our moral and spiritual shortcomings. We
learn that pride is a dangerous and deceptive vice, and that we must be wary
of it in our own hearts and lives.

Making judgments about the character of others can be very difficult,
given the fact that we cannot see into their hearts. We are warned to focus
on ourselves, and that the manner in which we judge others will be applied to us in some sense as well (see Matthew 7:1–5). But we do need to
make at least preliminary judgments about the character of others, without
condemning them. We must judge whether or not others have integrity, for
example, to make our way in the world. If a physician, nurse, teacher, or
banker behaves in dishonest ways, then reason and logic require that I take
this into account. As Jesus teaches us, "By their fruits you will know them"
(Matthew 7:16). In Luke 6:43–45, Jesus explains this truth in more detail:

No good tree bears bad fruit, nor does a bad tree bear good fruit.
Each tree is recognized by its own fruit. People do not pick figs
from thorn bushes, or grapes from briers. A good man brings
good things out of the good stored up in his heart, and an evil

man brings evil things out of the evil stored up in his heart. For the mouth speaks what the heart is full of.

This applies to our political leaders, including our current president. If he displays behavior that seems to be the fruit of a particular vice, then we have good reason for thinking that he possesses that vice, at least to a degree.

Of course, we should spend more time thinking through and seeking to correct our own character flaws. Yet when someone holds power over others, it would be irresponsible to ignore evidence of a flawed character. In light of this, consider an ancient Christian commentary on the prideful person:

> He must either talk or burst . . . He hungers and thirsts after hearers, to whom he may vaunt his vanities, to whom he may pour forth all his feelings, to whom his character and greatness may become known . . . Opinions fly around, weighty words resound. He interrupts a questioner, he answers one who does not ask. He himself puts the questions, he himself solves them, he cuts short his fellow speaker's unfinished words . . . He does not care to teach you, or to learn from you what he does not know, but to know that you know that he knows.[3]

A viewing of just one press conference[4] provides evidence of these dispositions in Trump, as does his behavior during the campaign and his term in office, the manner in which he conducts his rallies, not to mention his Twitter feed. It does not make me happy to say this. As an American, I want every president to succeed. As a Christian, I want all people to know and experience the love of God in its fullness, and be transformed by his grace.

The problem is that the vice of pride has the potential to hinder not only Trump's success in office, but the well-being of many in this nation and around the world. This is why character, especially the character of leaders, is so important. It can impact others in deep and lasting ways, for better or worse.

We have never had a perfect president, and we never will. But there are minimum moral standards one must meet to exercise power responsibly. We place great trust in the person who holds the office of the president. Godly wisdom dictates that all who hold the office be worthy of that trust. Sadly, the lack of humility and expansive presence of pride in the words

3. Bernard of Clairvaux, *The Steps of Humility* (Cambridge: Cambridge University Press, 1940), 205.

4. https://www.nytimes.com/2017/02/16/us/politics/donald-trump-press-conference-transcript.html?_r=0.

and deeds of Donald Trump make him unqualified to be president of the United States of America. He should not be given four more years to hold the highest political office in our land. Christians who ignore this not only undermine the present and future good of the nation, but also their witness to the gospel of Jesus Christ.

Chapter 6

The Trump Brand and the Mocking of Christian Values

Irene Fowler

MANY ARDENT, VOCIFEROUS TRUMP SUPPORTERS ARE LEADING FIGURES within the evangelical movement. They are quick to claim that Trump is a Christian who shares their core values as followers of Christ and are just as quick to criticize those who would dare to suggest otherwise. We must avoid arrogance in commenting on this situation but at this time speak honestly.

The Apostle Paul said: "I bear on my body the brand-marks of Jesus" (Galatians 6:17, NASB). As someone who prides himself on being a branding guru, Trump is fully cognizant of the importance of gaining and effectively representing the imprimatur of a brand. He however fails dismally to live by basic Christian values, and, sadly, his actions are antithetical to the tenets of the faith, if not an outright mockery.

Trump has certainly weighed in on this issue, proudly proclaiming he has a "very great relationship with God."[1]

One might seriously question what "a very great relationship with God" means given that Trump has been married three times,[2] been accused

---

1. https://www.independent.co.uk/news/world/americas/donald-trump-says-he
-has-a-great-relationship-with-god-a6818011.html.

2. https://www.metro.us/president-trump/how-many-times-has-donald-trump
-been-married.

by more than two dozen women of being a serial sexual assaulter,[3] cheated on all of his wives,[4] been sued dozens of times for not paying vendors,[5] forced to shut down his self-dealing charity for misappropriation of funds,[6] ordered to pay twenty-five million dollars to former students of Trump University after a judge determined it was a sham,[7] called the twenty-five or so women who have accused him of sexual assault "liars,"[8] and was impeached for shaking down a foreign country for dirt on a political rival.[9]

How can anyone say with a straight face he or she has a great relationship with God when they live their lives in such a godless manner? Trump may think he has a great relationship with God, but one can genuinely question if God thinks he has a great relationship with Trump.

This is a different issue from whether or not Trump is a Christian. Only God truly knows who his "sheep" are (John 10:14), and it would be wrong to weigh in on Trump's spiritual status with Christ as to whether or not he is a true follower. At the same time, the Bible provides a number of markers for discerning whether or not a person holds to the core values of Christianity. If a man or a woman does not cling to these values in how they live their life, they are not going to be able to run the country very well and are certainly not worthy of our vote.

What Are the Core Values of Christianity?

It would take volumes to adequately examine the core values of Christianity. Here, I want to explore what seem to be some of the most important values that a follower of Christ tries to adhere to in how they live their lives.

Humbly aware of your sins and the need for forgiveness. One of the most important values of Christianity is humble awareness of your sins and

3. https://www.independent.co.uk/news/world/americas/us-politics/trump-sexual-assault-allegations-all-list-misconduct-karen-johnson-how-many-a9149216.html.

4. https://www.newsweek.com/how-many-times-trump-cheated-wives-780550.

5. https://www.foxnews.com/politics/dozens-of-lawsuits-accuse-trump-of-not-paying-his-bills-reports-claim.

6. https://www.washingtonpost.com/politics/trump-agrees-to-shut-down-his-charity-amid-allegations-he-used-it-for-personal-and-political-benefit/2018/12/18/dd3f5030-021b-11e9-9122-82e98f91ee6f_story.html.

7. https://www.cnn.com/2018/04/10/politics/trump-university-settlement-finalized-trnd/index.html.

8. https://www.nytimes.com/2016/10/15/us/politics/donald-trump-campaign.html.

9. https://slate.com/news-and-politics/2019/11/trump-impeachment-ukraine-guide-evidence.html.

need for forgiveness. First John 1:8 says, "If we claim to be without sin, we deceive ourselves and the truth is not in us." If any of us is arrogant enough to believe we don't sin, or don't commit significant sins, we are deluding ourselves and not practicing humility before Christ.

Hunger and thirst for righteousness. Close on the heels of becoming more aware of our fallen moral state before God, Christians have a renewed desire for personal righteousness after their conversion to Christ. In the Sermon on the Mount, Christ said, "Blessed are those who hunger and thirst for righteousness" (Matthew 5:6). Being "born again" re-energizes our desire to live life in a morally healthy manner.

Love God and not the things of this world. We all struggle with what St. Augustine called "disordered love," loving people and things more than we love God. First John 2:15 says, "Do not love the world or anything in the world. If anyone loves the world, love for the Father is not in them." True followers of Christ *strive* to comply with Jesus' command, "Love the Lord your God with all your heart and with all your soul and with all your mind" (Matthew 22:37).

Love others. Another core value in Christianity is to love our fellow human beings. Jesus made the issue of loving others central to whether or not a person is one of his followers, saying, "A new command I give you: Love one another. As I have loved you, so you must love one another" (John 13:34). If you are frequently mean and cruel to others, you are not living out one of the most important core values of Christianity.

Glorify God, not yourself. Isaiah 42:8 says, "I am the LORD; that is my name! I will not yield my glory to another or my praise to idols." Another core value of Christianity is that Christ must increase and we must decrease. (John 3:30). All that we do is to glorify God and not ourselves.

Care for the hurting and oppressed. The true follower of Christ has a heart for the down and out. They are focused on how they can help a suffering world be better off, not themselves. James 1:27 says, "Religion that God our Father accepts as pure and faultless is this: to look after orphans and widows in their distress and to keep oneself from being polluted by the world." In a me-me-me world, Christians are committed to living out the core value of helping those who are suffering and in need.

Dedicated to truth. The enemy is a liar and the father of lies, and it is his native tongue to speak lies (John 8:44). A core value in Christianity is that you tell the truth. You are never supposed to lie to others in what you say, even if the truth comes back negatively on you and there are consequences to be endured. Christ always spoke truth when he interacted with others, and he wants his followers to do the same.

The Core Values of Christianity and Trump

Christ was clear that we must take the plank out of our own eye before we presume to judge the speck in another person's eye (Matthew 7:5). That is no easy task. All of us, certainly me included, would all be wise to practice this command from the Lord before we ever turn our gaze elsewhere and judge another person by their actions. But given that Trump is the president of the United States and claims to be a follower of Christ, it is biblically appropriate to judge his observable actions in an effort to honestly assess whether or not he fundamentally lives his life by the core values of Christianity.

Is Trump aware of his sins and the need for forgiveness? Trump said in an interview with CNN's Anderson Cooper, "I go to communion and that's asking forgiveness, you know, it's a form of asking forgiveness." He went on to say he "likes to work where he doesn't have to ask forgiveness," "I try not to make mistakes where I have to ask forgiveness," "I think repenting is terrific," and "Why do I have to repent or ask for forgiveness, if I am not making mistakes?"[10]

Does that suggest someone who is aware of his sinfulness and the need for God's grace and forgiveness?

Does Trump hunger and thirst for righteousness? Trump not only doesn't ever talk about needing to work on any character flaws or defects: displaying one of the markers of being a narcissist, he defensively doubles down when challenged about the wrong things he does. As one example, examine the phone call he made to President Zelensky of Ukraine. People on both sides of the aisle had more than a few problems with what Trump did in trying to get dirt from a foreign country on a potential political opponent. Yet, to hear Trump talk about it, the phone call was "perfect" and he did absolutely nothing wrong in making it.[11]

Is that the attitude of someone hungering and thirsting after righteousness?

Does Trump love God more than the things of this world? Trump, through his actions over many decades, has made it clear he can never have enough money, power, or sex. Trump said greed is a good thing,[12] not-so-jokingly kidded about staying in office much longer than the law

10. https://www.cnn.com/2015/07/18/politics/trump-has-never-sought-forgiveness/index.html.

11. https://www.nbcnews.com/politics/donald-trump/trump-goes-tweet-offensive-about-whistleblower-his-perfect-call-liddle-n1059636.

12. https://www.dailywire.com/news/donald-trump-says-greed-good-aaron-bandler.

allows and accruing more power as president,[13] and his track record of sexual assaults and affairs would seem to suggest that he is compulsive when it comes to sex.[14]

Does all that suggest Trump loves God or money, power, and sex?

Does Trump love others? In Dr. Bandy Lee's book, *The Dangerous Case of Donald Trump: 37 Leading Mental Health Experts Assess a President*, there is agreement among many in the mental health field that Trump is a narcissist.[15]

Narcissists are *incapable* of healthily loving others because they are malignantly in love with themselves. This may be what the Bible is referring to when it says in 2 Timothy 3:1, "But mark this: There will be terrible times in the last days. People will be *lovers of themselves*." Does Trump genuinely love others, or is he too narcissistically in love with himself to be able to love others?

Does Trump glorify God or himself? How many more rallies is Trump going to have where the primary focus is on him basking in the adoration of his base?[16]

How many more cabinet meetings is he going to have where people go around the room telling Trump how awesome he is and what a pleasure it is to work for him?[17]

How many more times is he going to talk about how great of a brain he possesses?[18]

How many more times are we going to have to suffer through Trump saying how much of an expert he is about things and that he knows more about them than the people who are actually experts in these areas?[19]

How many more times are we going to have to watch as Trump's coalition of faith praises him in the Oval Office as God's chosen man to lead the

13. http://nymag.com/intelligencer/2018/03/trump-jokes-about-staying-in-power-indefinitely.html.

14. https://www.thesun.co.uk/news/1957545/donald-trump-brags-about-sex-life-and-admits-he-only-stays-with-his-wife-for-her-breasts-in-shocking-new-tapes/.

15. Bandy Lee, ed., *The Dangerous Case of Donald Trump* (New York: Thomas Dunne, 2019).

16. https://billingsgazette.com/opinion/columnists/guest-opinion-trump-s-rally-obsession-bad-for-america/article_e6570430-47c8-542e-b2a9-3f526600bf41.html.

17. https://www.vanityfair.com/news/2017/06/donald-trump-cabinet-meeting.

18. https://www.salon.com/2017/05/02/lessons-in-history-from-donald-trump-who-has-a-very-good-brain-and-is-one-of-the-smartest-people-anywhere-in-the-world/.

19. https://www.axios.com/everything-trump-says-he-knows-more-about-than-anybody-b278b592-cff0-47dc-a75f-5767f42bcf1e.html.

country out of its moral decline? Does any of that sound like someone who wants to glorify God rather than glorify himself?

Does Trump store up treasure in heaven or here on earth? Trump frequently boasts about how much money he has and all the world-class properties he owns. In 1988, Trump went on a hypomanic buying spree, buying chunks of stock of companies he wanted to own, glitzing up his gaudy yacht, overpaying for the Park Plaza Hotel and the Eastern Shuttle, and fighting with game-show tycoon Merv Griffin for ownership of the most expensive casino in Atlantic City, the Trump Taj Mahal.[20]

Does that sound like someone laying up treasure in heaven by living in a godly manner or someone laying up treasure on earth by living in a greedy and insatiable manner?

Does Trump care for the hurting and oppressed? There are many examples of how Trump doesn't truly care for the hurting and oppressed, only for the wealthy and the white. You only need look at one of the most egregious actions Trump has taken since assuming office to address this issue, his southern border policy where he egregiously ripped children out of their parents' arms. Trump has little if any heartfelt empathy for people who are truly suffering but seems to have a lot of fondness for despots and the uber-rich. Trump loves to talk derisively about people on our southern border who want to immigrate to this country, calling them "animals."[21]

Is Trump someone who has a heart for the suffering so many poor and oppressed people experience on a day-to-day basis?

Does Trump speak the truth in love? Since taking office, Trump has made over 16,000 false or misleading statements.[22]

Sixteen-thousand! Previous presidents were roundly criticized and condemned for being caught in making any lies at all. Does Trump value the truth? His actions would say that he clearly doesn't. And, when Trump speaks, does he do so in an effort to love others or demean and denigrate them? Far too many of his words are meant to hurt those at whom they are targeted.

There are many other core values of Christianity that we could have explored. We are often told to not look at what people say but how they act. Based on Trump's *actions* since assuming the presidency, could a case be

---

20. https://www.politico.com/magazine/story/2016/03/1988-the-year-donald-lost-his-mind-213721.

21. https://www.usatoday.com/story/news/politics/2018/05/16/trump-immigrants-animals-mexico-democrats-sanctuary-cities/617252002/.

22. https://www.washingtonpost.com/politics/2020/01/20/president-trump-made-16241-false-or-misleading-claims-his-first-three-years/.

made that he lives his life by the core values of Christianity or by the core values of a malignant narcissist?

Core Christian Values and the Presidency

We can't know whether or not Donald Trump is a follower of Christ. Only God knows that. What we can know from his observable behavior is that there is little evidence he lives by the core values of Christianity—being aware of his sins and need for forgiveness, hungering and thirsting after righteousness, loving God more than the things of this world, caring about others, glorifying God rather than himself, laying up treasure in heaven rather than here on earth, caring for the oppressed and hurting, and speaking the truth in love.

Trump is cunning enough to know that without evangelical support, he would have never ascended to the presidency in 2016. Trump is also shrewd enough to know that without evangelical support in 2020, he isn't going to get re-elected. Doesn't it make sense that someone like Trump is masquerading as a follower of Christ (2 Corinthians 11:13) so he can get evangelicals to vote for him and continue to indulge his love for wealth, fame, and power?

The Bible seems to be talking about people like Trump when it says, "But mark this: There will be terrible times in the last days. People will be lovers of themselves, lovers of money, boastful, proud, abusive, disobedient to their parents, ungrateful, unholy, without love, unforgiving, slanderous, without self-control, brutal, not lovers of the good, treacherous, rash, conceited, lovers of pleasure rather than lovers of God—having a form of godliness but denying its power. Have nothing to do with such people" (2 Timothy 3:2–5). Isn't that a biblical description of our current president? Shouldn't we be deeply concerned that the Bible warns us to not have anything to do with someone like this?

If this passage is a description of Trump, does that not raise questions about whether Christians should support him? If Trump portrays himself as a Christian and says he holds to Christian values, shouldn't Christians be the first to demand his actions are in keeping with biblical values?

Chapter 7

---

10 Reasons Christians Should Reconsider
Their Support of Trump

Christopher Pieper
& Matt Henderson

As sociologists of religion, we are intrigued by the surprisingly large number of self-identified Christians, especially evangelicals, who support Donald Trump and have voted for him. In past elections, such voters were motivated by moral convictions around abortion, same-sex marriage, and the perceived deterioration of traditional values, and voted predictably for candidates such as Huckabee, Santorum, and most consequentially, George W. Bush. These issues and their equivalents have never been central features of Trump's life history, let alone his presidency, and on many of them he has confused, moderate, or unclear positions. Whatever the appeal of Trump to evangelicals might be, it is not due to these conventional stances.

It would take a good bit more research and analysis than the current space permits to adequately understand this head-scratcher. And, to be frank, it is not our central concern to do so. The clear and present danger of another Trump administration impels us to skip over the thoroughness we would normally dedicate to investigation. And more precisely, our consciences demand that we address voters not primarily as scientists, but as citizens and as people of faith. Our audience is that perplexingly large group of Christians who likewise identify as followers of Jesus Christ but plan to vote for and support Donald Trump.

For awhile, his opponents have seemed willing to ignore Trump, perhaps as a disciplined tact to suffocate his bloviations of the oxygen they need to burn. We have come to feel, however, that this approach has ultimately proven naive. However shallow and unserious anyone may find him, the nation is despairingly at a moment where we must take his ongoing harm seriously, especially as people committed to following Jesus.

So, at the risk of spilling more useless ink, as we approach the 2020 election, we offer an appeal to our fellow Christians or anyone concerned with the potential moral consequences of a continued Trump presidency to prayerfully consider how supporting him squares with Christian commitment.

Our argument is simple: A Christian who supports Trump either does not understand this person and his positions, or supports him in spite of their Christian convictions.

In the same way that a person cannot love the Yankees and the Red Sox or follow veganism and frequently devour a steak, one cannot really love Jesus and wish to follow him and also vote for a person who so clearly embodies the opposite of everything Christ taught, died for, and demands of us.

We organize our remarks around ideas central to social life, but especially to that of the Christian: character, relationships, and values.

Character

He lacks compassion

"As God's chosen ones, holy and beloved, clothe yourselves with compassion, kindness, humility, meekness, and patience" (Colossians 3:12).

On this point, we could cite Mr. Trump's many instances of inflammatory rhetoric against immigrants and Muslims, his record of discriminatory housing practices, his public cruelty to ex-spouses, or his sensational and mean-spirited feuds with other celebrities as evidence of his lack of compassion. But consider an AP-GfK poll back in 2015 showing that *among Republicans*, Trump is largely believed to lack compassion.[1]

And bear in mind, these are the people most likely to view him favorably. Many of those voters polled expressed this was not a concern. But for

1. https://www.realclearpolitics.com/articles/2015/12/11/republican_voters_on_trump_no_compassion_no_problem_129009.html.

Christians, an unrepentant lack of compassion suggests that the man does not seek to please God or lead according to his will.

He appeals to fear and anger

"There is no fear in love, but perfect love casts out fear; for fear has to do with punishment, and whoever fears has not reached perfection in love"(1 John 4:18). "But I say to you that if you are angry with a brother or sister, you will be liable to judgment; and if you insult a brother or sister, you will be liable to the council; and if you say, 'You fool,' you will be liable to the hell of fire" (Matthew 5:22).

Americans are finding the changing economy an increasingly hostile and unforgiving place. Their fears are existential and not without warrant. But Christians are called to love without fear. Mr. Trump has chosen to make immigration and the economy central themes of his campaign and his rhetoric surrounding these issues consistently appeals to fear and anger, absent appeals to love. Most notoriously, he chose to characterize Hispanic immigrants as rapists.[2]

Regardless of our policy convictions around the place of undocumented immigrants, this broad characterization is cynically aimed to incite fear and anger. His endorsement by the white supremacist American Freedom Party is the fruit of this rhetoric.[3]

It is also a callous and hostile way to characterize people, some of whom are our brothers and sisters in Christ, all of whom are God's children.

> He is enamored with "greatness" and ego, but has no concern for "goodness" or service

"Blessed are the meek, for they will inherit the earth. Blessed are those who hunger and thirst for righteousness, for they will be filled. Blessed are the merciful, for they will receive mercy. Blessed are the pure in heart, for they will see God" (Matthew 5:5–8).

In *The Narcissist Next Door,* author Jeffrey Kluger suggests Trump is a classic narcissist.[4]

---

2. https://www.huffpost.com/entry/donald-trump-racist-examples_n_56d47177e4 b03260bf777e83.

3. https://www.thedailybeast.com/white-power-party-swears-loyalty-to-president -trump.

4. Jeffrey Kluger, *The Narcissist Next Door: Understanding the Monster in Your Family, in Your Office, in Your Bed—in Your World* (New York: Riverhead, 2014).

Some might say that being elected president of the United States only further emboldens a person's narcissism. But narcissism may be the most dangerous condition for a Christian—without humility and self-effacement, we are incapable of modeling Jesus' behavior, we allow no space for the Holy Spirit to bless our relationships, and we are unable to receive or revel in the goodness of God. Ask yourself the last time you saw a public expression of humility from Mr. Trump.

He lies—a lot

"Beware then of useless grumbling, and keep your tongue from slander; because no secret word is without result, and a lying mouth destroys the soul" (Wisdom 1:11).

According to Pulitzer Prize-winning truth-checkers *Politifact*, a firm which compares each candidate's statements to evidence, Trump's statements were verifiably false 76 percent of the time when he ran for office in 2016.[5]

Among these is this infamous lie about 9/11: "I watched in Jersey City, N.J., where thousands and thousands of people were cheering as [the World Trade Center] was coming down. Thousands of people were cheering." This pattern of lying has only gotten worse over time during Trump's presidency.[6]

Not only is this pattern of dishonesty troubling for religious believers, it should disturb any citizen contemplating a vote for the most powerful office on the planet. Lying was enough to get two presidents impeached. Christian or not, a president telling the truth less than one-quarter of the time is the reddest of flags.

Relationships

He is hostile to women

"But now you must get rid of all such things—anger, wrath, malice, slander, and abusive language from your mouth" (Colossians 3:8).

Trump's feud with Fox News host Megyn Kelly is now the stuff of legend, but what prompted the tension initially were his documented remarks about women, which Kelly reiterated during the August 6 GOP debate:

5. https://www.usnews.com/news/articles/2015−12−21/fact-checking-website-donald-trump-lies-76-percent-of-the-time.

6. https://www.nbcnews.com/think/opinion/trump-s-lying-seems-be-getting-worse-psychology-suggests-there-ncna876486.

"You've called women you don't like 'fat pigs,' 'dogs,' 'slobs,' and 'disgusting animals,'" which Trump said was taken out of context.[7]

Consider instead perhaps this Trump tweet: "If Hillary Clinton can't satisfy her husband what makes her think she can satisfy America?" @realDonaldTrump #2016president.[8]

What kind of person constantly denigrates women? Trump is an old-school misogynist and has no remorse about being so.

He speaks about his daughter in a disrespectful and sexualized way

"Do you have daughters? Be concerned for their chastity, and do not show yourself too indulgent with them" (Sirach 7:24).

In a 2006 interview with *Rolling Stone,* when asked about the idea of his daughter posing for *Playboy,* Trump replied, "I've said if Ivanka weren't my daughter, perhaps I'd be dating her."[9]

For a self-identified Presbyterian, such a statement is hard to square with Calvinist sexual ethics.

He does not attempt to love his enemies, but instead cultivates antagonism

"You have heard that it was said, 'You shall love your neighbor and hate your enemy.' But I say to you, Love your enemies and pray for those who persecute you, so that you may be children of your Father in heaven; for he makes his sun rise on the evil and on the good, and sends rain on the righteous and on the unrighteous" (Matthew 5:43–48).

Trump's "plans" for dealing with adversaries involve heavy and immediate use of force. Regarding ISIS, he told *Fox & Friends,* "I would knock the hell out of ISIS . . . [and] when you get these terrorists, you have to take out their families."[10]

Most military and diplomatic experts quickly retorted that such tactics used a decade ago were precisely what created ISIS. This love for bloodshed and recklessness was again recently demonstrated by the unlawful

7. https://abcnews.go.com/Politics/history-donald-trump-megyn-kelly-feud/story?id=36526503.

8. https://www.dailymail.co.uk/news/article-3043861/Claim-Hillary-Clinton-t-satisfy-husband-winds-Donald-Trump-s-Twitter-account-staffer-retweets-it.html.

9. https://www.independent.co.uk/news/world/americas/us-elections/donald-trump-ivanka-trump-creepiest-most-unsettling-comments-a-roundup-a7353876.html.

10. https://time.com/4132368/donald-trump-isis-bombing/.

assassination of a top military official of a sovereign nation, Iranian General Qasem Soleimani. Apart from the strategic factors, such an approach to handling enemies, one that vindictively aims to punish the potentially innocent, is 100 percent counter to one of the core tenets of Jesus' teaching.

He does not model sacrifice or altruism

"But many who are first will be last, and the last will be first" (Matthew 19:30).

Perhaps Mr. Trump's most credible qualification for the presidency is his *supposed* prodigious business success, about which he never fails to remind us. However, Christians must consider how he made his fortune. Rather than invest in companies that provide goods and services which contribute to the prosperity of the Americans he seeks to lead, he has invested heavily in casino gambling.[11]

He gave his name to a sham university, defrauding students in the process.[12]

He has lobbied for and exploited imminent domain laws to muscle people off their property, most notably a New Jersey widow.[13]

Much has been made of his companies' multiple bankruptcies; more damning, though, is the fact that when his mortgage company failed, he denied responsibility, saying that he only let the company use his name.[14]

His business dealings do not suggest a willingness to place the fortunes of others ahead of his own, nor the integrity to accept responsibility.

Values

He doesn't seem to care about the poor

"Jesus said to him, 'If you wish to be perfect, go, sell your possessions, and give the money to the poor, and you will have treasure in heaven; then come, follow me'" (Matthew 19:21).

11. https://www.washingtonpost.com/investigations/trumps-bad-bet-how-too-much-debt-drove-his-biggest-casino-aground/2016/01/18/f67cedc2-9ac8-11e5-8917-653b65c809eb_story.html.

12. https://www.nationalreview.com/corner/trump-university-scam/.

13. https://www.washingtonpost.com/news/volokh-conspiracy/wp/2015/08/19/donald-trumps-abuse-of-eminent-domain/.

14. https://www.independent.co.uk/news/world/americas/donald-trump-mortgage-economy-2006-2008-crash-a6904796.html.

Trump's policy ideas across the board are shockingly thin, typical of demagogues. On the issues of poverty, hunger, and oppression, topics everyone from Jesus to Jeremiah cared a great deal about, Trump is deafeningly silent. This alone is unacceptable. To be fair, though, here is one of Trump's few but fairly specific plans for helping the disadvantaged: "Teenage mothers [shouldn't] get public assistance unless they jump through some pretty small hoops. Making them live in group homes makes sense."[15]

More recently, his deliberately callous and cruel treatment of refugee children at the southern border is strong evidence of his apathy toward the "least of these," the group most beloved by Jesus. In sum, his best twenty-first-century idea is the worst of eighteenth-century ideas.

His love of money is more apparent than his love of God or others

"No one can serve two masters, for either he will hate the one and love the other, or he will be devoted to the one and despise the other. You cannot serve God and money" (Matthew 6:24).

"My whole life I've been greedy, greedy, greedy," Trump said at a rally. "I've grabbed all the money I could get. I'm so greedy."[16]

The spiritual concern here is not so much greed, but the misplaced priorities that his statement reveals. He has made the pursuit of material wealth an idol and worshiped it his entire life. Trump has forgotten the source of all wealth, the Creator of all abundance, and instead deifies the gifts of God rather than God himself. No moral offense receives so many warnings in both the Old and New Testament as idolatry. Trump's confession of this addiction is a good first step, but he hardly seems repentant. On many campaign issues, he appears to have recently found religion—but apparently not this one.

It's a free country, thank God. You can vote for whoever you want. But for the Christian, this freedom is always constrained. Followers of Christ have taken up a yoke. And though it is light, it is not easy or common. This yoke ties all Christians, in all their perplexing diversity, to love, mercy, sacrifice, and justice. Voting, often thought of as a mere civic duty, is in this light, also a sacred act. It is the most powerful public expression of private values that most of us will ever harness. Let us cast all of our votes for love.

15. Donald Trump, *The America We Deserve* (Los Angeles: Renaissance, 2000), 107–8.

16. https://www.huffpost.com/entry/donald-trump-my-whole-life-ive-been-greedy-_b_11406288.

Author Note: This chapter is a revised version of an op-ed originally published in *The Dallas Morning News*, February 27, 2016.

Chapter 8

President Trump
and the COVID-19 Epidemic

RONALD J. SIDER

As I write this on April 9, there have been 435,780 cases of COVID-19 in the US and 14,865 deaths—with vastly more to come.

Repeatedly, until March 29, President Trump had downplayed the threat: "We have it very much under control," he repeatedly assured Americans.

Here are some of his statements—and the facts. You can judge for yourself whether or not this represents wise, courageous, science-based leadership.

On March 29, President Trump and his scientific advisors solemnly informed the nation that 100,000 to 240,000 Americans would die of COVID-19. But for much of the preceding three months, the President had assured us that all was well.

Very soon after January 3, American spy agencies began sending warnings to the President's Daily Brief about the seriousness of the problem. But most of the next seventy days were wasted in inaction and misinformation.[1] The president kept assuring the nation that all was well and that he had everything under control.

---

1. See Yasmeen Abutaleb, Josh Dawsey, Ellen Nakashima, and Greg Miller, "70 Days: U.S. Response to Virus Beset By Denial and Dysfunction," *Philadelphia Inquirer*, April 5, 2020.

On January 18, the Secretary of Health and Human Services, Alex Azar, finally—after a few unsuccessful attempts—managed to briefly talk to the president about the problem. But before Azar could start discussing the coronavirus, the president interrupted to criticize Azar for the way Azar was handling the issue of vaping.

On January 22, in President Trump's first public comment on the problem, a reporter asked if he was worried that there might be a potential pandemic. The president's answer: "No. Not at all. And we have it totally under control. It's one person coming in from China . . . It's going to be just fine"[2]

On January 24, Trump tweeted: "It will all work out well." In a speech four days later, he said: "We have it very well under control. We have very little problem in this country at this time—five. And these people are all recuperating successfully."[3]

On January 30, President Trump said in a speech in Michigan: "We think we have it very well under control. We have very little problem in this country at this moment—five—and those people are all recuperating successfully. . . . We think it's going to have a very good ending for us. . . . That I can assure you."[4]

On January 31, the president did bar any non-US citizens who had been in China in the previous two weeks from coming to the United States.

By late January, Matthew Pottinger (deputy to National Security Advisor Robert O'Brien) had been placed in charge of the US response to the developing problem. By the end of January, Pottinger pushed for a ban on travelers from countries in Europe where the coronavirus was spreading rapidly. But the Treasury Secretary and others concerned with the US economy objected and the president sided with his economic advisers. Not until a full month later—after hundreds of thousands from Europe had flown to the US—did the president ban arrivals from Europe.[5]

By early February, Health and Human Services Secretary Azar asked the White House to ask Congress for a supplemental appropriation of $4 billion to fund the stockpiling of supplies for a worst-case scenario. The White House Office of Management and Budget rejected that as too much and eventually the administration asked Congress for $2.5 billion. Congress,

2. Abutaleb et al., "70 Days."

3. David Leonhardt, "A Complete List of Trump's Attempts to Play Down the Coronavirus," *New York Times*, March 15, 2020, https://www.nytimes.com/2020/03/15/opinion/trump-coronavirus.html.

4. Rem Rieder, "Trump's Statement About the Coronavirus," March 19, 2020, https://www.factcheck.org/20203/trumps-statements-about-the-coronavirus/.

5. Abutaleb et al., "70 Days."

however, increased it to $8 billion. Tragically, President Trump only signed
the bill on March 5, a month after the secretary of Health and Human Services had asked for the money.[6] Crucial time had been wasted.

Meanwhile, the President was assuring the country that all was well.
On February 10, he said in a speech to governors and in a big rally, that
warm weather would kill the virus: "Looks like by April, you know, in theory, when it gets a little warmer, it miraculously goes away."[7] On February
19, Trump told a Phoenix TV station: "I think the numbers are going to get
progressively better as we go along." And four days later he said: "We had
twelve, at one point. And now they've gotten very much better. Many of
them are fully recovered." Four days later, the World Health Organization
reported that there were 78,811 confirmed cases in thirty countries.[8]

On February 24, the president tweeted: "The Coronavirus is very
much under control in the USA. We are in contact with everyone and all
relevant countries. . . . Stock market starting to look very good to me!"[9] The
day before, Trump had told reporters: "We have it very much under control
in this country."[10]

On February 26 at a coronavirus task force briefing, the president said:
"We're going very substantially down, not up." That was as the number of
infected Americans had grown to sixty. But Trump said that day: "When
you have fifteen people and the fifteen within a couple days is going to be
down to close to zero, that's a pretty good job we've done."[11]

That same day, someone at a press conference asked the president if
the schools in the United States should be preparing for the spread of the
coronavirus. He answered: "I don't think it's going to come to that, especially
with the fact that we're going down, not up. We're going very substantially
down, not up. "[12]

On February 29, speaking at a conservative conference, Trump said:
"And I've gotten to know these professionals. They're incredible. And everything is under control . . . Everything is really under control."[13]

6. Abutaleb et al., "70 Days."

7. Leonhardt, "A Complete List of Trump's Attempts to Play Down Coronavirus."

8. Leonhardt, "A Complete List of Trump's Attempts to Play Down Coronavirus."

9. Libby Cathey, "How Trump has Contradicted Himself," https://abcnews.go.com/
Politics/trump-contradicted-words-coronavirus-crisis/story?id=69918658.

10. Rieder, "Trump's Statements About the Coronavirus."

11. Cathey, "How Trump Has Contradicted Himself."

12. Rieder, "Trump's Statements About the Coronavirus."

13. Rieder, "Trump's Statements About the Coronavirus."

At a White House news conference on February 26, the president commented on the first reported cases in the US: "We're going to be pretty soon at only five people. And we could be just one or two people over the next short period of time. So we've had very good luck." And the next day at a meeting in the White House: "It's going to disappear. One day—it's like a miracle—it will disappear." And on March 7, he was asked if he was worried that the virus could spread to Washington, DC. His answer: "No, I am not concerned at all. No, I'm not. No, we've done a great job.[14]

On March 2, Trump said the pharmaceutical companies are going "to have vaccines, I think, relatively soon." Earlier that same day, the president's experts told him during a meeting with pharmaceutical leaders that the vaccine could take a year to eighteen months to develop.[15]

On March 6, a group of epidemiologists at the Imperial College London gave the White House coronavirus task force their terrifying projections for the US. (The virus was already in twenty-eight states in the US.) They compared COVID-19 to the disastrous 1918 influenza pandemic that killed 50 million people. And they said their scientific modeling indicated that if nothing was done to halt the spread of the virus in the US, within weeks it would infect 81 percent of the US population, eviscerate the health system, and kill as many as 22 million Americans.[16]

But three days later, President Trump compared COVID-19 to the annual flu. By that time, many parts of the American economy were shutting down and the stock market had plummeted. But Trump said the flu regularly killed thousands without the economy being closed. He tweeted on March 9: "So last year 37,000 Americans died from the common flu. It averages between 27,000 and 70,000 per year. Nothing is shut down, life and the economy go on. At this moment there are 541 confirmed cases of coronavirus, with 22 deaths. Think about that." And the next day he told Republican senators: "And we're prepared, and we're doing a great job with it. And it will go away. Just stay calm. It will go away."[17]

On March 6 (the same day the British scientists issued their terrifying predictions), the president visited the Centers for Disease Control in Atlanta wearing a "Keep America Great" hat. The number of COVID-19 cases in the US had doubled in the previous week. But the number of actual

14. Katie Rogers, "Saying He Long Saw Pandemic, Trump Rewrites History," *New York Times*, March 18, 2020.

15. Christian Paz, "All the President's Lies," https://www.theatlantic.com/politics/archive/2020/04/trumps-lies-about-coronavirus/608647/.

16. https://www.theguardian.com/us-news/2020/apr/04/trump-coronavirus-science-analysis.

17. Rieder, "Trump's Statements About the Coronavirus."

cases was very uncertain because there had been major problems with the tests. The Centers for Disease Control's initial tests were faulty and then the supply was inadequate. The day before the president visited the Centers for Disease Control, Vice President Mike Pence said, "We don't have enough tests today to meet what we anticipate will be the demand going forward." The states were begging for more test kits. But Trump said that day at the Centers for Disease Control: "Anybody who needs a test gets a test . . . They have the tests and the tests are beautiful."

In Atlanta that day, the president also commented on the cruise ship *Grand Princess*. It was docked in San Francisco but the passengers had not been allowed to disembark because there were twenty-one confirmed cases of COVID-19 on board. The president said he wanted the passengers to stay on board because if they disembarked, that would increase the number of COVID-19 cases in the US! "I would rather [that they stay on board] because I like the numbers being where they are. I don't need to have the numbers double because of one ship that wasn't our fault. I'd rather have them stay on, personally."

At the end of the press conference at the Centers for Disease Control, the president said the tests "are all perfect, like the letter was perfect, the transcript was perfect." He was referring to the transcript of his conversation where he asked the Ukrainian president, Volodymyr Zelensky, to investigate the Bidens. (Trump was expecting Vice President Joe Biden to be his opponent in the presidential election in the fall and he was hoping to have something to use against Biden.)[18]

At the press conference that day at the Centers for Disease Control, the president also boasted about his knowledge about COVID-19: "I like this stuff. I really get it. People are surprised that I understand it. Every one of these doctors said, 'How do you know so much about this?' Maybe I have a natural ability. Maybe I should have done that instead of running for president."[19]

By March 10, even the very conservative magazine *The National Review* sharply condemned the president's leadership in a biting piece by the editors. They noted that COVID-19 was likely to be the "most acute public health crisis Americans have had to face at home in decades." Then they pointedly criticized President Trump:

> So far in this crisis, Donald Trump himself has obviously failed to rise to the challenge of leadership, and it does no one any

18. Catherine Kim, "Trump's Visit to the CDC," https://www.vox.com/policy-and-politics/2020/3/7/21169233/coronavirus-trump-cdc-visit-covid-19.

19. Leonhardt, "A Complete List of Trump's Attempts to Play Down Coronavirus."

favors to pretend otherwise. . . . The failures of leadership at the top, however, show no sign of being corrected. In a serious public-health crisis, the public has the right to expect the government's chief executive to lead in a number of crucial ways: by prioritizing the problem properly, by deferring to subject-matter experts when appropriate while making key decisions in informed and sensible ways, by providing honest and careful information to the country, by calming fears and setting expectations, and by addressing mistakes and setbacks. Trump so far hasn't passed muster on any of these metrics. He resisted making the response to the epidemic a priority for as long as he could—refusing briefings, downplaying the problem, and wasting precious time. He has failed to properly empower his subordinates and refused to trust the information they provided him—often offering up unsubstantiated claims and figures from cable television instead. He has spoken about the crisis in crude political and personal terms. He has stood in the way of public understanding of the plausible course of the epidemic, trafficking instead in dismissive clichés. He has denied his administration's missteps, making it more difficult to address them.[20]

By mid-March however, the virus had spread to more and more states. Governors across the country were closing schools and businesses and demanding social distancing. The US economy was shutting down.

For the first time, on March 17, President Trump declared the situation a pandemic—and promptly claimed he had known that all along. That day he said: "I've always known this is real—this is a pandemic. I felt it was a pandemic long before it was called a pandemic. I've always viewed it as very serious."[21]

But the president continued to express concerns about the economic shutdown. On March 23, March 24, and March 29, he said that if the economic shutdown continued, the deaths by suicide "definitely would be far greater numbers than the numbers that we're talking about" for COVID-19 deaths.[22]

On Wednesday, March 25, as more than 650 Americans had already died, as the death toll continued to rise, as New York reported that the epidemic threatened to overrun its healthcare system, and as federal health officials called for greater restrictions on public interactions, President Trump

---

20. https://www.nationalreview.com/2020/03/president-trump-needs-to-step-up-on-the-coronavirus/.

21. Paz, "All the President's Lies."

22. Paz, "All the President's Lies."

announced that he hoped the US would be open by Easter—a little more than two weeks away. "I would love to have the country opened up and just roaring to go by Easter," he said on Fox News. "Wouldn't it be great to have all the churches full?" And in another interview, he said: "You'll have packed churches all over the country." In a town hall from the Rose Garden, he said thousands of Americans die every year of the flu and automobile accidents and "we don't turn the country off. . . . This cure is worse than the problem. . . . We have to go back to work, much sooner than people think." Trump's medical experts, on the other hand, promptly cautioned against quickly reducing the restrictions. Later in the same press briefing, Dr. Anthony Fauci (the nation's leading expert on infectious diseases and Trump's medical advisor) said: "No one is going to want to tone down anything when you see what is going on in a place like New York City."[23]

In the last week of March, Jerry Falwell, Jr., the president of Liberty University and a strong supporter of the president, followed through on Trump's call by inviting the university's students to return to campus—to the horror of local authorities.[24]

Finally, by Sunday, March 29, the president's medical experts had convinced him that the situation demanded drastic action. Some 142,000 Americans had already been infected and about 2,500 had died. Dr. Fauci told the president that even with aggressive action across the country, the American death toll could reach 200,000. On Sunday, a very sober president reflected on the devastation in New York City and elsewhere. He extended the guidelines on social distancing and closure of all nonessential services through the end of April—and perhaps June.[25] He stopped suggesting the cure of economic shutdown could be worse than the disease. Instead, he clearly stated on March 30 that the economy was only his second concern. His first priority was now saving lives.

As I finish this essay on April 9, COVID-19 has sickened 435,780 Americans and 14,865 have died. No one knows what those figures will be in three, six, or twelve months.

But one thing is clear. On November 3 of this year, Americans will have to decide who should be their president for the next four years. Reflection

23. Zeke Miller and Darlene Superville, "Trump Happy to See US Economy Reopened By Easter Amid Virus," March 25, 2020, https://apnews.com/87e9fad01d7b9ed96c83f992f429ee46.

24. McKay Coppins, "The Social Distancing Culture War," March 30, 2020, https://www.theatlantic.com/politics/archive.2020/03/social-distancing-culture/609019/.

25. Michael D. Shear, "Trump Extends Virus Guidelines One More Month," *New York Times*, March 30, 2020.

on the facts about how President Trump has dealt with the worst pandemic in a century should be an important factor in our decision.

PART II

ON EVANGELICAL SUPPORT
OF TRUMP

Chapter 9

The Deepening Crisis
in Evangelical Christianity

PETER WEHNER

SUPPORT FOR TRUMP COMES AT A HIGH COST FOR CHRISTIAN WITNESS. In the summer of 2019 Ralph Reed, the Faith and Freedom Coalition's founder and chairman, told the group, "There has never been anyone who has defended us and who has fought for us, who we have loved more than Donald J. Trump. No one!"

Reed is partially right; for many evangelical Christians, there is no political figure whom they have loved more than Donald Trump.

I exchanged emails with a pro-Trump figure who attended the president's reelection rally in Orlando, Florida in June 2019. (He spoke to me on the condition of anonymity, so as to avoid personal or professional repercussions.) He had interviewed scores of people, many of them evangelical Christians. "I have never witnessed the kind of excitement and enthusiasm for a political figure in my life," he told me. "I honestly couldn't believe the unwavering support they have. And to a person, it was all about 'the fight.' There is a very strong sense (I believe justified, you disagree) that he has been wronged. Wronged by [Robert] Mueller, wronged by the media, wronged by the anti-Trump forces. A passionate belief that he never gets credit for anything."

The rallygoers, he said, told him that Trump's era "is spiritually driven." When I asked whether he meant by this that Trump's supporters believe

God's hand is on Trump, this moment and at the election—that Donald Trump is God's man, in effect—he told me, "Yes—a number of people said they believe there is no other way to explain his victories. Starting with the election and continuing with the conclusion of the Mueller report. Many said God has chosen him and is protecting him."

The data seem to bear this out. In 2019 approval for President Trump among white evangelical Protestants was twenty-five points higher than the national average. And according to a Pew Research Center survey, "White evangelical Protestants who regularly attend church (that is, once a week or more) approve of Trump at rates matching or exceeding those of white evangelicals who attend church less often." Indeed, during the period from July 2018 to January 2019, 70 percent of white evangelicals who attend church at least once a week approved of Trump, versus 65 percent of those who attend religious services less often.

The enthusiastic, uncritical embrace of President Trump by white evangelicals is among the most mind-blowing developments of the Trump era. How can a group that for decades—and especially during the Bill Clinton presidency—insisted that character counts and that personal integrity is an essential component of presidential leadership not only turn a blind eye to the ethical and moral transgressions of Donald Trump, but also constantly defend him? Why are those who have been on the vanguard of "family values" so eager to give a man with a sordid personal and sexual history a mulligan?

Part of the answer is their belief that they are engaged in an existential struggle against a wicked enemy—not Russia, not North Korea, not Iran, but rather American liberals and the left. If you listen to Trump supporters who are evangelical (and non-evangelicals, like the radio talk-show host Mark Levin), you will hear adjectives applied to those on the left that could easily be used to describe a Stalinist regime. (Ask yourself how many evangelicals have publicly criticized Trump for his lavish praise of Kim Jong Un, the leader of perhaps the most savage regime in the world and the worst persecutor of Christians in the world.)

Many white evangelical Christians, then, are deeply fearful of what a Trump loss would mean for America, American culture, and American Christianity. If a Democrat is elected president, they believe, it might all come crashing down around us. During the 2016 election, for example, the influential evangelical author and radio talk-show host Eric Metaxas said, "In all of our years, we faced all kinds of struggles. The only time we faced an existential struggle like this was in the Civil War and in the Revolution when the nation began . . . We are on the verge of losing it as we could have lost it in the Civil War." A friend of mine described that outlook to me this way: "It's the Flight 93 election. FOREVER."

Many evangelical Christians are also filled with grievances and resentments because they feel they have been mocked, scorned, and dishonored by the elite culture over the years. (Some of those feelings are understandable and warranted.) For them, Trump is a man who will not only push their agenda on issues such as the courts and abortion; he will be ruthless against those they view as threats to all they know and love. For a growing number of evangelicals, Trump's dehumanizing tactics and cruelty aren't a bug, they are a feature. Trump "owns the libs," and they love it. He'll bring a Glock to a cultural knife fight, and they relish that.

Jerry Falwell, Jr., the president of Liberty University, one of the largest Christian universities in the world, put it this way: "Conservatives & Christians need to stop electing 'nice guys.' They might make great Christian leaders but the United States needs street fighters like @realDonaldTrump at every level of government b/c the liberal fascists Dems are playing for keeps & many Repub leaders are a bunch of wimps!"

There's a very high cost to our politics for celebrating the Trump style, but what is most personally painful to me as a person of the Christian faith is the cost to the Christian witness. Nonchalantly jettisoning the ethic of Jesus in favor of a political leader who embraces the ethic of Thrasymachus and Nietzsche—might makes right, the strong should rule over the weak, justice has no intrinsic worth, moral values are socially constructed and subjective—is troubling enough.

But there is also the undeniable hypocrisy of people who once made moral character, and especially sexual fidelity, central to their political calculus and who are now embracing a man of boundless corruptions. Don't forget: Trump was essentially named an unindicted co-conspirator ("Individual 1") in a scheme to make hush-money payments to a porn star who alleged she'd had an affair with him while he was married to his third wife, who had just given birth to their son.

While visiting the Pacific Coast, I had lunch with Karel Coppock, whom I have known for many years and who has played an important role in my Christian pilgrimage. In speaking about the widespread, reflexive evangelical support for the president, Coppock—who is theologically orthodox and generally sympathetic to conservatism—lamented the effect this moral freak show is having, especially on the younger generation. With unusual passion, he told me, "We're losing an entire generation. They're just gone. It's one of the worst things to happen to the church."

Coppock mentioned to me the powerful example of St. Ambrose, the bishop of Milan, who was willing to rebuke the Roman Emperor

Theodosius for the latter's role in massacring civilians as punishment for the murder of one of his generals. Ambrose refused to allow the church to become a political prop, despite concerns that doing so might endanger him. Ambrose spoke truth to power. (Theodosius ended up seeking penance, and Ambrose went on to teach, convert, and baptize St. Augustine.) Proximity to power is fine for Christians, Coppock told me, but only so long as it does not corrupt their moral sense, only so long as they don't allow their faith to become politically weaponized. Yet that is precisely what's happening today.

Evangelical Christians need another model for cultural and political engagement, and one of the best I am aware of has been articulated by the artist Makoto Fujimura, who speaks about "culture care" instead of "culture war."

According to Fujimura, "Culture care is an act of generosity to our neighbors and culture. Culture care is to see our world not as a battle zone in which we're all vying for limited resources, but to see the world of abundant possibilities and promise." What Fujimura is talking about is a set of sensibilities and dispositions that are fundamentally different from what we see embodied in many white evangelical leaders who frequently speak out on culture and politics. The sensibilities and dispositions Fujimura is describing are characterized by a commitment to grace, beauty, and creativity, not antipathy, disdain, and pulsating anger. It's the difference between an open hand and a mailed fist.

Building on this theme, Mark Labberton, a colleague of Fujimura's and the president of Fuller Theological Seminary, the largest multidenominational seminary in the world, has spoken about a distinct way for Christians to conceive of their calling, from seeing themselves as living in a promised land and "demanding it back" to living a "faithful, exilic life."

Labberton speaks about what it means to live as people in exile, trying to find the capacity to love in unexpected ways; to see the enemy, the foreigner, the stranger, and the alien, and to go toward rather than away from them. He asks what a life of faithfulness looks like while one lives in a world of fear. He adds, "The church is in one of its deepest moments of crisis—not because of some election result or not, but because of what has been exposed to be the poverty of the American church in its capacity to be able to see and love and serve and engage in ways in which we simply fail to do. And that vocation is the vocation that must be recovered and must be made real in tangible action."

There are countless examples of how such tangible action can be manifest. But as a starting point, evangelical Christians should acknowledge the profound damage that's being done to their movement by its braided political relationship—its love affair, to bring us back to the words of Ralph

Reed—with a president who is an ethical and moral wreck. Until that is undone—until followers of Jesus are once again willing to speak truth to power rather than act like court pastors—the crisis in American Christianity will only deepen, its public testimony only dim, its effort to be a healing agent in a broken world only weaken.

At this point, I can't help but wonder whether that really matters to many of Donald Trump's besotted evangelical supporters.

Author Note: This piece was originally published July 5, 2019, in *The Atlantic*, © Peter Wehner.

Chapter 10

Donald Trump and the Death
of Evangelicalism

RANDALL BALMER

AFTER A LONG AND LINGERING ILLNESS, EVANGELICALISM DIED ON NOVEM-
ber 8, 2016. On that day, 81 percent of white American evangelicals who
for decades claimed to be concerned about "family values" registered their
votes for a twice-divorced, thrice-married, self-confessed sexual predator
whose understanding of the faith is so truncated that he can't even fake religious literacy.

Before we sound the requiem for this movement, it might be instruc-
tive to chart its storied history—if for no other reason than to appreciate
how far it had fallen before its demise.

First, let's dispense with a definition of terms. Some scholars of evangelicalism peddle complex, theologically recondite definitions, which I'm
sure have their place in the realm of scholarly discourse. I prefer a functional,
three-part—*trinitarian*—definition. An evangelical is someone who takes
the Bible seriously as God's revelation to humanity. Such individuals view
the Bible as authoritative and therefore profess to interpret it literally, when
in fact they routinely engage in what I call the ruse of selective literalism.

Second, evangelicals believe in the centrality of a conversion or "born
again" experience. This derives from the Gospel of John where Nicodemus,
the Jewish leader, visits Jesus under cover of darkness to ask how he might
be admitted into the kingdom of heaven. Jesus replies that Nicodemus must

be "born again," although some translations render the text "born from above." Many evangelicals understand conversion as a datable moment that marks the difference between sin and salvation, hell and heaven. Most evangelicals, furthermore, subscribe to a "baptist" (lower case) understanding of conversion. They reject what they call baptismal regeneration.

Finally, evangelicals believe in *evangelism*, bringing others into the faith. This derives from the so-called Great Commission at the end of the Gospel of Matthew, when Jesus enjoins his followers to "go and make disciples of all nations, baptizing them in the name of the Father and of the Son and of the Holy Spirit." With very few exceptions, evangelicals will acknowledge their responsibility to spread the faith, although it's my observation over the last fifty years or so that evangelicals hire professionals to do this for them—missionaries, visitation pastors, and the like.[1]

This three-part definition—the Bible as God's revelation to humanity, the centrality of conversion, and the responsibility to evangelize—is a broad one, and intentionally so. In the United States, surveys suggest that this definition of evangelicalism would encompass approximately one-third of the population. Within this capacious definition, of course, reside several strains of evangelicals: fundamentalists, pentecostals, holiness people, neoevangelicals, and others.

Historically, evangelicalism emerged in North America in the middle decades of the eighteenth century from the confluence of three Ps: the vestiges of New England Puritanism, Continental Pietism, especially in the Middle Colonies, and Scots-Irish Presbyterianism. (Baptists, with their suspicion of church-state entanglement that they inherited from Roger Williams, founder of the Baptist tradition in America, emerged a bit later, especially in New England and Virginia.)

I think it's still possible to discern vestiges of the three Ps in contemporary evangelicalism. From the Puritans evangelicals inherited spiritual introspection; just as the Puritans kept diaries to chart the progress of their spiritual pilgrimages, evangelicals are constantly looking inward to assess their piety. Evangelicals took from Presbyterians the importance of doctrinal precisionism. Finally, from the Pietists evangelicals derived the importance of a warmhearted faith. It's not enough to hold specific beliefs; religious affections also play a central role in the life of a believer. These emphases vary by group, by ethnicity, and by region, of course, and also in various periods of history.

If a peculiar North American form of evangelicalism emerged during what historians call the Great Awakening in the middle decades of the

1. Matthew 28:19 (NIV).

eighteenth century, it found its public voice during the Second Awakening in the decades surrounding the turn of the nineteenth century. Evangelical revivals torched three theaters of the new nation: New England, emanating from Yale College; the so-called Great Revival centered in the Cumberland Valley of Kentucky; and upstate New York, the area opened to settlement by the construction of the Erie Canal, which was completed in 1825.

Especially in the North, evangelical optimism about individual regeneration unleashed programs of social amelioration. Animated by postmillennialism, the notion that believers could bring about the millennium—one thousand years of righteousness—by dint of their collective efforts, evangelicals sought to reshape society according to the norms of godliness. Their ambitions, as well as the results, were truly astonishing—and they stand in vivid contrast to the agenda of the Religious Right in recent years.

Charles Grandison Finney, the lawyer turned evangelist who by any measure was the most influential evangelical of the nineteenth century, believed that evangelicalism entailed more than mere conversions. A regenerated individual, in obedience to the teachings of Jesus, bore responsibility for the improvement of society and especially the interests of those most vulnerable. Finney, in fact, understood benevolence toward others as a necessary corollary of faith. "God's rule requires universal benevolence," he wrote. "I abhor a piety which has no humanity with it and in it," he added. "God loves both piety and humanity."[2]

The engines of evangelical social reform were remarkable for their comprehensiveness and for their innovation. Benevolence took many forms, including education, prison reform, and advocacy for the poor and for the rights of women. Many evangelicals, seeking to obey the commands of Jesus to love their enemies and turn the other cheek, enlisted in efforts to oppose war. Still others, including Finney, took a dim view of capitalism and business practices. Even though the evangelical obsession with temperance looks presumptuous and paternalistic in hindsight, the temperance movement was a response to the very real depredations and suffering, including child and spousal abuse, caused by excessive alcohol consumption.[3]

While it is true that Southern evangelicals, notably James Henley Thornwell and Robert Lewis Dabney, defended slavery, evangelicals in the North worked to abolish the scourge of slavery. Some evangelicals harbored nativist sentiments, but a far greater number supported "common schools" as a means of upward mobility for the children of immigrants; evangelical

2. Charles G. Finney, *Sermons on Gospel Themes* (Oberlin, OH: E. J. Goodrich, 1876), 348, 356.

3. W. J. Rorabaugh, *The Alcoholic Republic* (New York: Oxford University Press, 1979).

ministers often headed organizations and agencies dedicated to public education.

Antebellum evangelicals saw universal public education as a means of advancing the fortunes of the poor. "Common Schools are the glory of our land," a writer declared in the *Christian Spectator*, "where even the beggar's child is taught to read, and write, and think, for himself." Evangelicals well understood the target of their efforts, both among Native Americans and in the cities: "children of the extremely indigent" and "people of color." There can be little doubt that an unhealthy dose of paternalism tainted evangelical educational efforts, but their conviction that education for those less privileged provided the first step on the ladder of upward mobility contrasts with recent evangelical schemes to defend segregated educational institutions and undermine public schools.[4]

Antebellum evangelicals embraced equal rights for women, including voting rights and access to education commensurate with men. To the question "what are woman's rights and duties?" James H. Fairchild, an ordained minister and professor at Oberlin College, a major center of evangelical life in the mid-nineteenth century, replied, "the same, in general as those of all other human beings, because she possesses the common attributes of humanity." Fairchild argued for equality of wages for equal work. "The laborer is worthy of his hire," he said, "and it is desirable that woman should receive according to the work she does."[5]

Many evangelical sentiments in the antebellum period would be considered radical by the standards of both the twentieth and twenty-first centuries. Finney's understanding of the Christian faith and duty led him to a suspicion of capitalism because it was suffused with avarice and selfishness. Finney allowed that "the business aims and practices of business men are almost universally an abomination in the sight of God." What are the principles of those who engage in business? Finney asked. "Seeking their own ends; doing something not for others, but for self."[6]

Elsewhere, Finney preached explicitly against the mores of business. "The whole course of business in the world is governed and regulated by the maxims of supreme and unmixed selfishness," he said. Finney indicted capitalism itself, arguing that the "whole system recognizes only the love

---

4. "Thoughts on the Importance and Improvement of Common Schools," *Christian Spectator*, n.s., 1 (February 1827), 85; "On Sabbath Schools—Letter II," *Christian Spectator*, 1 (August 1829), 403.

5. James H. Fairchild, "Woman's Rights and Duties," *Oberlin Quarterly Review*, 4 (July 1849), 236–37, 346. The pagination in this fascicle appears to be haphazard.

6. Charles G. Finney, *Sermons on Gospel Themes* (Oberlin, OH: E. J. Goodrich, 1876), 352, 354. Finney upheld Bible societies as business models.

of self," and "the rules by which business is done in the world, are directly opposite to the gospel of Jesus Christ, and the spirit he exhibited." The man of business, by contrast, lives by the maxim: "Look out for number one."[7]

Evangelicals condemned usury and the corrosive effects of affluence. "The prosperity of the times in the business world threatens to endanger the piety of the church," a writer in the *New-York Evangelist* declared. "Can the heart be sanctified by constant contact with goods and merchandize, bills and invoices, notes and monies, checks and drafts?" The *Christian Chronicle* expressed similar reservations. "Riches, alas! are often amassed by the arts of oppression, extortion and deceit," the article warned. "Thus acquired, the blessing of heaven cannot rest upon them."[8]

These evangelical reservations about capitalism couldn't be more different from Jerry Falwell's declaration in 1984: "I believe in capitalism and the free enterprise system and private property ownership."[9]

Antebellum evangelicals supported prison reform, believing that "compassion must be mingled with severity." A group of evangelicals organized the New-York Peace Society in 1815. "The Society originated with a few individuals," the organization's annual report recalled three years later, "from the conviction that war is inconsistent with the Christian religion, immoral in its acts, and repugnant to the true interests of mankind." Members of the society worked toward the day when "these sentiments would become universal" and "men would beat their swords into ploughshares, and their spears into pruning hooks, and learn war no more." The Vermont Peace Society opened its membership to "Any person of good moral character, who receives the Bible as the rule of his faith."[10]

As evangelicals in the North worked for abolition, some Southern evangelicals, notably James Henry Thornwell and Robert Lewis Dabney, offered theological defenses of slavery. But Southern evangelicals understood the enormity of slavery, even as they differed from Northern evangelicals on how to end it. A writer in the *Virginia Evangelical & Literary Magazine* acknowledged slavery as "the greatest political evil which has ever entered the United States" and the slave trade as an "object of general detestation."

7. "Mr. Finney's Lectures on Christian Duty," *New-York Evangelist*, February 13, 1836, 26.

8. "The Moral Influence of 'Money-Making,'" *New-York Evangelist*, March 12, 1836, 41; "Reflections on Wealth," *Christian Chronicle*, November 7, 1818, 314.

9. Jerry Falwell, *Wisdom for Living* (Wheaton, IL: Victor, 1984), 131.

10. "New-York Peace Society," *Christian Spectator*, 1 (April 1819), 210; "From the Vermont Journal," *Christian Chronicle*, December 19, 1818, 391ff.; "Dying Confession of Joseph Hare, Remarks on the Penitentiary, &c," *Virginia Evangelical & Literary Magazine*, 1 (December 1818), 553, 554–55.

But, like other Southerners, he dismissed the notion of outright abolition. He urged support for colonization efforts in Africa and, in the meantime, advocated educational efforts for slaves to prepare them "for forming a prosperous colony." A writer from North Carolina sent a dispatch to the editor of the *Evangelical Witness* with a similar suspicion of abolition, even as he acknowledged that, "The intelligent part of the southern section of the United States, have long regarded slavery both as a moral and political evil, as it exists in our country."[11]

Paradoxically, the aversion of evangelicals in the North toward the scourge of slavery would lead the nation inexorably toward the expression of violence that many evangelicals found repugnant. The reforming impulses of evangelicalism in the North, especially opposition to slavery, finally drove an angry South to secession. By the time Confederate guns blazed against Fort Sumter in the early morning hours of April 12, 1861, evangelical piety in the South had turned inward, while evangelicalism north of the Mason-Dixon line held out for a benevolent empire that encompassed virtually all elements of life, from personal morality to public policy, from individual comportment to economic systems and international relations. The vision of society articulated by Charles Finney and other evangelicals took special notice of those on the margins of society—women, slaves, the victims of war and abuse, prisoners, the poor—those Jesus called "the least of these."

This vision of nineteenth-century evangelicalism stands in marked contrast to the political agenda of the majority of evangelicals at the turn of the twenty-first century. To be sure, some evangelicals in the earlier era took a dim view of social reform, either because of contrary political leanings or because they feared that it diverted attention from evangelism. But in contrast to the predilections of evangelicals late in the twentieth century, the dominant nineteenth-century agenda was reformist, directed toward the benefit of those on the margins. Whereas antebellum evangelicals supported common schools as a democratizing influence and a vehicle of upward mobility for those less fortunate, many contemporary evangelicals decry public education and seek taxpayer support for sectarian schools.

Evangelicals worked for the cessation of wars in the early decades of the nineteenth century, whereas evangelicals early in the twenty-first century overwhelmingly supported the invasion of both Iraq and Afghanistan. Nineteenth-century evangelicals advocated equal rights for women, but many evangelicals late in the twentieth century resisted the proposed Equal Rights Amendment to the Constitution. In the early decades of the

11. "Thoughts on Slavery," *Virginia Evangelical & Literary Magazine*, 2 (July 1819), 293, 294, 295; "Negro Slavery," *Evangelical Witness*, 2 (April 1824), 410.

twenty-first century, politicians with evangelical sympathies regularly tout their "pro-business" and "free enterprise" credentials. Many—possibly most—evangelicals of an earlier age, however, criticized "the rules by which business is done in the world" as "directly opposite to the gospel of Jesus Christ."[12]

Although few evangelicals could have suspected it at the time, the evangelical benevolent empire reached its apotheosis by 1860. With the onset of the Civil War, the shining aspirations of evangelical social amelioration began to dim for several decades as Americans coped with the devastation of the war and addressed the delicate task of mending the torn fabric of the republic. Even then, however, evangelicals were active in various freedman's associations, seeking to provide education and integration of African Americans into American life. In the waning decades of the nineteenth century, evangelical benevolence shifted toward the newly burgeoning cities with their roiling labor unrest and teeming, squalid tenements.

Many evangelicals joined with more theologically liberal Protestants in a movement known as Social Christianity, or the Social Gospel, which held that Jesus is capable of redeeming not only sinful individuals but sinful social institutions as well. They organized "slum brigades" and rescue missions and recreational opportunities, but they also sought to reform the systemic abuses that lay behind human misery. Advocates of the Social Gospel worked hand in hand with political progressives on behalf of child-labor laws, housing reform, and the six-day work week. They battled against alcohol abuse and corrupt political machines.

Evangelical support for Prohibition and worries about "godless communism" during the Cold War pushed evangelicals toward the political right during the twentieth century. Opposition on the part of some to Franklin Roosevelt's New Deal led to attenuated suspicions of capitalism and eventually to an embrace of commerce.

The 1970s proved to be the turning point in evangelicalism's divestment of its social conscience. A small group of evangelicals, meeting in Chicago, hammered out the Chicago Declaration of Evangelical Social Concern in November 1973. Meeting at the YMCA on Wabash Street, these evangelical leaders crafted a document remarkably consistent with the agenda of nineteenth-century evangelicals. The Chicago Declaration bemoaned the persistence of racism and militarism in American society. It decried the growing chasm between rich and poor and noted the scandal of hunger in

---

12. "Mr. Finney's Lectures on Christian Duty," *New-York Evangelist*, February 13, 1836, 26.

an affluent society. Finally, the Chicago Declaration affirmed evangelicalism's historic support for women's equality.

By no means did the Chicago Declaration speak for a majority of white evangelicals; following the lead of Billy Graham, they had overwhelmingly supported Richard Nixon over George McGovern the previous year. But progressive evangelicalism, as defined by nineteenth-century evangelicals and as reiterated in the Chicago Declaration, made one last stand in the candidacy of one of their own, Jimmy Carter, in 1976. Carter, a "born again" Sunday school teacher, was unabashed about his faith, and had it not been for his misbegotten *Playboy* interview, which hit the newsstands just weeks before the election, he likely would have won in a landslide. Instead, he squeaked into the White House.

The standard, albeit false, narrative is that evangelical concerns over legalized abortion prompted evangelicals' political engagement in the 1970s. This abortion myth, however, collapses under closer scrutiny. Evangelicals considered abortion a "Catholic issue" in the 1970s; the Southern Baptist Convention called for the legalization of abortion in 1971, and evangelical leaders, including W. A. Criswell of First Baptist Church in Dallas, applauded the *Roe v. Wade* decision of 1973.

The catalyst for the emergence of the Religious Right was not abortion. It was defense of tax exemptions for racially segregated schools—"segregation academies"—and Bob Jones University, which lost its tax exemption on January 19, 1976, because of its racial policies. Jerry Falwell, who had founded his own segregation academy in 1967, along with other evangelical preachers, banded together at the behest of Paul Weyrich and threw their support behind Reagan.

By the 1980 election, recognizing that support for segregation alone would not galvanize grassroots evangelicals, Falwell and the Religious Right began to lament what they characterized as moral decay in America, including gay rights and legalized abortion. Reagan, who opened his 1980 general election campaign with a speech about "states' rights" in Nashoba County, Mississippi, where three civil rights workers had been murdered by the Ku Klux Klan sixteen years earlier, became their champion, despite the fact that, as governor of California, he had signed into law the most liberal abortion bill in the country.

That alliance between Reagan and the Religious Right proved pivotal. Not only were evangelicals forced to abandon their long-standing opposition to divorce (Reagan was divorced and remarried), they gravitated toward the far-right precincts of the Republican Party. A movement that once identified with the poor and the marginalized supported tax cuts for the affluent, and it is no accident that the so-called prosperity gospel, a kind of spiritualized Reaganism, became all the rage among evangelicals in the 1980s. Whereas evangelicals in the early nineteenth century populated peace movements, by the early years of the twenty-first century they had become George W. Bush's biggest cheerleaders for his military adventures in Iraq and Afghanistan, invasions that would not meet even the barest of "just war" criteria.

Evangelical support for Trump in 2016, then, looks less like an aberration than the terminus of a slippery slope, or to shift the metaphor, the tragic culmination of a long illness evangelicals contracted in the late 1970s. The 2016 election allowed white evangelicals finally to abandon all pretense that theirs was a movement about "family values." The election also allowed the Religious Right to circle back to its founding principle, racism, for as history has proven time and time again, unaddressed racism festers and becomes malignant.

The death of evangelicalism leaves a gaping hole in American political discourse. Evangelicals in previous generations, from Charles Finney and Frances Willard to William Jennings Bryan, Mark Hatfield, and Jimmy Carter, called Americans to their better selves and people of faith to the front lines of social amelioration. Benevolence toward others, they believed, mandated actions on behalf of those on the margins. By contrast, the triumph of misguided prophets—Franklin Graham, Robert Jeffress, Tony Perkins, Jerry Falwell, Jr.—and their unblinking embrace of a mendacious politician leaves behind a movement utterly devoid of moral conscience or credibility.

But is the death of evangelicalism in 2016 the end of the story? I suspect it is, although we must never give up hope. Jesus, after all, raised Lazarus from the dead, even though, the Gospels tell us, his body had already begun to decay.

One of the tenets of evangelical theology is redemption. Evangelicals don't have the formalized process of confession and absolution that Catholics enjoy, but they believe in the possibility of forgiveness and amendment of life. In the realm of politics, every election offers a fresh chance.

If pressed, I would have to concede that I don't have much confidence that evangelicalism can rise again from the ashes of its self-immolation. Evangelicals, lacking sacramental theology, liturgical rubrics, or ecclesiastical hierarchies, are too susceptible to the cult of personality, and the unholy alliance between white evangelicals and the hard-right precincts of the Republican Party has calcified over the past four decades. But if I were to search for glimmers of hope, I'd look to evangelical women and to younger evangelicals willing to challenge the shibboleths of their elders and reclaim the faith.

Such reclamation would be an arduous process, one that would entail reconnecting with the Bible itself, which evangelicals claim as the basis for their authority. There they will find sobering words about care for the needy, clothing the poor, visiting the prisoners, and welcoming the foreigner as one of their own. Resuscitating evangelicalism would entail evangelicals reconnecting with their own past, especially the tradition of progressive evangelicalism. All of those evangelicals took biblical teachings seriously, but what set them apart was their willingness to transcend narrow, pinched interpretations in favor of a broader, more capacious understanding of the mandates of the gospel.

The Bible, after all, admits of many interpretations. As Jimmy Carter noted about his fellow Southern Baptists, the leaders of his denomination have the option of cherry-picking verses from the Bible to justify restrictions on women's ministry, or they could take the larger view, which would countenance such evidence as how Jesus himself treated women or Paul's declaration that in Christ there is no distinction between slave or free, male or female. He might have added that the former, literalistic approach to the Bible was not all that different from the one employed for centuries to justify slavery.[13]

Progressive evangelicalism generally has aspired to the broader view and, in so doing, the tradition has challenged not only those with more cramped readings of the Bible but also, in many cases, the prevailing social norms. When Charles Finney welcomed women to testify publicly in religious gatherings, for example, he was defying the social conventions of his day. When he and other evangelicals condemned the excesses of capitalism, advocating a moral economy rather than a market economy, they set themselves against the regnant economic thinking of the nineteenth century. The evangelical advocates for peace or common schools or prison reform or labor rights had little to gain personally from their causes, and their advocacy very often aligned them against powerful interests, but they persevered because they believed they were obeying the mandates of the gospel and the command of Jesus to care for "the least of these."

The death of evangelicalism is not irreversible. Evangelicals, after all, believe in the power of conversion. They also believe that Jesus raised Lazarus from the dead.

---

13. The Pauline reference is Galatians 3:28.

Chapter 11

Will the Evangelical Center
Remain Silent in 2020?

RONALD J. SIDER

MAJOR POLITICAL DISAGREEMENTS ARE REGULARLY DIFFICULT. MAJOR PO-
litical disagreements among Christians are often especially complicated and
painful. In addition, the greater the theological agreement among Christians disagreeing vigorously about politics, the greater the potential for pain
and tragedy.

Whenever Christians believe we must disagree publicly, we should begin with our common commitment to Christ. That is especially true when
the disagreement is over politics. Political discussions are almost infinitely
complex, and our knowledge and wisdom are painfully finite. Consequently, we must be humble about all our political judgments, confessing that we
might be wrong.

Furthermore, and far more important, all Christians—no matter how
large and pointed our political disagreements—confess one Lord and Savior. We all want Jesus Christ to be Lord of all our life, including our politics.
We all (hopefully) confess that our oneness in the one body of Christ is far
more important than our political disagreements. Therefore, we all know,
we ought to listen carefully to each other, pray together for God's guidance
in our political decisions, and be especially careful to state accurately without distortion the specific areas where we disagree.

In 2020, I feel compelled to disagree publicly with some evangelical Christians about the appropriate political choice for president this year. As I do that, here and elsewhere, however, I pray that God will help me to pray for, listen to, and fairly describe the views of those brothers and sisters in Christ with whom I disagree.

In 2016, a few evangelical leaders dared to say publicly that Donald Trump violated so many biblical principles and norms that Christians should not vote for him. Russell Moore, head of the Southern Baptist's official public policy organization (the Ethics and Religious Liberty Commission) said in *The New York Times* (September 17, 2015) that "to back Mr. Trump, these voters must repudiate everything they believe." Moore condemned Donald Trump's attitude toward women as "that of a Bronze Age warlord" and lamented the fact that Trump in his books "revels in the fact that he gets to sleep with some of the 'top women in the world.'" Peter Wehner, a distinguished Republican who served in important government positions in the administrations of Presidents Ronald Reagan, George H. W. Bush, and George W. Bush, condemned Trump as a "moral degenerate" and a "comprehensive and unrepentant liar." Even famous evangelical author Max Lucado (who had never spoken publicly about presidential candidates) warned against Donald Trump.

But the number of these courageous evangelical leaders was very small. Almost all who agreed with Moore, Wehner, and Lucado remained silent.

In September 2016, I talked with a very prominent evangelical leader whom I deeply respect. This person told me that he did not know anyone in his huge board of directors of more than fifty prominent evangelical leaders who supported Donald Trump for president. But those evangelical leaders said nothing publicly.

And their people voted for Trump! Eighty-one percent of white evangelicals supported Donald Trump on November 8, 2016.

Already in 2016, we knew that Donald Trump lied regularly and made frequent racist and sexist statements. We already knew that Trump lived a sexual life that was fundamentally contrary to biblical ethics. ("Grab them by the pussy," Trump said, in a statement listened to by millions.) We already knew in 2016 that Donald Trump's actions violated numerous biblical principles.

Today, four years later, the evidence is much more abundant and clear.

The president has referred to Haiti and certain African nations as "shit-hole countries." He has called Mexicans seeking asylum "rapists." Instead of condemning the white nationalist and Nazi sympathizers in the Charlottesville, Virginia, 2017 march, President Trump insisted there were fine people on "both sides." *The Washington Post* reported on January 20,

2020 that President Trump had made 16,200 false or misleading claims since becoming president (see Chris Thurman's chapter for massive documentation). Long-time Republican Peter Wehner labels President Trump a "compulsive liar." When globally respected newspapers like *The New York Times* print stories he dislikes, President Trump denounces their stories as fake news. He denies the overwhelming scientific consensus on global warming. No democracy can thrive (or even survive) if its political leaders reject the distinction between truth and falsehood and refuse to base their policy decisions on the best knowledge available.

At least as troublesome as his personal immoral behavior is his long list of public policies that are both dangerously wrong and fundamentally unjust by biblical standards.

Despite the ever-stronger scientific consensus that global warming will produce devastating climate change unless the world rapidly reduces carbon emissions, President Trump has reversed numerous measures that had begun to deal with the problem. He pulled the United States out of the 2015 Paris Agreement where almost all the nations of the world finally agreed to start taking substantial (although still not adequate) steps to reduce carbon emissions. By this action, President Trump has substantially stalled the essential changes we must make if our children and grandchildren are to inherit a livable planet. He promotes the mining of coal (the worst carbon polluter), reversed measures to demand more gasoline efficient cars, and weakened other important environmental policies.

President Trump's much vaunted tax bill gave the vast amount of its benefits to the richest Americans. (The tax bill did include a commendable expansion of the child tax credit, but this provision was written in such a way that most of the additional benefits go, not to poor Americans, but to more wealthy Americans.)

Trump's tax bill increased the already dangerously unequal distribution of wealth and income in the United States. The richest 1 percent of Americans own more wealth than the bottom 80 percent.[1]

Already from 1993 to 2007, more than half of all the population adjusted increase in the nation's income went to the richest 1 percent. And from 2002 to 2007, two-thirds of increased total US income went to the richest 1 percent.[2]

And the inequality has increased since then.

---

1. https://www.brookings.edu/blog/up-front/2019/06/25/six-facts-about-wealth -in-the-united-states/.

2. See my *Fixing the Moral Deficit* (Downers Grove, IL: InterVarsity, 2012), 26 and 151n12.

The average income of the richest 1 percent has increased by $800,000 since 1970. But the vast number of workers have not enjoyed much of an increase in income. After inflation is taken into account, the average hourly wage for non-management private sector workers is almost the same as it was in 1970![3]

The distribution of wealth in the US today is more unequal than at any time since just before the beginning of the great depression in 1929—and this growth in inequality fosters more injustice and seriously undermines democracy. President Trump's tax bill has added to that injustice—and greatly increased the national debt as well.

At the same time, President Trump has repeatedly moved to cut effective programs to empower poor people here and abroad—thus ignoring the central biblical teaching that God demands justice for all, especially the poor. (As evangelical leader Rick Warren has insisted, there are hundreds and hundreds of biblical verses about God's concern for the poor.)[4]

Trump has slashed foreign aid designed to help poor nations overcome poverty. He has tried (with some success) to cut food stamps which help poor Americans afford adequate food. His 2021 budget proposal contains deep cuts in student loan assistance, affordable housing programs, food stamps, and Medicaid (healthcare for poor Americans).

Healthcare for all is a central part of any biblically informed pro-life agenda. Careful studies show that people without health insurance fail to seek medical attention as soon as they should and, as a result, die younger. "Health insurance saves lives: the odds of dying among the insured, relative to the uninsured, is 0.71 to 0.97."[5]

In the richest nation on earth, good healthcare for everyone should be a basic demand of all Christians who respect the sanctity of every human life. But President Trump has done all he could to attack, weaken, and destroy the Affordable Care Act of 2010. As a result, millions have lost their health insurance. And he has vigorously tried (unsuccessfully thus far) to totally repeal that act, which provided health insurance to about 20 million more Americans and reduced the number of uninsured Americans to the smallest number in modern history. And, despite promises, he has not offered any alternative health plan.

---

3. https://www.pewresearch.org/fact-tank/2018/08/07/for-most-us-workers-real-wages-have-barely-budged-for-decades/.

4. See the almost 200 pages of biblical texts on this topic in Ronald J. Sider, ed., *For They Shall Be Fed* (Dallas: Word, 1997).

5. Steffie Woodlander and David U. Himmelstein, "The Relationship of Health Insurance and Mortality: Is Lack of Insurance Deadly?" *Annals of Internal Medicine*, 167 (6) (2017), 424–31.

One of the central biblical teachings is that God and God's people must have a special concern for the "sojourner" and "alien" (e.g., Deuteronomy 10:17–19). That means the immigrant! In Matthew 25:35–44, Jesus says that when we care for the "stranger," we actually care for Christ himself! But President Trump has attacked people seeking asylum as "rapists." Historically the United States has generously accepted large numbers of desperate refugees (people forced to flee from their homeland because of war or persecution). But President Trump has slashed the number of people admitted as refugees to the lowest point in many decades. Some 85,000 refugees were admitted in President Obama's last year in office. President Trump has drastically cut that number to 18,000. His policies have separated thousands of children from their parents at the border—causing agony and lifelong psychological damage.

I do not mean that the US should accept everyone who wants to come here. But biblical Christians should demand that our policies toward asylum-seekers and refugees be shaped by biblical teaching about how God wants us to treat the "sojourner."

What about President Trump's "America first" agenda? And the idea that America is a Christian nation with a special relationship to God that no other nation has? The Bible teaches that every person of every nation is made in the image of God and loved equally by God. God cares equally about every nation. For the biblical Christian, any politician who places the well-being of Americans above all else is flatly violating central biblical teaching.

Racism—the devastation of Native Americans; the centuries of slavery; the decades of lynching and legal discrimination against African Americans after the Civil War; and the decades of continuing discrimination in schools, housing, and jobs even after Dr. King's courageous civil rights movement—racism and its history continue to plague our nation. Our best political leaders have spoken and acted to lead us to a better future that transcends the racism of the past. President Trump has used subtle and not very subtle appeals to white racists. Peter Wehner cites studies in his book, *The Death of Politics*, that show that a major factor in the vote in 2016 of white, male Christians was their anxiety about losing their cultural dominance in this country.[6]

That was even more important than economic anxiety! (Sometime around the year 2015, the people who said they were "white" and "Christian" became a minority in America for the first time in our history.)

6. Peter Wehner, *The Death of Politics* (New York: HarperOne, 2019), 15–18.

Many of these white Christians men apparently feel that they face more discrimination in the United States than minorities, Muslims, and women! Instead of urging his followers to embrace the biblical view that all persons are created in the image of God and are equally loved by God, President Trump has blatantly stoked racist attitudes and failed to condemn the dangerous growing movement of militant white nationalism.

I acknowledge that some things President Trump has done will, in the short run, promote things I care about. His Supreme Court appointments will probably lead to decisions that move in the right direction on abortion and religious freedom. (But the new appointments will also very likely make decisions that hinder progress on ending racial discrimination, gerrymandering in politics, and unlimited political expenditures by very wealthy people [which fundamentally undermines our democratic process].)

Furthermore, as evangelical pastor and Republican candidate for Congress in 2018 Robb Ryerse says: "To vote for him because he sees the political expediency of supporting restrictions on abortion [Trump supported abortion before he ran for president] is a Faustian deal with the devil that is ultimately more likely to exact greater cost than reward."[7]

Clearly President Trump lies constantly, encourages white racists, models sexual immorality, and ignores factual, scientific knowledge. His policies in numerous areas—the environment, immigration, economic justice, taxes, policies that empower the poor, racial justice—violate fundamental biblical norms. And his vision of "America first" approaches idolatry.

So, What Should Evangelicals Do?

In 2008, an important book was published showing that in the years around 2000, an evangelical center had emerged.[8] This evangelical center rejected a narrow focus primarily on just abortion and marriage and instead adopted a much broader agenda that included abortion and marriage but also embraced a concern to end racism, promote economic justice, environmental concerns, and immigration reform. Composing this new evangelical center were evangelical organizations like InterVarsity Christian Fellowship, the National Association of Evangelicals, the Council for Christian Colleges and Universities, *Christianity Today*, Evangelicals for Social Action, evangelical relief and development agencies like World Vision and Compassion, International Justice Mission, black and Hispanic evangelicals, the Center

7. https://time.com/5775440/donald-trump-evangelicals-opposition/.

8. David P. Gushee, *The Future of Faith in American Politics* (Waco, TX: Baylor University Press, 2008), 87–117.

for Public Justice, evangelical publishing houses like Baker and IVP, and mega-church pastors like Rick Warren and Joel Hunter.

Perhaps the best single illustration of this new evangelical center was the official public policy document, *For the Health of the Nation,* unanimously adopted by the huge board of the National Association of Evangelicals. (The National Association of Evangelicals represents the largest evangelical network in the United States. Most evangelical denominations—Reformed, Wesleyan, Pentecostal—are members. And many heads of those denominations serve on its board.) *For the Health of the Nation* spells out the official public policy of the National Association of Evangelicals. And since 2004, the NAE has sought to work on all the positions endorsed in this document. In 2019 this document was updated and reaffirmed.

In the section on the "Method for Christian Civic Engagement," the document insists that "faithful evangelical civic engagement and witness must champion a biblically balanced agenda" (p. 13). "The Bible makes clear that God cares a great deal about the well-being of marriage and family, the sanctity of human life, justice for the poor, human rights, care for creation, peace, religious freedom and racial justice" (p. 13). Then it goes on to develop eight different issues in the section called "Principles of Christian Political Engagement" that are necessary for a "biblically balanced agenda." They are: religious liberty, the sanctity of human life (abortion and euthanasia), marriage, justice and compassion for the poor, human rights, racial justice, peace, and care for creation.

This consensus evangelical document insists that faithful evangelical engagement must be based on "the best available factual information" (p. 12). It also rejects an "America first" agenda, insisting that "we must advocate for policies that offer the most potential for creating the conditions of human flourishing, not only for Americans, but also for all those in the human community" (p. 18). That means that "the reduction of global poverty should be a central concern of American foreign-policy" (p. 34).

We must "welcome refugees and others who seek protection and opportunity within our nation" (pp. 18–19). "Immigration policies should prioritize family unity and avoid separating families by deportation or detention" (p. 34).

The document also calls Christians to "reject white supremacy" (p. 42).

"God identifies with the poor . . . Jesus said that those who do not care for the needy and the imprisoned demonstrate by such lack of action that they are not his followers (Matthew 25:31–46) . . . God measures societies by how they treat the vulnerable and powerless" (p. 33).

Both by his words and his policies, Donald Trump contradicts and violates many of the biblical principles and concrete applications of this consensus document of the most representative evangelical organization in the United States. Despite that, 81 percent of white evangelicals voted for Donald Trump and the vast majority still support him. And with a few notable exceptions, the white evangelical leaders of the evangelical center remain largely silent.

I believe a major test of biblical fidelity and courageous leadership in 2020 will be whether this large body of evangelical leaders in the center will dare to break their silence. Will they dare to say that biblical Christians demand truth and submission to the "best factual information"—including that on global warming? Will they dare to say that biblical faith demands a commitment not only to defend the sanctity of human life and religious freedom, but also to oppose racism and white supremacy, promote economic justice for the poor, welcome refugees, and care for creation?

That does not mean that I think most evangelical leaders should explicitly condemn Donald Trump and urge their people not to vote for him (although some, including this writer, will do that). And it does not mean they must urge their people to vote for Trump's Democratic opponent. But what they must do, if they do not want to repeat their timid, unfaithful silence of 2016, is to clearly and publicly call their people to support the candidate who embraces an agenda that comes closer, on balance, than other candidates, to reflecting a "biblically balanced agenda." "One-issue" voting contradicts the consensus public policy document of the evangelical center. My hope and prayer are that the leaders of the evangelical center will have the courage in 2020, clearly and publicly, to call their people to use their own official public policy document to decide how to vote in 2020.

Chapter 12

Voices from the Global
Evangelical Community

J. SAMUEL ESCOBAR,
DAVID S. LIM,
& D ZAC NIRINGIYE

THE DAY BEFORE THE INAUGURATION OF DONALD TRUMP, THE FORTY-fifth President of the United States, the International Fellowship for Mission as Transformation (INFEMIT) issued a call for biblical faithfulness to the radical implications of the gospel. Its message was for the church world-wide, but especially for the church in the United States. It called for biblical faithfulness amid what it identified as "the new fascism," words which many at the time deemed too harsh. Tragically, the words, policies, and actions of the Trump administration over the last four years have lived up to the charge. The possibility of a second Trumpian term compels us to reprint the Call, along with follow-up voices from Latin America, Asia, and Africa.

A Call for Biblical Faithfulness Amid the New Fascism[1]

A new form of dangerous political leadership is emerging in different parts of the world. Although this is not the first, and likely not the last time, the threat today of what can be called the new

1. INFEMIT, https://infemit.org/call-biblical-faithfulness/.

96

fascism is real. As an ideology characterized by fundamental-ist, militant, nationalistic, and racist policies, fascism threatens especially the "other," be it the poor, the oppressed, or the disen-franchised people for whom God has a special concern.

As members of the global evangelical community, we, the undersigned, feel compelled by the Spirit to call the church worldwide, first and foremost ourselves, to hear the clarion call of the Gospel to radical biblical faithfulness amid the new fas-cism and to renew its commitment to live out the peace, justice, and hope of the kingdom of God in Jesus Christ.

Though we witness this form of dangerous political leader-ship emerging in other parts of the world, we are issuing this statement around the inauguration of Donald J. Trump as the 45th President of the United States, because of that nation's global influence. We are keenly aware of the anxiety and fear being caused around the world by the actions, stated positions, and inflammatory foreign policy remarks of the President-elect.

As followers of Jesus, we also feel compelled to issue this call because we find it disturbing that many self-identified evan-gelicals in their respective countries contributed in no small part to the new fascism by the way they voted in a number of recent referenda (e.g., Colombia, United Kingdom) and national elec-tions (e.g., Philippines, United States). In the case of the U.S., we mourn the reduction of the gospel that resulted in single-issue voting, even as we acknowledge the complexity of the political process and the agony of many over the options available. It is true that for many evangelicals, their vote was more *against* the other candidates than it was *for* the one they elected. None-theless, we grieve the part that evangelicals played in electing a person whose character, values, and actions are antithetical to the Gospel. Furthermore, we find it inadmissible that some high-profile evangelical leaders have hailed the President-elect as a Christian and a prophet. It does not surprise us that many people, especially from the younger generation, are abandoning the evangelical world altogether.

As representative members of the global evangelical com-munity, we stand with all who oppose violence, racism, mi-sogyny, and religious, sexual and political discrimination by resisting the leadership of a person whose life, deeds and words have normalized and even glorified these postures. Our voices represent solidarity with them both in their grief over the results of the elections and in their resolve to speak to power in word and deed in these troubling times.

As a challenge to the new fascism, we call the whole church to biblical faithfulness in:

- the merciful and just treatment of immigrants, refugees, strangers, and racial and religious minorities.

- the rejection of all sorts of objectification of women and commercialization of sex.

- the responsible and just regard for the care of God's creation, including taking seriously the reality and dangers of climate change.

- the commitment to world peace in the face of the war industry, military rhetoric and action.

- the courageous and self-sacrificing pursuit of the welfare of the poor, marginalized, people with disabilities, and other vulnerable groups, including children and youth.

Finally, we call to account the incoming U.S. President and his administration in the power of the Gospel, warning them that God holds each nation, each leader, and each individual responsible for how they act on behalf of the poor and the oppressed. And we encourage all God's people to pray for the United States and its leaders, for the sake of the welfare not only of U.S. citizens but of all people around the world.

J. Samuel Escobar (Lima, Peru)

I believe that in good conscience, both as a Latin American evangelical and as an American citizen, I cannot support President Trump. For me it would be supporting a pagan war-maker in clear contrast with a Christian peacemaker. Trump is a pagan, and this is demonstrated by a behavior in which wealth, sex, and power were the dominant values in his life. I see no evidence that his moving close to the conservative Protestant side of the American scene is the result of a conversion to Christ either in speech or in behavior.

Of course, this places me in an uncomfortable position as a citizen. Is there a possibility that a Christian peacemaker may enter in the political arena of the USA today and be elected as president? Or is that unthinkable? I am aware that even evangelicals who share theological convictions and political principles may not agree in answering these questions.

In the year 2005 and as a result of his experience as President of the United States, Jimmy Carter wrote: "Americans cherish the greatness of our homeland, but many do not realize how extensive and profound are the transformations that are now taking place in our nation's basic moral values, public discourse and political philosophy."[2]

For me, the way in which the policies as well as the discourse of President Trump have developed in these years that he has been in office, show the accuracy as well as the relevance of what Carter predicted in 2005. He said: "Narrowly defined theological beliefs have been adopted as the rigid agenda of a political party. Powerful lobbyists, both inside and outside government, have distorted an admirable belief in free enterprise into the right of extremely rich citizens to accumulate and retain more and more wealth and pass all of it on to descendants. Profits from stock trading and income from dividends are being given privileged tax status. To quote a Christian friend, the new economic philosophy in Washington is that a rising tide raises all yachts."[3]

I am not writing as a Democratic voter but as a Christian pondering the reflections of another Christian with great political experience. What do his reflections tell me about what I, as a missiologist, can learn from them as to the way God acts in history and expects Christians to act?

In 1985 Jimmy Carter published his book *The Blood of Abraham*. As he tells us in the initial pages of the book, it is an effort to which Carter dedicated several years.[4]

It has a historical chronology of the region which goes from 9,000 before Christ to 1985, and five excellent maps that include Abraham's trip to the birth of the State of Israel as well as the situation up to 1984. Carter wants his readers to understand a really complex situation. With his wife Rosalynn and with Kenneth Stain, he traveled through Egypt, Israel, Jordan, Saudi Arabia, Syria, Lebanon, and Morocco. A chapter is dedicated to each and in every one of them the Carters interviewed statesmen, scholars, and authorities.

I have come to the conclusion that by his way of life, his commitment to Christian truth and the quality of his testimony, President Jimmy Carter showed that it was possible for a Christian to hold such a position acting as a Christian peacemaker and not as a pagan war seeker.

2. Jimmy Carter, *Our Endangered Values* (New York: Simon and Shuster, 2005), 3.

3. Carter, *Endangered*, 4.

4. Jimmy Carter, *The Blood of Abraham* (Boston: Houghton Mifflin Company, 1985), vii–viii.

David S. Lim (Manila, Philippines)

Why not reelect Trump? Eight reasons. I share my political views as a representative voice of the evangelical movement in Asia, having been in the leadership teams of the Lausanne Movement in the Philippines since 2007 and in Asia (especially Southeast Asia) since 2008.

As a vocal critic of the Trump-like Philippine President Rodrigo Duterte, I would like to call all evangelical citizens of the USA to campaign as vehemently as possible to oppose the reelection of President Donald Trump. Trump's election with the strong backing of white Evangelicals has shown that US Evangelicalism has fallen into the worst-case scenario that I wrote about thirty-five years ago.[5]

Here in brief are the eight main reasons why I urge Americans, especially evangelicals, not to vote for Trump again.

Personal integrity matters

Above all, leadership, especially world leadership, must be by example. Over the past three years Trump has proven that his character and leadership have no moral fiber. His values and behavior have been antithetical to biblical standards and even plain simple ethics. His life, deeds, and words have enhanced racism (particularly white supremacy), misogyny, sexual and political discrimination, and gun violence. He has been devoid of empathy and compassion for the poor and marginalized (especially minorities and refugees) and even of decency in speech (most notably the vulgarity in his tweets). He has made false and misleading statements routinely and unapologetically.[6] He has yet to apologize for any lie, mistake, or sin that he has said or done.

Leadership style matters

Secondly, Trump has practiced a Machiavellian (or dictatorial) style of leadership and has shown his high regard for contemporary dictators like Russia's Putin, China's Xi, and North Korea's Kim. Politics thus becomes amoral—any means however unscrupulous can justifiably be used to achieve and maintain power. His governance has been unprincipled and manipulative, often unethical and dishonest, showing no respect for human

5. David Fraser, ed., *The Evangelical Round Table, II: Evangelicalism: Surviving Its Success* (Princeton, NJ: Princeton University Press), 210–36.

6. Cf. "Veracity of Statements by Donald Trump," *Wikipedia*.

rights and rule of law. No one can trust any tweet he posts or any word he says. This is far from the model of President "Honest Abe" Lincoln.

This is also seen in his "transactional politics" based on personal vendetta. If one treats him badly, Trump will hit back even more badly. If another treats him well, Trump will reward him doubly. He has been petty, making decisions based on personal hurt feelings. This narcissistic pattern is seen in his hostility to any criticism from any person (including his appointed staff and advisers, and even his party mates) in any media (including his favorite Fox News)

National unity matters

Thirdly, rather than working for national unity, Trump has encouraged worse public divisions. Perhaps he is just riding on the global trend towards populist politics, like China's Xi, India's Modi, the UK's Johnson, Philippines' Duterte, etc. But this has not been the case in many other countries, like Germany, France, Sweden, Finland, New Zealand, Japan, Singapore, etc. Populisms claim to represent the common people and use narrow nationalistic sentiments (like building walls and discriminating against minorities) to gain loyalty and votes. This is shown in Trump's persistent use of personalization of issues, thereby building a personality cult around himself. This has resulted in the heated polarization of the citizenry, seen in the voters' choice based on loyalty (or disloyalty) to his person rather than his party platform and/or national policies.

Just policies matter

Fourthly, since the 1963 March on Washington, the USA has made great strides in fulfilling the ideals on which the country was founded. But the fight for true equality continues today.[7]

Trump rolled back previous regimes' regulations and pushed through a corporate tax cut while boosting military spending, thereby putting unemployment to a record low, yet driving inequality worse.

Due to these and other "anti-poor" policies, more than 1.5 million US public school students were homeless at some point over the past three years, according to data from the 2017–2018 academic year published in

---

7. Cf. "Equality now," *Time*, March 2–9, 2020, 28–83.

January 29, 2020 by the National Center for Homeless Education. That is more than double the number from 2004–2005.[8]

Foreign policies matter

Fifthly, cancelling or changing trade deals and military pacts has made the USA appear like a rogue superpower that wants to bully weaker nations, while China has been making friends with its Belt and Road Initiative and generous loans. Trump even reversed Obama's "pivot to Asia" policy! Today, no one (not even Trump himself) knows what his overall foreign master plan is!

In the Middle East, Trump unilaterally recognized the divided Jerusalem as the capital and disputed Golan Heights as a sovereign part of Israel, thereby raising the "rumors of war." And in Syria, the USA should be using her diplomatic power to "insist on a cease-fire and a negotiated peace based on some measure of political participation, accountability and the conditions for the safe return of refugees."[9]

Instead his sudden personal decision to pull strategic troops out of Syria has left a leadership vacuum that Russia and Turkey have gladly filled.

Climate crisis matters

Sixthly, confronting the challenge of climate change needs resolute leadership based on "*the* Science." At the mid-February Davos 2020 event, teenage activist Greta Thunberg rightly said, "Pretty much nothing has been done since the global emissions" of carbon dioxide have not been reduced. In fact global temperatures will rise far beyond the desired level even if governments follow through on their current commitments in the Paris Agreement.[10]

G20 reports that it is Trump's USA that is the only member that opposes the issuance of a clear statement to take serious steps to address the climate emergency. We need global leaders who are not "climate deniers," but "creation care" advocates to minimize if not eradicate this catastrophe for generations to come.

8. "News Ticker: Students face record homelessness," *Time*, February 10, 2020, 10.

9. Angelina Jolie, "The price of inaction in Syria," *Time*, March 2–9, 2020, 18.

10. Justin Worland, "The world of finance groggily awakens to climate change," *Time*, February 10, 2020, 16 and 18.

US leadership matters

Seventhly, in a world where Communist China has risen rapidly to become "the superpower" by 2030 if not earlier, the USA has to have a clear blueprint on what to do, particularly on trade deals and military pacts, and a strategic chart toward attaining world peace. But so far Trump has shown that he has no such master plan and no intention of following the wisdom of the Pentagon or the multilateral decisions of the United Nations and other global bodies.

As the commander-in-chief of still the world's superpower (and its allies, especially the Philippines, Taiwan, South Korea, and Japan in Asia), Trump has made USA into an unpredictable bully nation, behaving like the tough "Ugly American" depicted in the 1958 book of Eugene Burdick and William Lederer.[11]

He has made the world more vulnerable, uncertain, unsafe, and insecure. Trump's slogan to "make America great again" sounds so hollow and laughable!

Evangelical brand matters

Eighth and lastly, with white evangelicals being the key supporters of Trump and his regime, the identity and reputation of American (and global) evangelicalism is at stake. And with the above seven reasons, it has been an embarrassing and shameful downward slide. As a key leaders of the Philippine and Asian partner-members of the Lausanne Movement, my colleagues and I have started to label ourselves as "post-evangelical" and white evangelicalism as "fundamentalist"! We long to return to being called simply "evangelicals" (with white American "fundamentalists" on board, too) as soon as possible.

In short, you need to redeem the damage of bringing embarrassment (if not dishonor) to your country's status (and to Christ's name) in Trump's first term. Trumpism has been a great disaster. Trump made American degraded, debased, and decadent! For the above eight reasons, therefore, I plead with American voters by the mercies of God, please vote for the next presidential candidate who is "anti-Trump"! Let history not show that you are ignorant accomplices to your past shameful deed of enabling and supporting the worst president of the USA who made your country ugly (and uglier) again! "In God (alone) we trust."

---

11. That American ambassador's "loud and ostentatious" behavior was offensive to the local people.

Bishop D Zac Niringiye (Kampala, Uganda)

Two reasons compel me to share my thoughts about the political situation in the United States. First, I was a signatory to INFEMIT's Call to Biblical Faithfulness. I consider this a further opportunity to share my angst and sense of a *kairos* moment that the Trump Presidency and candidature presents. Second and more importantly, I belong to the body of Christ and therefore, as a fellow pilgrim with brothers and sisters in the USA and indeed all over the world (past, present, and future), it behooves me to share in their struggles, hopes, dreams and fears. It is a shared journey, in Christ, in the world.

There will be some who question the second motivation. They ask: What business does a citizen of another country (in this case Uganda) have with the business of citizens in another country (USA), who exercised and will be exercising their responsibility in making a choice on by whom and how they are governed? Indeed, there is a lot that could be said in favor of this objection. But, as the gospel of Christ teaches us, although we belong and dwell in *different countries*, we dwell on the *one earth*; and although we belong to *different nations*, we also belong together as the *one human family*, created in the image of God. We are all "God's offspring" (Acts 17:28). Therefore, whether we like it or not, we are unavoidably interdependent: one human family, in a single habitat (the earth).

Moreover, those of us who invoke the name of Jesus of Nazareth as the Christ of God, the Lord and Savior of all creation, as the ground for our identity and location in the world, know that irrespective of where we are and what citizenship we hold, we share together in the citizenship of the kingdom of God. That is why *The Call* was addressed primarily to "the church worldwide, first and foremost ourselves, to hear the clarion call of the Gospel to radical biblical faithfulness . . ." Each location, in time and geography, and the perspective from that location, adds to the developing wisdom of the worldwide church.

There are some who have questioned *The Call*'s reference to a "new fascism" and its timing "around the inauguration of Donald J. Trump as the 45th President of the United States, because of that nation's global influence." Certainly, there is need to continue to evaluate the correlation of the "new fascism" with the current president of the USA, because *The Call* itself stands or falls on this. The question should therefore be what it is about the "Trump phenomenon" that justifies *The Call*'s placing Trump in the category of "the new fascism." And why should it matter to all of us (American and non-American, Christian or non-Christian, evangelical or whatever shade of Christianity) whether that critique is grounded in the gospel?

I was having a conversation over lunch one afternoon with my friend Valerie from Burkina Faso, who was visiting Uganda for a conference. We talked with each other about the hopes and fears of Africa and her people, as we surveyed the dismal performance (to say the least) of contemporary political leadership across the continent. We agreed that the exception proves the rule. We also spoke about the external influences and pressures, particularly from the USA, Europe, and China. I then shared with her my assignment to write this reflection. She was very quick to interject: "Let me tell you why I like President Trump." I was startled. I prepared myself to hear from her what I had heard from many Christians in different parts of Africa, why they (like the majority of American evangelicals) like Trump: that he is chosen by God, according to Romans 13; the "King Cyrus" of our times; a man who is committed to defend and protect Christianity from Islam, secular humanists, and other "enemies"; and one who has shown commitment to fight for the promotion of family values, against abortionists and the LGBTIQ agenda. But Valerie likes Trump for a different reason: because he presents to the world, and in particular to the USA an opportunity for critical self-examination. "President Trump is like a mirror. He is a reflection of the society that voted him into power," Valerie clarified. She explained to me that in her view the presidency of Donald J. Trump provided the opportunity for America generally and evangelical America in particular to see itself for what it really is; and that, looking toward the next election, the question should not be about the terrifying prospect of his reelection, but rather whether America and in particular evangelical America has yet come to terms with the America and world that affirms the Trump narrative. I couldn't agree with her more.

The critical issue therefore is to come to grips with the story that the Trump phenomenon tells: the story that "the Trump base" (that includes American evangelicals) tells to itself and to America and the world; its roots and shoots in American history and society; and its resonance with narratives in different countries and contexts elsewhere in the world. Who we are and how we self-identify and make sense of our location in the world, are the stories we have imbibed and tell ourselves and the world. Stories have a way of not only making the past present, but also creating individual and societal imaginations of the future.

I suggest that the story that Trump lives and is indeed the central feature of the Trump phenomenon, is fear. Fear is the story he embodies, projects, and presents. Fear is what he hopes will shape the present and the future of America and the world. As I read his tweets and addresses, his executive orders, his hiring and firing of various members in his administration, how he interacts with other world leaders, and what he says of other nations and their relationship with the USA, the story line is one of fear. It was epitomized in his signature election pledge to the American people: building a wall on the whole length of the US-Mexico border. The performance of fear is evident in the relentless pursuit of nationalism—what John Stott called "a blinkered and exaggerated loyalty to 'my country right or wrong,'"[12] which is rooted in structures of race and racism. Nationalism thrives on intolerance of "the other" and is the very antithesis of the motif of one human family, in a single habitat. These three traits—fear, nationalism, and intolerance—are what define what *The Call* named as "the new fascism."

Thus, when America voted for Trump, they voted for fear. The fact that the majority of white American evangelicals voted for Trump should be seen in the same light: a vote in favor of fear of the other. That now provides the meaning of "evangelical" identity and location in America and the world. *The Call* rightly points out that this is a form of dangerous political leadership that is emerging in different parts of the world. It did not surprise me when Yoweri Museveni, the military dictator, who this year is entering his thirty-fifth year as president of Uganda, praised Trump as "one of the best presidents ever" for America. This was two weeks after Trump described African nations, along with Haiti and El Salvador, as "shithole countries" whose inhabitants were not desirable as immigrants to the United States.[13]

Narratives grounded in fear are the very antithesis of the gospel story because the essence and logic of the gospel is love: "For God so loved the world that he gave his one and only Son, that whoever believes in him shall not perish but have eternal life" (John 3:16). Jesus himself said: "'Love the Lord your God with all your heart and with all your soul and with all your mind' and . . . 'Love your neighbor as yourself'" (Matthew 22:37, 39). The Apostle John captured it very well: "There is no fear in love. But perfect love drives out fear" (1 John 4:18). Therefore, in my view, the question that the next US general election presents to evangelical Christians in the USA is whether to grasp the opportunity to repent of fear and seek a path of love. Will American evangelicals repent of the pursuit of building walls and choose building bridges (justice, peace, and reconciliation)? Will you move beyond narratives of fear, to the hard and joyful work of love?

---

12. John Stott, *Issues Facing Christians Today*, 4th ed. (Grand Rapids: Zondervan, 2006), 180.

13. https://www.washingtonpost.com/news/worldviews/wp/2018/01/23/ugandan-president-says-he-loves-trump-he-talks-to-africans-frankly/.

Chapter 13

"If You Board the Wrong Train . . ."

American Christians, Dietrich Bonhoeffer, and Donald Trump

STEPHEN HAYNES

I HAVE LONG ARGUED THAT THE GERMAN PASTOR-THEOLOGIAN DIETRICH Bonhoeffer (1906–1945) occupies a unique place in the American imagination. In 2004, I wrote a book—*The Bonhoeffer Phenomenon: Portraits of a Protestant Saint*—that detailed the various ways Bonhoeffer has been adopted, adapted, and domesticated by American Christians. The book described competing portraits of Bonhoeffer in which his admirers cast him as a radical theologian, a liberationist, a pacifist, a righteous Gentile, a martyr of conscience, and a model of mature faith. *The Bonhoeffer Phenomenon* also included a chapter on the "evangelical Bonhoeffer" that detailed the pastor-theologian's growing stature among conservative Christians.

Still, until four years ago, I could not have imagined the words "American Christians, Dietrich Bonhoeffer, and Donald Trump" in the same sentence. Support for "the Donald" among otherwise sane and law-abiding Christians? It would have seemed preposterous. True, at the end of *The Bonhoeffer Phenomenon,* in order to highlight the perils associated with emulating Bonhoeffer in contemporary America, I noted that some radical pro-lifers had used Bonhoeffer's role in an assassination plot against Hitler to justify the murder of abortion providers. But the Bonhoeffer-inspired abortion activists of the 1990s were fringe figures. By 2004 those who were not dead or in prison were complaining of their abandonment by pro-life Christians, most of whom had repudiated them. By comparison, Trump's Christian supporters are eminently mainstream. They include Eric Metaxas, a Yale-educated author and syndicated radio show host who made his reputation with a bestselling biography of Bonhoeffer.

So here we are in 2020. Well-known evangelicals, led by men with surnames like Graham and Falwell, not to mention leaders of prominent churches in established denominations, are backing Donald Trump with an enthusiasm and confidence few of us could have predicted four years ago. Encouraged by these thought leaders, lesser lights have come forward to celebrate Trump's "Christ-like sense of boldness," assert that he is "chosen" by God, and claim that Jesus himself would vote for him. Meanwhile rank-and-file evangelicals use letters to the editor, op-ed pieces, blogs and podcasts to make their own "Christian case for Trump," often invoking Bonhoeffer in the process.

By itself, Bonhoeffer's ubiquity in American public discourse is not surprising. As I discuss in *The Battle for Bonhoeffer: Debating Discipleship in the Age of Trump* (2018), Americans are often drawn to Bonhoeffer during periods of political or social conflict. Over the last decade, in fact, conservatives have coined the phrase "Bonhoeffer moment" to express their conviction that America faces an imminent moral crisis. The first to invoke the phrase in making such a case was Metaxas, who at the National Prayer Breakfast in Washington in 2012 linked abortion with slavery and Nazism. While Metaxas's presumption in lecturing President Obama and other government officials on the evils of abortion was surprising, his recruitment of Bonhoeffer to the pro-life cause was not. The German pastor-theologian had long been a hero of American abortion opponents, based on some strong words on abortion as "murder" in his *Ethics*.

Nor was it surprising three years later when, in anticipation of the Supreme Court's decision in *Obergefell v. Hodges*, a "Bonhoeffer moment" was proclaimed by conservative Christians who believed the imminent legalization of same-sex marriage should trigger cultural resistance. These evangelicals rightly saw in the pending Supreme Court decision evidence of a sea change in attitudes toward traditional marriage, a threat to religious freedom (which for them included the right to refuse service to same-sex couples), and a warning that their enemies in the culture war were on the verge of a stunning victory.

But how did we get from invoking Bonhoeffer to undergird a principled moral stance in opposition to same-sex marriage to using him to marshal support for a presidential candidate whose record with regard to traditional marriage was, let us say, mixed? This is precisely where we had arrived by October 2016 when, responding to Trump's misogynist rant caught on tape by *Access Hollywood*, Metaxas defended the presidential candidate in a *Wall Street Journal* op-ed piece. Stunningly, he did so by directly comparing Trump to Bonhoeffer, who, according to Metaxas, "also did things most Christians of his day were disgusted by."

How did evangelical Christians go from declaring that shifting moral boundaries constituted a "Bonhoeffer moment" for Bible-believing Christians to climbing aboard the bandwagon of the least moral presidential candidate in memory? One thing is for certain, once aboard the Trump train, evangelical leaders have adamantly defended their decision to ride, despite a cascade of troubling revelations about the president's character. In fact, there seems to be an implicit competition among Trump's Christian supporters on who will be the first to double down when a new crisis emerges. Currently Metaxas seems to have taken the lead, based on a January 2020 piece in *The Wall Street Journal* titled "The Christian Case for Trump" and a recent radio show in which he compared the president's impeachment to the mass psychosis that brought Hitler to power.

So how do we explain this shift in American evangelicals' use of the Bonhoeffer legacy? The answer one is most likely to hear is that Bonhoeffer was against abortion and Trump promises to stack the Supreme Court enough to overturn *Roe v. Wade*. Fair enough. But here is where Bonhoeffer-loving evangelicals need to look more carefully at the German pastor-theologian's own commitments.

Even if we assume Bonhoeffer would have opposed legal abortion as it exists in America (which is not self-evident), or that he would have opposed same-sex marriage (even less self-evident)—that is, even if we assume that the "Bonhoeffer moments" declared by conservatives in recent years align to some degree with Bonhoeffer's own concerns—we are a far cry from exhausting Bonhoeffer's meaning for the present day. Abortion and marriage were simply not at the heart of his theological concerns. Nor do the issues on which anti-Trumpers tend to apply Bonhoeffer—the Muslim ban, failure to condemn white supremacy, draconian immigration policies—fully capture his relevance for us. All these attempts to demonstrate Bonhoeffer's relevance in contemporary America are faithful to his legacy as far as they go, but they miss the theological concern at the center of his own life and work: the German church's failure to resist political co-optation.

After 1933, Bonhoeffer's life was dedicated to defining and maintaining authentic Christian existence under totalitarianism. He believed the individual was called to do so by following Christ at all costs, while the church, although it had no direct role in political life, was called to preach the gospel while defending itself from encroachment by alien ideologies.

From 1933 until he joined the anti-Hitler resistance around 1940, Bonhoeffer's mission was to protect the church's independence from a totalitarian state that would usurp Christ's role as "God's vigorous announcement of his claim upon our whole life" (as the Barmen Declaration put it). It was in service of this calling that he moved to England in 1933, joined the Confessing Church in 1934, wrote *Discipleship* in 1935, took over the directorship of an illegal seminary in 1937, maintained "collective pastorates" when the seminary closed, and returned from America to Germany in 1939.

The implication for us is clear enough. If American Christians desire to extend Bonhoeffer's legacy, at the heart of their vision must be a determination to resist the "false doctrine," repudiated in the Barmen Declaration, that the church recognize "other events, powers, historic figures and truths as God's revelation." Bonhoeffer's earliest and most singular contribution to the German Church Struggle was his insistence that if the church adjusted its constitution by excluding "non-Aryans" from the German Reich Church, it would succumb to precisely this kind of false doctrine. In theological terms, Bonhoeffer stressed that adopting a racial qualification for church membership was not *adiaphora* (something about which sincere Christians could disagree), but a *status confessionis* (a situation demanding an unequivocal confession of faith). In the "confessional situation" precipitated by attempts to coordinate the Christian message with Nazism through adoption of the "Aryan Paragraph," the church's very substance was at stake.

In this sense, the thing that most concerned Bonhoeffer was not Nazism per se, but his fellow Christians' determination to bring the church into "alignment" with it. In fact, as Michael DeJonge has recently shown, the ecclesiastical concept of *status confessionis* Bonhoeffer worked out in 1933 was fundamental to the theology of resistance that informed his entire career.[1]

This is why it is so alarming to see American Christians claiming to revere Bonhoeffer while committing the very theological error he was determined to resist—willingly conforming Christian faith to a popular political movement.

With regard to Trump and Trumpism, this process of conformation is most evident in the shift in evangelical attitudes regarding a candidate's personal morality. While in 2011 only 30 percent of American evangelicals believed "an elected official who commits an immoral act in their personal

---

1. See Michael DeJonge, *Bonhoeffer on Resistance* (Oxford: Oxford University Press, 2018).

life can still behave ethically and fulfill their duties in their public and professional life," by October 2016 the number was 70 percent.[2]

Then after the election, as hope faded that the presidency would calibrate Trump's moral compass, his evangelical supporters began to claim they really didn't need moral leaders at all, citing the example of Persian King Cyrus as proof that even godless autocrats can be instruments of the divine will.

The Cyrus analogy appeals to evangelicals precisely because it implies that God works through "imperfect vessels," particularly if they are engaged in a larger task of "restoration." But claims to see the "hand of God" in Trump's election have eerie parallels with the Nazi era. Hitler's unlikely breakthrough after years of struggle convinced many German Christians he had been placed in power through a graceful act of divine intervention. Here are a few examples of how they interpreted God's role in Hitler's rise:

- ". . . No one could welcome January 30, 1933 [the date of Hitler's accession to power] more profoundly or more joyfully than the German Christian leadership."

- "Adolf Hitler, with his faith in Germany, as the instrument of our God became the framer of German destiny and the liberator of our people from their spiritual misery and division."

- "[Hitler is] the best man imaginable, a man shaped in a mold made of unity, piety, energy and strength of character."

- "[Hitler], the most German man, is also the most faithful, a believing Christian. We know that he begins and ends the course of his day with prayer, that he has found in the Gospel the deepest source of his strength."

- "If the German who truly believed in Jesus could find the Spirit of the kingdom of God anywhere, he could find it in Adolf Hitler's movement."

- ". . . in the pitch-black night of Christian church history, Hitler became like a wonderful transparency for our time, a window through which light fell upon the history of Christianity."

- "[God has granted us an] hour of grace . . . through Adolf Hitler."

- "God has once again raised his voice in a singular individual."[3]

2. "POLL: White Evangelicals Have Warmed To Politicians Who Commit 'Immoral' Acts," *npr.com*, https://www.npr.org/2016/10/23/498890836/poll-white-evangelicals-have-warmed-to-politicians-who-commit-immoral-acts).

3. Mary Solberg, ed., *A Church Undone* (Minneapolis: Fortress, 2015) 145, 197, 246,

Note the similar language used by these American Christians in response to Trump's election:

- "God raised up . . . Donald Trump" (Michele Bachmann).

- "God has righteously chosen [Trump] to affect the way that this nation goes forward" (Chuck Pierce).

- "Donald Trump represents a supernatural answer to prayer" (James Robison).

- "Donald Trump actively seeks God's guidance in his life" (James Dobson).

- Trump's victory "showed clear evidence of 'the hand of God' on the election" (Franklin Graham).

- "[Trump is] a bold man, a strong man, and an obedient man" (Kenneth Copeland).

- "I see this as a last-minute reprieve for America, and the Church" (Rodney Howard-Browne).

- "[Trump] does look like he's the last hope" (Phyllis Schlafly).

- "God was raising up Donald Trump as he did the Persian king Cyrus the Great" (Lance Wallnau)

- "God had raised up [Trump] for such a time as this" (Stephen Strang).

- "In the midst of . . . despair, came November the 8th, 2016. It was on that day . . . that God declared that the people, not the pollsters, were gonna choose the next president of the United States. And they chose Donald Trump" (Robert Jeffress).

- "We thank God every day that he gave us a leader like President Trump" (Robert Jeffress)[4]

Given how evangelical Christians have come to revere the German Confessing Church, the Barmen Declaration, and men like Bonhoeffer and Karl Barth, it is ironic that so many of them have blithely recapitulated the mistakes committed by German Christians in the wake of the Nazi revolution. Like those naïve and desperate Germans, many of our Christian leaders, convinced that God was at work in Trump's unlikely accession to power, have been willing to interpret whatever Trump says and does as in keeping with the divine plan.

302, 333, 347, 353, 358.

4. Stephen E. Strang, *God and Donald Trump* (Lake Mary, FL: FrontLine, 2017), 4, 15, 17, 22, 25, 30, 60, 64, 65, 65, 75, 76, 107, 131, 150, 169, 170, 176.

I doubt if Christian Trump supporters will be convinced by this analogy, but here is an easy way for them to disprove it: Tell the rest of us what
Trump would have to do to lose their support. How far would he have to
slide into immorality/corruption/unconstitutionality to convince them that
God is not on Trump's side, that he is not the "chosen one," that he is doing
more to undermine than to restore the moral order?

Here's why we need to know: The so-called falsifiability principle,
which has applications in philosophy and science, holds that if a claim cannot be falsified—that is, if one can't identify the conditions under which it
would be disproved—then that claim is based in blind faith and cannot be
taken seriously. I would challenge Christian admirers of Trump with this
version of the falsifiability principle. If your support for the president is to
be considered something other than class or race resentment, tribalism,
religious bigotry, or simple stubbornness, then you must identify the conditions under which it would be withdrawn.

Trump has (jokingly?) claimed that he could shoot someone in public
without alienating his base. I suspect this is the case for many of his Christian supporters, although only they can say for sure. So tell us: if there are no
circumstances under which your support for Trump would be withdrawn,
the rest of us can conclude with confidence what we've come to suspect—
that your Trumpism is not a serious political commitment but the sort of
no-turning-back, all-or-nothing, fatal embrace that Christians have often
offered political leaders who catered to them.

One would have thought a breaking point was reached with the *Access Hollywood* tapes; or with reports that Trump carried on an affair with a
porn star while Melania was at home with their child, and then bought the
woman's silence; or when it became clear that he put his own interests before those of the country in the Ukraine scandal. But because none of these
revelations has seemed to affect evangelical support for Trump, it would not
be surprising if evangelicals simply cannot imagine a circumstance in which
they would abandon the "chosen one." If this is true, we have prima facie
evidence that their support is nothing more than instinct or prejudice and
thus lacks the moral and spiritual seriousness that is supposed to characterize Christian life.

Another thing for Christian supporters of Trump to consider is
whether their support for a president who attracts allegiance from white
supremacists belies their claim that they have learned the requisite lessons
from eras when Christianity was on the wrong side of history. Many evangelicals are determined never to repeat the mistakes of American Christians
who established "biblical" cases for slavery and segregation, for example.
They decry the Dred Scott Supreme Court decision, quote from the sermons

of Martin Luther King, Jr., and refer to the brave souls at Selma, all in order to differentiate themselves from the white Christians who defended slavery, excluded blacks from their churches, and stood by while civil rights warriors were vilified and attacked.

I suspect this desire to demonstrate Christianity's moral credibility is part of the reason evangelical Christians are attracted to the courage and witness of Dietrich Bonhoeffer. But one cannot repudiate the American church's implication in white supremacy while giving it tacit approval by supporting Trump. Whether or not the president himself is a racist, it is beyond debate that he has enabled the forces of hate and intolerance in our country. The longer evangelical Trump supporters fail to condemn these forces, the more difficult it is to take seriously their claim to represent a different kind of Christianity.

So, what to do in 2020? I know some Christians could not bring themselves to vote for Hillary in 2016. So, they took a chance on Trump, convinced he was the *lesser* of two evils. But now that the scale of Trump's "evil" has become terrifyingly clear, Christians are obliged to do their part in neutralizing it. This will probably require voting for someone they feel uneasy about, someone they suspect is only marginally better than Trump. And they will have to be prepared, depending on how this person governs, to renounce him or her, precisely the thing evangelicals have thus far refused to do with Trump.

There is no other way forward for Christians who would take seriously their political responsibilities. "If you board the wrong train," Bonhoeffer famously said, "it's no use running along the corridor in the opposite direction." This was his response to those who thought they could remain loyal to Christ while working to reform the nazified German Reich Church "from within." Christians who support Trump face an equally stark choice: If they have boarded the Trump train, they have hitched their spiritual wagons to a man who is "pretty much the human embodiment of the question 'What would Jesus not do?'"[5]

For that reason, following Christ while riding that train will look a lot like trying to run down the corridor in the opposite direction. Doing so may cause one to feel better; but the only thing outsiders will see is a naïve Christian being taken for a ride.

If I seem adamant in my belief that Christian support for Trump is a mistake, it is not because I am a "cultural Marxist" (as Eric Metaxas recently referred to me and other board members of the International Bonhoeffer

5. Amy Sullivan, "America's New Religion: Fox Evangelicalism," *The New York Times*), https://www.nytimes.com/2017/12/15/opinion/sunday/war-christmas-evangelicals.html?_r=0.

Society who called for an end to Trump's presidency). It's because I grew up in an evangelical church that taught me an important lesson about the church's efforts to align itself with a popular political movement.

I grew up in the early 1970s in Key Biscayne, Florida, an island off the coast of Miami where President Richard Nixon maintained a residence he called the "Winter White House." Often when he was in town, Nixon graced us by worshiping at our church. In time, members of the church became Nixon fans in every sense—we liked his politics and we loved that he was willing to take time from his busy schedule to attend church with his family. We were impressed that Billy Graham was Nixon's "spiritual advisor," and even more impressed when he befriended our pastor, John Huffman. Huffman was invited to the Nixon "compound" and on several occasions to the White House itself. At the president's request, our church held a special service to honor the Paris Peace Accords, which was televised live on the major television networks.

As you can imagine, Nixon's fall from grace and the disclosure of how duplicitous he had been were devastating for all of us. No one was devastated more than John Huffman, who when the Watergate scandal broke asked Nixon directly if he had known about the break-in. When Nixon swore to him that he had not, Huffman continued to defend him. But when the transcripts of Nixon's White House recordings were released, Huffman was understandably shocked and outraged. "If President Nixon claims to be a Christian," he told *Time*, "he needs to repent of both the language used and the attitudes expressed toward people in those tapes." In an interview with *The New York Times*, Huffman went further, questioning "the moral qualifications for the presidency of a person who cannot be trusted to tell the truth."[6]

As a fourteen-year-old evangelical Christian, I took two valuable lessons from this experience. First, I learned how embarrassing and demoralizing it was for a pastor I trusted and loved to realize he had been "played" by a master manipulator who masked his quest for power with the veneer of evangelical Christianity. As a recent biographer of Nixon concludes, there was always a self-serving element in the president's relationships with evangelical leaders whom he believed could help him politically. "When he knew he was going to run for president, he wooed them and they wooed him," the author writes.[7]

6. John A. Huffman, Jr., *A Most Amazing Call* (n.p.: 2011).

7. Kelsey Dallas, "Q&A: Did Richard Nixon Have a Religious Side?" *Deseret News*, https://www.deseretnews.com/article/865680780/QA-Did-Richard-Nixon-have-a-religious-side.html. This description of Nixon's religiosity is that of John A. Farrell, author of *Richard Nixon: The Life* (New York: Doubleday, 2017).

I guess such things are easier to recognize in hindsight.

Second, I learned a lesson in Christian humility from John Huffman, who had the courage to admit he had been wrong about Nixon and the integrity to repudiate Nixon's unchristian actions in no uncertain terms, despite the high personal cost of doing so. The whole experience made me suspicious of politicians who use piety to construct their public persona, especially if I suspect they are doing so to solicit Christian support. It also instilled in me an abiding respect for religious leaders who are willing to speak truth to power, particularly when there are consequences for doing so.

Having the most powerful man in the free world worship alongside us in our small sanctuary was heady stuff. We believed that we—and our pastor—had been chosen by God to make a difference in the way he governed. In retrospect, however, it is painfully clear that our president was Nixonizing us more than we were Christainizing him. I believe the same is true of Christian support for Donald Trump. His evangelical supporters may have given up on Christianizing Trump; yet no one can dispute that he has succeeded in Trumpifying American Christianity.

Chapter 14

Hymn for the 81%

Daniel Deitrich

In 2016, 81 percent of white evangelical Christians voted for Donald Trump after hearing an audio recording of him bragging about sexually assaulting women.

In the years since, even after enacting the deliberately cruel Zero Tolerance policy which ripped families apart and put children in cages at the southern border, evangelical support is as fervent as ever.

This phenomenon hits close to home because I was raised in the evangelical world. Countless hours in church services, youth group gatherings, retreats, and summer camps shaped me. I was taught to take the words of Jesus seriously: love God, love your neighbor, feed the hungry, fight against injustice. I was taught that things like love, peace, kindness, gentleness, and self-control matter. That's why I have been so confused and deeply saddened by the unflinching loyalty to a man who so clearly embodies the opposite of these values.

With this mix of sadness and confusion, even anger and betrayal, I sat down with my guitar and pen. What came out is both a lament and rebuke. Inspired by the words of Jesus and the Prophets, it doesn't sugar-coat the critique, but it does come from a deep well of love for the faith tradition I was raised in.

Hymn for the 81%
By Daniel Deitrich

I grew up in your churches
Sunday morning and evening service
Knelt in tears at the foot of the rugged cross
You taught me every life is sacred
Feed the hungry, clothe the naked
I learned from you the highest law is Love
I believed you when you said
That I should trust the words in red
To guide my steps through a wicked world
I assumed you'd do the same
So imagine my dismay
When I watched you lead the sheep to the wolves

You said to love the lost
So I'm loving you now
You said to speak the truth
So I'm calling you out
Why don't you live the words
That you put in my mouth
May love overcome and justice roll down

They started putting kids in cages
Ripping mothers from their babies
And I looked to you to speak on their behalf
But all I heard was silence
Or worse you justified it
Singing glory hallelujah raise the flag
Your fear had turned to hatred
But you baptized it with language
torn from the pages of the good book
You weaponized religion
And you wonder why I'm leaving
To find Jesus on the wrong side of your walls

You said to love the lost
So I'm loving you now
You said to speak the truth
So I'm calling you out
Why don't you live the words
That you put in my mouth
May love overcome and justice roll down

Come home, come home

You're better than this
You taught me better than this
Come home, come home
You're better than this
You taught me better than this

You said to love the lost
I'm trying to love you now
You said to speak the truth
So I'm calling you out
Why don't you live the words
That you put in my mouth
May love overcome and justice roll down
May love overcome and justice roll down
May love overcome and justice roll down

I've watched good people with strong faith forced to defend not just the president's personal moral failings, but his harmful policies as well. With each new shocking tweet or soundbite, I think to myself, surely this is the last straw. Surely, they will condemn the mocking of a disabled reporter or the slandering of revered war hero and POW, John McCain. There's no way they'll stay silent as Trump betrays our Kurdish allies or pardons war criminals. Surely all Christians will rise up to condemn locking children in cold cages without beds or blankets or soap or toothbrushes.

"We didn't elect a pastor-in-chief," they say instead.

"Obama did it first"—as if that makes it ok?

"No one is perfect!" "Who are you to judge!" "Romans 13!"

They'll go as far as to say "God appointed Trump and to criticize him is a sin."

For a group of people who claim the Bible as their end-all-be-all anchor, white evangelicals seem woefully (or willfully) ignorant of the huge swaths of Scripture that critique those in power—even those "appointed by God." The prophets of the Hebrew Bible were constantly calling out the nation of Israel and its kings any time they strayed from the path of God. And what was the metric by which they were judged? It wasn't the economy. It wasn't the size or strength of their army. The people of God were called out—verbally eviscerated really—when they failed to care for the widow, the orphan, the immigrant.

Isaiah 58:6–7(NIV) reads,

Is not this the kind of fasting I have chosen:
to loose the chains of injustice
    and untie the cords of the yoke,
to set the oppressed free
    and break every yoke?
Is it not to share your food with the hungry?
    and to provide the poor wanderer with shelter—
when you see the naked, to clothe them,
    and not to turn away from your own flesh and blood?

I can imagine these words from Amos 5:23–24 (New Living Translation) ruffling a few feathers:

Away with your noisy hymns of praise!
    I will not listen to the music of your harps.
Instead, I want to see a mighty flood of justice,
    an endless river of righteous living.

Kings were not immune to these critiques. If anything, they were held to a higher standard. Trump supporters will point to King David as a shining example of a flawed leader with a questionable moral track record who nonetheless became "a man after God's own heart." What is always omitted in the comparison is the scathing rebuke of David's behavior by the prophet Nathan and David's subsequent repentance. Trump has stated he has never asked for God's forgiveness for anything ever in his life and shows no signs of changing his behavior.

Modern Western Christianity, white evangelicalism specifically, has been weaponized and the list of casualties is long. While Trump didn't start the fire, he gladly threw gasoline on it. There's so much work to do to combat white supremacy, homophobia, transphobia, sexism—all the ways in which people are treated as less than the children of God that they are. The church could—and should—be leading the charge in these battles for justice and dignity for those on the margins, but we have largely abdicated our prophetic role. We've traded prophetic fire for what Dr. Martin Luther King called an "obnoxious peace," marked by complacency and passivity.

I'm far from perfect and have so much learning and growing to do. I'm not comparing myself to the prophets or Jesus, but simply pointing out that all of us can and should learn from their example. When our elected officials are not wielding their power to help the marginalized and oppressed, we must call them to a higher standard or vote them out. When the laws and systems of our society only work for those who are white and male, we must break and rebuild those laws and systems. And when outright evil is done on our watch—no matter what political party is in power—we must not only speak out but actively work to bring justice and shalom to a hurting world. As Dr. King said, "If peace means keeping my mouth shut in the midst of injustice and evil, I don't want it."

This is the way of Jesus.

Chapter 15

Trump, the Last Temptation

GEORGE YANCEY

WHEN DONALD TRUMP CAME DOWN THAT ESCALATOR IN 2015, I HAD nothing but contempt for the man. I had heard him a couple of times delivering "political" commentary on Fox News and soon learned to go to CNN or MSNBC as soon as he came on (I watch news across the political spectrum). I had heard of his show *The Apprentice* which also did not inspire much respect for him. I figured that he, like many nonpolitician presidential candidates, would be the candidate of the week for the Republicans and then we would get to the more serious candidates.

As his lead persisted in the Republican party, I became more worried. I wanted two viable candidates for president. I used my Facebook page to deride him and tried to convince some of my conservative friends to not support him. When he won the nomination, it was disheartening to think that one of the major political parties would have such an incompetent candidate. I assumed he would lose but discouraged my Christian friends from voting for him as much as possible. I even placed articles in *The Stream*, a conservative Christian online magazine largely favorable to Trump to discourage Christian support. I knew my effort would have little influence, but I wanted to be able to tell my kids years later that I did my part in stopping Trump from becoming president.

On election night I settled in to watch Clinton become president. That prospect did not make me happy as her many flaws were quite apparent.[1]

But at least she was not Trump and overall, I felt the country was better off having her as president. As I watched the returns at around 8 PM it began to dawn on me that Trump could become president. Ashen faced, I told that to my wife, who stared at me in disbelief. I did not think he could win until that moment. About an hour later the possibility became reality and I knew that Donald Trump would be the next president of the United States.

I had hopes that perhaps Trump was elected president without outsized support from Christians. That hope was dashed when I learned that a higher percentage of white evangelicals supported Trump than supported previous Republican presidential candidates.[2]

I expected more white evangelicals to vote for Trump than Clinton as they are Republicans. But to support Trump more than other Republican presidential candidates blew my mind. I did not know what just happened. I still wonder how a crude, incompetent, race-baiting sexist could win the presidency of our country.

Ultimately what I think happened was that Trump had spoken to needs among evangelicals that were not being addressed by other political candidates. One of the most important issues can be seen in my research on Christianophobia, or the unreasonable hatred or fear of Christians.[3]

Many evangelical Christians see Trump as someone who will save them from Christianophobia. So, I first want to make certain that I understand and respect the nature of their fears. In fact, I share them. But then I want to argue why I believe that Trump is not only not a solution to these issues but in the long run he will make things worse.

Is Christianophobia a Problem?

When the topic of Christianophobia comes up there are those who argue that it is merely Christians who have lost their privilege. Yet is it a privilege

---

1. As such I voted for Mike Maturen, the American Solidarity Party candidate.

2. Randall Balmer, Kate Bowler, Anthea Butler, Maura Jane Farrelly, Wes Markofski, Robert Orsi, Jerry Z. Park, James Clark Davidson, Matthew Avery Sutton, and Grace Yukich, "Studying Religion in the Age of Trump," *Religion and American Culture* 27 (1) (2017), 2–56.

3. George Yancey, *Hostile Environment* (Downers Grove, IL: InterVarsity, 2015); and George Yancey and David A. Williamson, *So Many Christians, So Few Lions* (Lanham, MD: Rowman & Littlefield, 2014).

to be able to obtain a job in academia free of religious bias? Some of my research has documented that bias.[4]

Is it a privilege to have religious leaders in student organizations who believe in their religion? The development of all-comers policies and the way they have been used to target Christian groups has revealed this threat to freedom of association.[5]

Outside of academia there are episodes of a lay-pastor being fired from his position as a district health director due to his sermon and a fire chief being fired due to a Christian book he wrote.[6]

It is more reasonable to see these events as rights, rather than privileges, being denied to certain Christians.

My research shows that those with anti-Christian hatred tend to be white, wealthy, educated, and male.[7]

They also tend to be politically progressive and irreligious. I suspect that they are quite powerful in cultural centers of our society such as academia, media, and entertainment. Many Christians, especially conservative Christians, see evidence of Christianophobia in their lives yet see no attempt in our cultural institutions to document it. It is the frustration that comes from this disconnect from their experiences and the way it is not portrayed in the larger culture that led some to Trump. Indeed, when I talked to many of my friends who voted for Trump, one common phrase I heard was, "Well, he may be bad but at least he does not hate me and will leave me alone. Clinton hates me and will not leave me alone."

I want to say to my Christian friends, especially the evangelical ones who most support Trump: I hear you. Christianophobia is real. I have studied it and debated with those who do not believe it exists. Trump has promised to protect Christians. The seeking of political control is one way to try to deal with Christianophobia. But it is the wrong way.

The Problem Is the Culture

Trump cannot fix what troubles Christians because at best, even if he is competent, he can only offer a political solution. The issue is the culture. What

4. George Yancey, *Compromising Scholarship* (Waco, TX: Baylor University Press, 2011).

5. Zachary R. Cormier, "Christian Legal Society v. Martinez: The Death Knell of Associational Freedom on the College Campus," *Texas Wesleyan Law Review* 17 (2010), 287.

6. David Jeremiah, *Is This the End?(with Bonus Content)* (Nashville: Thomas Nelson, 2016).

7. Yancey and Williamson, *So Many Christians, So Few Lions.*

Trump can do is make the situation worse by turning the culture against us further. We tend to underestimate just how powerful cultural influences are. Look at how culture has shaped race in our society. Slavery was accepted because our culture accepted it. Only when the forces of abolition were able to move our society to reject slavery could we have a war that stopped it. Interracial marriage was not accepted until our cultural values changed. How we envision racial issues is largely shaped by the cultural values we have.

Likewise, how Christians are perceived in our society is going to be shaped by cultural values. Decades ago, Christians had a powerful, perhaps even dominant, position in our society. While there may have been individual episodes of anti-Christian events, systemically it was better to be a Christian in our society than not. Anti-Christian hostility was generally discouraged. Today that is not the case. Indeed, for reasons that are not completely clear, anti-Christian attitudes have become more acceptable, particularly among the elite in institutions such as academia, the media, and entertainment. If these cultural values exist, Christianophobia will be acceptable in major sections in our society.

We do not change our culture with pure political power. Remember all the state laws that outlawed same-sex marriage? That was political power. Our culture has changed as it concerns acceptance of homosexuality. Whether the Supreme Court legalized it or not, same-sex marriage was going to be part of our society. Polls show the rising support of same-sex marriage and those state laws would not have lasted. The early political victories outlawing same-sex marriage could not survive the culture change of our attitudes about homosexuality. Christians are hoping that political power will help them to deal with the anti-Christian attitudes in our society. They look to Trump to help them maintain that power. But lessons about same-sex marriage show us that such political victories are temporary if there are not also cultural changes to support them.

We may not know exactly what has led to the rise of anti-Christian attitudes, but we do know the arguments used to support it. Many of those with such attitudes envision Christians as bigoted, intolerant, racist, unthinking, and crude.[8]

These are also qualities that are tied, with good reason, to President Trump. To have Christians seen as supportive of Trump is to reinforce some of the Christianophobic stereotypes. Support of Trump will ironically reinforce many of the cultural stereotypes working against Christians in the long run. I do not doubt that in the short term there are protections gained by Trump. But that is shortsighted. In the long term any legal protection

---

8. Yancey and Williamson, *So Many Christians, So Few Lions*.

gained because of Trump will be overturned by a culture that is more anti-Christian because of current evangelical support of Trump.

Let me deal with a couple of arguments I encountered when presenting this argument. One argument is that we should look at what President Trump is doing to the courts. If there is one area where he has shown some degree of competence, it is his naming of judges and the ability of Senator Majority Leader Mitch McConnell to get them appointed. Certainly, these judges can prosecute the political issues that conservative Christians care about. I will stipulate that President Trump has been good for those issues in the short term. And of course, Federal, and Supreme Court judges are appointed for a lifetime so it is fair to say that this short term can last quite a while.

But even lifetime appointments come to an end. If our culture changes so much to widely accept Christianophobia then those cultural sentiments will outlast those judges. Eventually they will be replaced by judges who are more in line with those hostile sentiments. All the achievements can be overturned just like the state political victories against same-sex marriage. With a culture deeply ingrained with Christianophobia, it is uncertain if the changes brought about by judges and justices with less sympathy to Christians will ever be remedied if that type of religious bigotry is accepted. Trump's judges and justices may protect Christians alive today. But our children and grandchildren will have to suffer the brunt of the hostility the support of Trump has generated. Working on cultural change is the proper long-term play.

The second major pushback I receive is that those who hate Christians will continue to hate us regardless of whether we support Trump or not. True. Some people have such hatred in their hearts that nothing we do short of capitulating to all their political and social causes will satisfy them. But thankfully, they do not make up most of the country. A lot of folks do not hate or love Christians. They live their lives not thinking much about Christians. But when they see Christians massively supporting a race-baiting, bombastic, sexist, and sexually immoral president, they can naturally begin to think of Christians as hypocrites. They can also become more open to Christianophobic arguments when frustrated by having a president with those qualities and blame Christians for putting him into office. Whether we support Trump or not will not matter to those who already have high levels of anti-Christian animosity, but it can raise that animosity in those who previously had a neutral attitude towards Christians but are turned off by the vices of Trump. It is a mistake to think everyone's mind is made up about what they think of evangelicals. There are many people who will still be influenced by the support evangelicals have given to Trump.

Political Leaders and Scripture

To deal with Christianophobia, we must challenge the cultural values emerging from this type of intolerance. But in a very practical manner the evangelical support of Trump is making our culture even more toxic for Christians. For utilitarian reasons alone, Christians should not throw their support behind our current president.

But my argument is not limited to utilitarian concerns. The way Christians have come to support Trump does not fit with a proper understanding of the Scriptures. I acknowledge that I am not a trained theologian and so people may rightly argue with my interpretations. But I am confident that the evidence for Christians to be cautious about putting too much faith in their political issues is very strong.

Any fair assessment of the Old Testament and the trials of the children of Israel consistently comes back to the theme of relying on political figures instead of God. From the very beginning of the formation of Israel, Jews were warned about seeking a king to be the solution to their problems.[9]

And what where the problems that the Jews needed to address? They were a nation in the middle of other nations that did not like them. The idea was that a king could fight for them and they were jealous of the kings in other nations. And the problem of looking to political leaders was not limited to recruiting Saul as their first king. The children of Israel not only sought to rely on other Jews for the projection and leadership they wanted. They also looked to powerful foreign nations for protection.[10]

In other words, they believed more in the protection they could obtain from individuals who did not accept their God-given values than a God who has said he would protect them. Sound familiar?

I am not arguing that Christians should not get involved in politics. Christians should feel the freedom to engage in politics just as much as anyone else. And there is nothing sinful about advocating for issues of life, religious freedom, and justice. But when we become so loyal to a political party that we are afraid to correct the leaders of the party, then we are not merely participating in politics. We are looking to politics to save us. This explains not only the hesitation of many Christians to condemn some of the ugliness that comes from President Trump's mouth, his constant tweets, and administration, but also their willingness to change their attitudes about moral values. After the election of Trump, surveys have shown that conservative Christians went from those who were most supportive of requiring moral

9. 1 Samuel 8: 5–22.

10. Isaiah 31:1.

political leaders to the religious groups that least required such morality.[11] Efforts by Christians to placate President Trump suggest an undeserved level of loyalty.

I cannot help but think that this type of placating and loyalty is due to a sense of desperation within conservative Christians. In a society where they feel the effects of Christianophobia, they want to turn to a powerful political leader for protection. That sentiment may be understandable from a human point of view, but it is not in keeping with biblical commands to not live in fear[12] and to not prioritize human resources over God's resources.[13]

If we claim to have a power beyond what those outside of our faith enjoy, then we have to live it out. Looking for political muscle just like any other special interest group is the opposite of living out that faith.

Trump and the Split Among Christians

Beyond connecting Christians to some of the more unsavory parts of Trump, the danger of Trump is also the danger of division within the Christian church. Trump is especially unpopular among the young and people of color. There is evidence that even among evangelicals, younger persons are less likely to support Trump. At a time where it has become more important for Christians to hang together and deal with anti-Christian attitudes, President Trump has created even more division. To be sure, the division is our fault more than it is Trump's fault. The way some Christians have placed Trump on a pedestal has created a divisive situation considering the way he freely dehumanizes others. But it would not be fair to place the entire responsibility upon those defending Trump. I do not defend all the actions of those of us who have combatted Christian support of Trump. Whenever there is human division it is inevitable that members on both sides of the divide contribute to the conflict.

But it should not surprise us that a political leader who traffics in divisive rhetoric would produce followers who spread that type of division. I have heard again and again that some Christians not only fail to critique the dehumanizing comments of Trump, but they also like him because of that "tough man" approach. They often say that there is a need to go to war against progressives and Trump's hostility towards those progressives is

11. Robert P. Jones and Daniel Cox, "Clinton maintains double-digit lead (51% vs. 36%) over Trump," PRRI, October 19, 2016, https://www.prri.org/research/prri-brookings-oct-19-poll-politics-election-clinton-double-digit-leads-trump/.

12. 2 Timothy 1:7, Matthew 10:28.

13. Matthew 6:25–34.

welcomed. Let us admit that there are progressives who will mistreat Christians the first chance they get. Even in that situation, Trump's attitude is opposite of how we are to approach those progressives. We are not to treat them with the same type of dehumanization that we perceive them willing to direct against us. That does not mean we have to be a doormat, but there is a big difference between standing up for our own rights and seeking to destroy our political opponents by maligning them.

I fear that many of Trump's evangelical supporters have brought this "we are in a war" perspective into their interactions with other Christians. They are impatient with those of us who are not willing to sign up for this battle. We are seen as traitors. I have been accused of acting out of fear due to my opposition to Trump. Unfortunately, I have seen a good deal more fear on the part of those who support Trump. They are reacting out of fear because of what may happen if progressives take over our government. They fear a loss of their rights and passage of laws that they disapprove. Trump is seen as the solution to their fears. And out of those fears, they often lash out at those of us who will not support him. As such, while there is no doubt that at times Christians who oppose Trump have acted in ways that have made these divisions worse, many evangelical Trump supporters feel pressure to force those who will not support him to join in their pro-Trump agenda. Only when we can detach ourselves from an unholy alliance with our contentious president will we be able to turn down the temperature in this heated conflict and concentrate on building the Christian community we will need in a post-Christian world.

What to Do?

To some degree the damage has already been done. No matter what happens in 2020, the image of Christians putting Trump into power in 2016 will remain. However, it may be possible to limit the damage if we refuse to support him. Perhaps rejection of Trump will resonant with some individuals. In the Doug Jones/Roy Moore Alabama Senate race, there was a fear that Christians would overlook the problems connected to Moore and send him to the Senate. Instead they stayed home. They could not support Jones, but neither were they willing to back Moore. That removed the potential of Moore being yet another cultural noose around our neck. Perhaps with a noticeable drop of evangelical support and a Trump loss, we can lose some of the cultural baggage of the linking of Christians to Trump. But we should not be naïve about that possibility either. The damage may have already been done.

But perhaps even more troubling than the vote for Trump is the unwillingness of Christians to challenge him. It is one thing to argue that we must vote for Trump because of the alternative. There is a rational argument of selecting the lesser evil. But there is no rational argument for once having selected that evil, to go on to allow that evil to go unchecked. We have already seen that Christians have altered their stance on the morality of leaders to suit Trump. Perhaps most notably is the public statement of Robert Jeffries about giving Trump a sexual "mulligan." How much will we be willing to sully our reputation to protect Trump?

But it is not only his moral failings that Christians are too eager to defend. Too often I have encountered Christians who twist themselves in all sorts of knots in their efforts to defend Trump on his race-baiting. I had one encounter with a leading Christian supporter of Trump who insisted that Trump does not engage in race-baiting. When I pointed out that Trump had clearly lied about not knowing about David Duke and that he did this to pacify white nationalists, his response was that all politicians lie. I could not believe what he had just argued. Do politicians lie to make racists feel better? The denial of this person to see any problems with many of Trump's race-baiting statements indicate a desire to defend Trump no matter what he says or does. This must stop.

If Christians do not push back on the disturbing attributes of Trump, then we will own those attributes. For example, if enough Christians accept the perceptions of the leader in the previous paragraph, then our faith will become known for not caring about the race-baiting statements of our president. This will translate into Christians not caring about racism and people of color. The argument that we must vote for Trump as the less bad option will not save us from being labeled racist if we do not challenge Trump's race-baiting. Or let me put it this way. Many conservative Christians accuse Democratic Christians of endorsing abortion because they vote for pro-choice candidates. If those Christians stay silent on that issue, then they have a point. But if Democratic Christians vote for Democrats despite abortion and make it plain that they opposed that plank of their political party, then they do not own the pro-choice label. It is fairer to say that their vote is due to the reality that neither political party accurately reflects their overall political beliefs and they had to make the best of a bad situation. Likewise, if you cannot find it in yourself to not vote for Trump, although I really hope that you won't vote for him, I would urge you to hold him accountable by becoming vocal about his dehumanizing, race-baiting, and sexism. Too many evangelicals have supported Trump without condemning his vile speech and actions. That failure tars our faith with his actions. We dare not allow him to continue to poison the good name of Christians.

Chapter 16

Immoral, Spineless, Demonic, Prideful, Blind, Stupid, and Lacking in Grace?

CHRIS THURMAN

OVER THE LAST FEW YEARS, I HAVE FOUND MYSELF EXPERIENCING WAVES of anger, disappointment, confusion, and sadness in relation to the political landscape the Trump presidency has created. I feel angry about people's commitment to party over principle, disappointed by their alignment with a president who is militantly and unrepentantly immoral, confused by their denial of his disordered personality, and saddened that our country's most cherished institutions are taking such a huge hit.

Even more disturbing has been the widespread support of Trump by evangelicals, a number of them prominent. Some leading evangelicals have been especially enthusiastic in their backing of Trump, proudly proclaiming him to be a strong leader, someone chosen by God for this moment in history, and a good man who will make America great again by righting all the moral wrongs our nation has fallen into. If these well-known evangelicals had simply left it at that, many of us who believe the opposite to be true would have agreed to disagree and continued in our efforts to provide a biblical counter-narrative to their views in an effort to oppose the false belief that Trump is fit to lead the nation.

Unfortunately, that is not where some leading evangelicals left it. Instead, they have publicly demeaned Christians who oppose the president. In doing so, they acted as if there are no valid reasons for followers of Christ to oppose Trump. Large numbers of Christians know there are *many* theologically sound reasons to oppose this president, given his glaring mental and moral deficits. And, since Trump never admits to having any flaws or defects much less work on them, they also know that the numerous things wrong with the president are not going away and are only going to get worse.

Some leading evangelicals have taken it upon themselves to serve as Trump's spiritual advisory team, a religious defense team to be accurate. In doing so, they sometimes employ the same tactics Trump uses when he is criticized or disagreed with—attack the messenger *and* the message. From examining how they protect the president, it seems clear that some members of his spiritual advisory team cannot accept the fact that there are devoted followers of Christ who see Trump as a significant danger to our country, a man with no moral core, someone who is psychologically disturbed, a political and religious con artist, and the most incompetent president we have ever had.

Evangelical leaders who effusively support Trump only serve to embolden an already arrogant and out-of-control president to cause even greater damage to our nation, damage that will take years, possibly even decades, from which to recover. Even more tragically, evangelicals who enthusiastically back Trump only serve to empower the president to cause further damage to the reputation of Christ.

Trump's Most Prominent Evangelical Supporters

Several leading evangelicals have been at the forefront of supporting Donald Trump. At times, they have taken shots at Christians who oppose the president. *Using their own words*, five men have been especially vociferous in their support of Trump and egregious in denigrating followers of Christ who oppose him.

Ralph Reed, former head of the Christian Coalition and Founder and Chairman of the Faith and Freedom Coalition, boldly proclaimed that evangelicals "have a moral obligation to enthusiastically back" President Trump in the upcoming election.[1]

This may not strike you as Reed denigrating Christians who oppose Trump, but it is. The implication of what Reed is saying is that if you're a Christian and you oppose Trump, you're immoral. There are many evangelicals who believe just the opposite is true—that we have a moral obligation to *oppose* a president who is as disturbed as Trump and do everything we can

---

1. https://www.newsmax.com/newsfront/evangelicals-christians-ralph-reed-trump/2019/10/09/id/936344/.

to ensure his removal from office before he causes any further harm. Are Christians who oppose Trump sinfully violating their "moral obligation to enthusiastically back" the current President of the United States? According to Ralph Reed, the answer is yes.

Franklin Graham, President and CEO of Samaritan's Purse and the Billy Graham Evangelistic Association, stated during an interview with die-hard Trump supporter Eric Metaxas, there is "almost a demonic power" at work in opposition to Trump.[2]

The idea here is that if you're a Christian who opposes Trump, you're playing into the devil's hands, being exploited by demonic forces, and working against the cause of Christ. Are Christians who oppose Donald Trump playing into the hands of the devil and working against the cause of Christ? According to Franklin Graham, the answer is yes.

Jerry Falwell, Jr., President of Liberty University, criticized Mark Galli, former Editor-in-Chief of *Christianity Today,* for writing an op-ed in which Galli stated Trump should be removed from office because of his blatant and unrepentant immorality.[3]

Rather than respond in a biblically solid and respectful way to Galli's *opinion* about the president, Falwell attacked both the messenger and the magazine he worked for, saying "Although Christians have never had a better champion in the White House than President Trump, a so-called Christian media outlet is using its platform to echo the radical, progressive left in demanding his removal from office, stalking the Internet like a wolf in sheep's clothing."

Christianity Today isn't "a so-called Christian media outlet," it *is* a Christian media outlet—in fact, probably the most influential Christian magazine in the United States. Galli wasn't using the magazine "to echo the radical, progressive left in demanding his (Trump's) removal from office," he was exercising his freedom as an American citizen to say enough is enough when it comes to the president's flagrant and remorseless immorality. Finally, Galli is not a "wolf in sheep's clothing," he's a devoted Christian who had the courage to publicly rebuke a sitting president for his gross moral waywardness while at the same time challenging believers to remember who they are and that their allegiance is to Christ, not someone as overtly godless as Trump. Is a Christian who rebukes Trump for his immorality only a "so-called" Christian, someone echoing the radical left, and a "wolf in sheep's clothing"? According to Jerry Falwell, Jr., the answer is yes.

2. https://www.washingtonexaminer.com/news/franklin-graham-claims-demonic-power-behind-attacks-on-trump.

3. https://www.foxnews.com/opinion/jerry-falwell-jr-christianity-today-is-wrong-about-trump-he-is-a-champion-for-people-of-faith.

Jack Graham, senior pastor of Prestonwood Baptist Church in Dallas, is another evangelical who has been effusive in his praise of Trump. Graham wrote an op-ed in *The Christian Post,* "Why It Is Wise for Christians to Support President Trump."[4]

I don't want to be presumptuous here, but his op-ed may have been in response to one I wrote in *The Christian Post,* "You Foolish Evangelicals, Trump Has Bewitched You."[5]

In my op-ed, I expressed my *opinion* that evangelicals who support an immoral con artist who clearly doesn't share our Christians values are foolish for doing so. Graham stated, "Some Christians who think us foolish and gullible have met this effort with skepticism and cynicism, decidedly ignoring the many ways President Donald Trump has positively impacted our country and honored the beliefs that Americans and Christians hold dear. Our critics seem to have a theology with so little grace and they fail to recognize that someone with an unrighteous past can still make righteous decisions on behalf of those they lead."[6]

Graham is belittling anti-Trump Christians in two ways here. First, he is saying that we have a theology "with so little grace." I beg to differ. There are many of us who oppose Trump who are not lacking in grace but simply believe that grace shouldn't continue to abound toward a president who defiantly continues to sin. Second, Graham is saying Christians who oppose Trump are unwilling to see his current moral upside because we are too focused on his past moral downside. Let's be clear. Trump's moral downside isn't all in the past. Trump's lack of a moral core expresses itself in the here and now each and every day of his presidency. And, because he lacks remorse about it, Trump's moral decadence is getting worse. Are Christians who criticize and oppose Trump people with "so little grace" and unwilling to acknowledge when the president does something good? According to Jack Graham, the answer is yes.

Robert Jeffress, senior pastor of First Baptist Church in Dallas, is, perhaps, Trump's most enthusiastic evangelical supporter. Sadly, he has unapologetically called Christians who oppose Trump "spineless morons"[7]

---

4. https://www.christianpost.com/voices/why-it-is-wise-for-christians-to-support
-president-trump.html.

5. https://www.christianpost.com/voices/you-foolish-evangelicals-trump-has-be-
witched-you.html.

6. https://www.christianpost.com/voice/why-it-is-wise-for-christians-to-support
-president-trump.html.

7. https://www.huffpost.com/entry/robert-jeffress-trump-evangelicals-morons_n_
5c66eb5ee4b01757c36b2dcb.

and stated, "A very obvious reason they are against Trump is that they were wrong about Trump and their pride won't let them admit that."[8]

This kind of talk from a Trump-supporting evangelical, especially a pastor who ought to know better, is one reason Christ warned his followers, "Do not judge, or you too will be judged. For in the same way you judge others, you will be judged, and with the measure you use, it will be measured to you" (Matthew 7:1–2).

Jeffress is attacking anti-Trump Christians in three ways. First, we are "spineless," meaning he views us as cowards. Second, we are "morons," meaning he thinks we're stupid. Third, our pride won't let us admit we are wrong about Trump, meaning he thinks we're arrogant. The implication of the flip side of Jeffress's stance is that those who *support* Trump are courageous, smart, and humble, flattering himself and all those who agree with him in the process. From my perspective, it takes a great deal more courage, intelligence, and humility to oppose Trump than it does to support him. Are Christians who oppose Trump "spineless morons," too arrogant to admit they are wrong when it comes to how they view the president? According to Robert Jeffress, the answer is yes.

Why the attacks? Why would leading evangelicals belittle anti-Trump Christians this way? Why would they say that followers of Christ who oppose Trump are immoral, demonically influenced, spineless, ungracious, stupid, blind, and prideful for viewing the president the way they do?

Perhaps the answer we search for can be found in Peter Wehner's book *The Death of Politics*. In it, he suggests the answer to why evangelicals support someone as mentally and morally disturbed as Trump is a mistake people of faith have made throughout human history. Wehner insightfully writes, "Some evangelicals are giving in to the ancient temptation of being too close to political power, choosing to be court pastors to win the favor of the king. They are thrilled to be taken seriously, thrilled to be invited to the White House, thrilled to be seen as having influence in the highest ranks of political power."[9]

I think that pretty much explains it.

The Biblical Challenge to "Speak the Truth in Love"

The real issue when it comes to the different view's evangelicals have about Trump isn't that we disagree or that we call each other names. The real issue

8. https://capstonereport.com/2020/01/02/dr-jeffress-pride-keeps-beth-moore-never-trumpers-from-supporting-president/33682/.

9. Peter Wehner, *The Death of Politics* (New York: HarperOne, 2019), 81.

is about truth and whether or not the names we call each other are accurate and motivated by love. I know that sounds crazy, perhaps even unbiblical, but bear with me.

As Christians, we agree that our role model for how to treat others is Jesus Christ. I hope we also agree that there were times in the life of Christ when he treated people kindly and compassionately, and there were times when he was severe and rough. Given that Jesus Christ is the highest expression of love, it must be the case that agape love is sometimes soft and sometimes hard in how it is expressed.

On the hard side of love, Christ called the Pharisees, the religious leaders of his day, "hypocrites," "blind guides," "blind fools," "whitewashed tombs," "snakes," and a "brood of vipers" (Matthew 23:13–33). Was he being sinful to do so? No, we know that Christ was without sin. The reason it wasn't sinful for Christ to call the Pharisees harsh names was that they were true and he did it out of love. Christ called the Pharisees these negative things in a loving effort to help them come to their senses, to go from being in darkness to being in the light. Speaking the truth in love is among the most Christlike things we can do in interacting with others, whether they receive it that way or not.

Lest we think calling someone a name was reserved for Christ, keep in mind that Paul called the believers in Galatia "foolish" and "bewitched" (Galatians 3:1), Judaizers who opposed the gospel "dogs" and "evildoers" (Philippians 3:2), and people who taught something other than sound doctrine "conceited" (1 Timothy 6:4). Peter called false teachers "springs without waters and mists driven by a storm" (2 Peter 2:17) and those who deny that Christ is coming back "scoffers" (2 Peter 3:3). John called a person who denies that Jesus is the Christ a "liar" (1 John 2:22) and those who do not acknowledge Jesus Christ "deceivers" (2 John 1:7). Jude called unbelievers who had secretly slipped in among believers "ungodly" (Jude 1:4). Apparently, whether you are addressing Christians or non-Christians, it is permissible to call them some pretty bad names as long as you are being accurate and doing it to help them grow.

Here's the deal. I don't mind a brother or sister in Christ calling me or any other believer a coward, moron, blind, immoral, demonic, and lacking in grace *if it's true and motivated by love*. I mind it a great deal if it is untrue and motivated by meanness. Speaking an untruth about someone out of a desire to demean them is a twofold violation of the principle "speaking the truth in love" (Ephesians 4:15), not something a holy God takes too kindly to. It is also breaking the ninth commandment, "You shall not give false testimony against your neighbor" (Exodus 20:16). However you slice it, calling someone a name that is untrue in an effort to demean them is an unchristian thing to do.

From my perspective, Trump is in the group of people the Apostle Paul warned us about, "lovers of themselves, lovers of money, boastful, proud, abusive, disobedient to their parents, ungrateful, unholy, without love, unforgiving, slanderous, without self-control, brutal, not lovers of the good, treacherous, rash, conceited, lovers of pleasure rather that lovers of God—having a form of godliness but denying its power" (2 Timothy 3:1–5a). I further believe that God is clear about what he wants us to do with someone like this: "Have *nothing* to do with such people" (2 Timothy 3:5b, italics mine). Nothing means nothing. Because I believe this passage is an accurate description of Trump, I believe evangelicals are being foolish (Merriam-Webster: "showing a lack of good sense, judgment, or discretion") to have *anything* to do with him, much less enthusiastically support him.

I hope I'm wrong on this, I really do. I don't want a person running the country who God tells us to have nothing to do with. And, I don't want to call my Trump-supporting friends in Christ foolish if they are not. If I'm wrong about Trump, I'm going to owe my brothers and sisters in Christ an apology for calling them foolish to support him. If, in reality, Trump is actually the opposite of what's described in 2 Timothy 3:1–5—humble, grateful, loving, forgiving, self-controlled, kind, and a lover of God—I would hope evangelicals who enthusiastically support him would be upset that any Christian had the nerve to call them foolish for being in his corner. If Trump truly possesses these positive qualities, followers of Christ would be foolish *not* to support his presidency. Personally, I don't believe the *observable* facts of Trump's life justify coming to such a positive conclusion, and that's the main reason I believe all Christians should have nothing to do with him and choose someone else to lead the country.

There is a flip side to all this. If Trump is the kind of person described in 2 Timothy 3:1–5, I would hope my evangelical friends in Christ would admit it and stop supporting him. I quoted Robert Jeffress earlier saying that he believes we who oppose Trump are the ones making a big mistake and too prideful to admit it. Nevertheless, if Trump is an unbridled lover of himself, a lover of money, boastful, proud, abusive, ungrateful, unholy, without love, unforgiving, slanderous, without self-control, brutal, not a lover of the good, treacherous, rash, conceited, and a lover of pleasure rather than a lover of God (all the things an objective observer knows him to be), I would hope evangelicals who support him would be the ones to humbly admit they have hitched their wagon to the wrong horse and stop having anything to do with him.

We're All a Part of the Problem

Given that the God who created the universe lives inside of us via the Holy Spirit, we can all do a much better job improving our interactions with each other about the Trump presidency. That certainly includes me. If I could rewrite the op-eds I've written about Trump and his evangelical supporters, I wouldn't change *what* I said, but I would certainly change the *way* I said it. Some of the things I said in my op-eds were not said in love, something God has disciplined me about. I hope nothing I've said in this chapter is repeating the same mistake.

We must return to practicing three important principles in Scripture, "If it is possible, as far as depends on you, live at peace with everyone" (Romans 12:8); "Come now, and let us reason together (Isaiah 1:18, NASB); and "speaking the truth in love" (Ephesians 4:15). If we fail to do this, we are a much bigger part of the problem in our current political and spiritual climate than the president.

The stakes are incredibly high when it comes to how we, as Christians, view Trump and how we express those views. Will we assess him with eyes that are willing to see? Or, are we going to keep our blinders on? And, when we express what we think, are we going to do it lovingly or hatefully, truthfully or dishonestly?

I hope and pray we will humble ourselves and let two things and two things only determine where we land in supporting or opposing this or any other president—truth and love. The truth sets us free to be wiser and more discerning when it comes to who we support and who we don't. Love sets us free to take what we believe and express it in ways that further the growth and maturity of the body of Christ. If, in our pursuit of truth and love, we hold on to the views we have of Trump, move away from them, or some mixture of the two, at least we did it allowing the two most important things to run the show and can hold our heads high.

Our country has recovered from difficult and trying political times in the past, and it will do so again. My prayer is that we, as followers of Christ, will engage with each other about the Trump presidency the way God wants us to—truthfully, lovingly, graciously, firmly, gently, humbly, justly, and mercifully. Let's co-labor together to that end.

Author Note: The author would like to acknowledge the contribution of Tiffany Dang, MA, to this chapter.

Chapter 17

Setting Your Own Rules
and Cognitive Dissonance

*The Case of Donald Trump
and Conservative Christian Evangelicals*

EDWARD G. SIMMONS,
DAVID C. LUDDEN,
& J. COLIN HARRIS

THE HALLMARK OF THE TRUMP PRESIDENCY HAS BEEN INCREASINGLY CASTing off restraints. "Letting Trump be Trump" became the justification for this president to set his own rules, leading to accelerated trampling on laws and policies that got in his way. Lies and bold fabrications have steadily increased with the freeing of Donald Trump's gut feelings—along with demands for unquestioning loyalty of his cabinet and congressional supporters. Republican support held firmly as the prosecutions and findings of Special Prosecutor Robert Mueller were undermined and even when clearly documented efforts to extort an ally fighting Russia led to impeachment charges and a truncated Senate trial.

A paradox of the Trump presidency is that the most irreligious president in at least 100 years is being hailed in messianic language by conservative evangelical Christians who remain loyal despite prosecutions, corruption, and impeachment. Jesus, the biblically proclaimed Messiah, spoke of humility rather than a public display of righteousness (Matthew 6:5) and of loving and forgiving enemies as well as neighbors (Luke 6:27–28; Romans 12:14). Donald Trump, on the other hand, seems naturally to bypass traditional political and religious values, even to the point of mocking them at times. His rules feature shameless self-glorification, even to the extent of using messianic language about himself. After surviving impeachment, revenge against witnesses was openly carried out with claims of defending national security.

The political success of Trumpism is undeniable. Two puzzling questions are: How is it possible for conservative Christian groups to justify membership in the Trump base? And what mental processes underlie their support of a president who openly reflects the opposite of religious, moral, and compassionate values they would normally embrace with fervent passion?

Our purpose is to argue that too many conservative Christians make a habit of rejecting verifiable truth by giving priority to a sort of blind faith that justifies the cognitive dissonance they experience. This version of faith is associated with reliance on inflexible interpretations of religious beliefs and now includes a political agenda that is tied to a messianic pretender.[1]

We also believe there is a path to healing by prioritizing the pursuit of truth over varieties of blind faith. The initial steps involve repentance and humility in response to criticism—such as King David's reaction when confronted by the prophet Nathan over his affair with Bathsheba.

Justifying Membership in the Trump Base

During the campaign of 2016, Donald Trump made claims of exceptionalism that were almost messianic. Without having governmental or military experience, he asserted knowledge greater than experts or generals. "I alone can fix it," was a claim he made in campaign rallies. Once elected, he began obstructing investigations into his campaign and himself. As congressional investigations began to lead toward impeachment, he resisted all subpoenas and even claimed in a lawsuit that he was exempt from any form of investigation. Through one scandal after another involving the president and his

---

1. Using the term *conservative evangelical* in this chapter is not meant to imply that all Christian evangelicals are conservative or Trump supporters. Two of the authors have spent a career in the progressive side of the evangelical movement. A thorough review of the forty-year struggle of progressive evangelicals to reclaim Jesus but remain evangelical is found in Brantley W. Gasaway, "Making Evangelicals Great Again? American Evangelicals in the Age of Trump," *Evangelical Review of Theology: A Global Forum,* 43 (4), 293–311.

close associates, conservative evangelical groups continued to support and praise Donald Trump.

This leads to our first question: How do conservative Christians explain joining the base of someone whose example undermines their beliefs? Part of the answer is found in the 2017 Baylor Religion Survey.[2]

A team of sociologists used survey results to argue that Christian nationalism was the foundation of Trump's religious support. Opposition to Islam and keeping the United States a "Christian nation" was found to be more significant than biblical convictions.[3]

Yet prominent evangelical leaders have consistently appealed to Scripture for support, excusing Trump's shortcomings with references to King David's adultery and to the way Jesus associated with sinners. Since the Trump administration moved the American Embassy in Israel to Jerusalem, religious leaders have even begun using messianic-sounding language that Trump has encouraged.[4]

Many news stories provide examples of inconsistent use of Scripture to defend President Trump's actions. For example, accounts of pre-election efforts to cover up an affair with the porn star Stormy Daniels brought statements from Tony Perkins, president of the Family Research Council, about giving the president "a mulligan," which is a golf term for an extra swing after a bad golf shot. "We see right and wrong. We see good and evil, but also among evangelicals, there's an understanding that we are all fallen, and the idea of forgiveness is very prominent . . . And so, we understand that, yes, there is justice, but there is mercy." In the same *Politico* article, Perkins was asked about his hostile remarks about Barack Obama and whether it was appropriate to turn the other cheek. Perkins replied: "You know, you only

---

2. For information on the history and results of the survey, see Baylor University, Baylor Religion Surveys, https://www.baylor.edu/baylorreligionsurvey/.

3. Andrew L. Whitehead, Joseph O. Baker, and Samuel L. Perry, "Despite porn stars and Playboy models, white evangelicals aren't rejecting Trump. This is why," *The Washington Post*, March 26, 2018, https://www.washingtonpost.com/news/monkey -cage/wp/2018/03/26/despite-porn-stars-and-playboy-models-white-evangelicals-ar -ent-rejecting-trump-this-is-why/.

4. Jay Lowder, "I'm an evangelist and a Trump voter. But Trump as the 'second coming of God' is blasphemous," *The Washington Post*, August 22, 2019, https://www.wash -ingtonpost.com/religion/2019/08/22/im-an-evangelist-trump-voter-trump-second -coming-god-is-blasphemous/; Eugene Scott, "Comparing Trump to Jesus, and why some evangelicals believe Trump is God's chosen one," *The Washington Post*, December 18, 2019, https://www.washingtonpost.com/politics/2019/11/25/why-evangelicals-like -rick-perry-believe-that-trump-is-gods-chosen-one/.

have two cheeks. . . . Look, Christianity is not all about being a welcome mat which people can just stomp their feet on."[5]

This is an example of inconsistent use of Scripture, for Jesus is used to support unlimited passes for one president while the command to "turn the other cheek" limits forgiveness for a different president.

Statements by other Christian conservatives in the *Politico* article defended Donald Trump's policies as the basis for overlooking immoral behaviors. They acknowledged his personal flaws but consider him a God-sent champion of their religious-political agenda. That agenda was described at length in a letter to the editor of *Christianity Today* as Congress debated impeachment. Nearly 200 well known evangelical leaders objected to an editorial in *Christianity Today* that supported the removal of President Trump. (Note that Mark Galli's editorial did not explicitly call for impeachment.) Calling themselves "Bible-believing Christians and patriotic Americans," they listed eight policies they support, beginning with "the unborn" and religious freedom, and ending with support of Israel. They also claimed to follow the example of Jesus by associating with tax collectors and sinners and by giving to "Caesar what is Caesar's—our public service."[6]

Franklin Graham and Jerry Falwell, Jr., sons of prominent evangelical leaders of the late twentieth century, also attacked *Christianity Today* for supporting President Trump's removal. Graham announced that his father Billy voted for Trump and would be supporting him now if he were alive. Pro-life policies and defense of religious freedom were mentioned as important accomplishments. He dismissed the claims of immorality against the president by acknowledging that Trump is a sinner "as were all past presidents and as each one of us are."[7]

Even though conservative evangelicals are clearly pragmatic in supporting an openly immoral bully, they continue appealing to Scripture for support, most often using stories about Jesus and King David. However, their scriptural defenses ignore the obvious question of whether either Jesus or David fit the mold of leaders who set their own rules and violate sacred restraints.

5. Edward-Isaac Dovere, "Tony Perkins: Trump Gets 'a Mulligan' on Life, Stormy Daniels," interview of Tony Perkins in *Politico Magazine*, January 23, 2018, https://www.politico.com/magazine/story/2018/01/23/tony-perkins-evangelicals-donald-trump-stormy-daniels-216498.

6. Melissa Barnhart, "Nearly 200 evangelical leaders slam *Christianity Today* for questioning their Christian witness," *The Christian Post*, December 22, 2019, https://www.christianpost.com/news/nearly-200-evangelical-leaders-slam-christianity-today-for-questioning-their-christian-witness.html.

7. Caleb Parke, "Franklin Graham slams *Christianity Today* for invoking father's name in call for Trump's removal," Fox News, December 20, 2019, https://www.foxnews.com/media/trump-graham-christianity-today-remove-billy-franklin-impeach.

It is true that Pharisees accused Jesus of consorting with people they considered moral outcasts (Matthew 9:11; 11:16–19; Luke 19:5–7). Pharisees also criticized him for violating the technical requirements of the Sabbath (Matthew 12:10; Mark 3:2). Nevertheless, encounters with critics, such as these, were typical of the debates later recorded in Rabbinic texts. They were matters of interpretation, not arbitrary new rules trampling on universally accepted laws.

In Matthew's Sermon on the Mount, Jesus said clearly that he did not intend to undermine rules in the Torah (Matthew 5:17–20). Rather he sought to fulfill and improve them. He claimed a special relationship to God as he focused on going beyond externalities such as purity rituals. Motives, actions of compassion, forgiveness, and justice not tilted toward the rich were themes frequently repeated in Jesus' parables and teaching.

The Jesus known for healing through God's power and proclaiming the rule of God was the opposite of a charismatic leader who claims the right to set his own rules. Furthermore, excusing support for Trump as comparable to Jesus hanging out with sinners ignores the poverty and low social standing of those typically found in the company of Jesus. People who would be at home staying in the Trump Hotel in Washington or at properties such as Mar-a-Lago would rarely have been comfortable in the company of Jesus.

The adultery of David is also used as biblical evidence of God approving of someone with Trump's morals. The story of adultery with Bathsheba and the subsequent plot to kill her husband is well known. It features condemnation by the prophet Nathan and David's repentance in 2 Samuel 12. The humility of a repentant king, which can also be seen in many of the Psalms attributed to David, is as far from the usual Trumpian counterpunching response as can be imagined.

David is important because he established Jerusalem as capital and made it the religious center by moving the ark of the covenant there. The prophet Nathan plays a significant role in the narrative as a critic of the adultery with Bathsheba and as the agent declaring a special promise in response to David's wish to move the ark of the covenant from a tent to "a house of cedar." In 2 Samuel 7:11–16, Nathan tells David of God's veto of a temple by stating a larger promise that: "Your house and your kingdom shall be made sure before me; your throne shall be established forever." The adultery with Bathsheba came after this promise and modifying that promise was not mentioned in the accusation of adultery. The point that undermines evangelical use of these episodes is the radical expressions of guilt and pleas for forgiveness by David when attacked by the same man who had delivered the earlier promise. Where is the prophetic tone of Nathan in evangelical comments on Trump's morals? It is certainly clear that President Trump would not follow David's example if condemned by evangelical Nathans today.

Efforts to use scriptural support for membership in the Trump base become embarrassing when examined. Everything about Trump repudiates the teachings and example of Jesus. The closest parallels are Old Testament examples, namely the adulterous—but not the repentant—David, as well as the bullying Samson. Thus, we need to ask our second question: what mental processes can possibly justify such an embarrassing misuse of Scripture?

Living with Cognitive Dissonance

Timothy Dalrymple, president and CEO of *Christianity Today*, observed that evangelicals have gone too far in supporting the Trump administration.

> The problem is that we as evangelicals are also associated with President Trump's rampant immorality, greed, and corruption; his divisiveness and race-baiting; his cruelty and hostility to immigrants and refugees; and more. In other words, the problem is the wholeheartedness of the embrace.[8]

Dalrymple described a paradox of a religious group embracing a set of moral convictions and at the same time supporting a president who is a daily exception to many of those beliefs. When a person's behaviors contradict their deeply held beliefs, the result is an uncomfortable mental state that psychologists call cognitive dissonance.

How do the evangelicals mentioned by Dalrymple live with the cognitive dissonance that arises from ignoring moral values and denying evidentiary truth so apparent to most Americans? In all cases of cognitive dissonance, the mental discomfort can only be resolved by modifying either one's beliefs or one's behavior so that they once again come into alignment. In the case of Trump-supporting evangelicals, the resolution of cognitive dissonance appears to occur through the adoption of a closed-ended approach to faith that resists factual input. The problem is not faith itself, for human beings must be able to trust relationships and their perceptions of the world. However, blind faith is perilous because it rejects data from the external world that may limit the reliability of what is being trusted.

Earlier we mentioned a letter to the editor of *Christianity Today* in which nearly 200 evangelical leaders condemned an editorial supporting

---

8. Timothy Dalrymple, "The Flag in the Whirlwind: An Update from CT's President," *Christianity Today*, December 22, 2019, https://www.christianitytoday.com/ct/2019/december-web-only/trump-evangelicals-editorial-christianity-today-president.html.

the removal of President Trump. Like the president's defense in the Senate trial, the letter ignored the evidence of actions that prompted impeachment and the testimony of witnesses who braved presidential intimidation to carry out what they saw as their duty. Although it mentioned Trump's accomplishments and the example of Jesus, the letter adopted the overtly partisan language of President Trump in denouncing motives of those supporting impeachment and used the same hyper-partisan language in defending their own motives.[9]

In short, this letter is evidence of severe cognitive dissonance. Ignoring the evidence brought out in the trial and insulting the motives of opponents indicate faith in beliefs that are closed off and unreceptive to facts that would have carried much weight in a federal or state court proceeding.

The tone of the letter betrays the cognitive dissonance of these evangelical leaders as they behave in ways that contradict their essential beliefs. According to Carol Tavris and Elliott Aronson, cognitive dissonance "is about how people strive to make sense out of contradictory ideas and lead lives that are, at least in their own minds, consistent and meaningful." Defending things that make us uncomfortable can lead to behavior that is even more troubling as we convince ourselves we are right and justified. This is known as self-justification, through which people "convince themselves that what they did was the best thing they could have done." From this entirely natural process emerges a confirmation bias, an inclination to ignore or misinterpret fact-based evidence against the action.[10]

Another problem is that these evangelical leaders use faith to justify setting one's own rules. Faith itself is not the issue, but reliance on faith that is blind to data because of absolute allegiance to higher religious, political, social, or economic authorities inevitably leads to cognitive dissonance. Those who adopt blind faith attempt to resolve this cognitive dissonance by isolating themselves in silos that shield them from ever having to confront facts that challenge their cherished worldview. This mounting social division has laid the groundwork for the Trump presidency, with its strategy of accelerating national fear. This way of resolving cognitive dissonance promotes many varieties of tribalism as groups "live in bubbles." The result is mounting cognitive dissonance and social division—a problem that produced the Trump presidency and its strategy of accelerating national fear.

These conclusions become unfair when applied to all evangelical Christians, for there are large numbers who consider themselves more

---

9. Barnhart, "Nearly 200 evangelical leaders slam *Christianity Today.*"

10. Carol Tavris and Elliott Aronson, *Mistakes Were Made (But Not By Me)* (New York: Houghton Mifflin Harcourt Mariner, 2015), 5, 15–16, 21–23, 51.

progressive and open to factual input. Still, Bill Leonard's warning, in his *Baptist News* column describing the controversy surrounding the *Christianity Today* editorials about removal of President Trump, cautions advocates and critics of evangelical Christianity:

> American evangelicalism is certainly no monolith but involves a broad spectrum of participants proceeding from Appalachian Pentecostal serpent-handlers to Calvinist-oriented mega-churches; from Jim Wallis and *Sojourners* to James Dobson and Focus on the Family. In the broader society, however, those distinctions may be too nuanced . . . Like it or not, the evangelical dilemma has implications for the way much of Christianity is viewed throughout American culture . . .[11]

The article in the *Christian Post* on the letter to *Christianity Today* emphasized the large number of signers, thereby suggesting broad support in Christianity. Bill Leonard is right; the reputation of American Christianity is on the line when intemperate defenses of presidential misbehavior make headlines.

Social Healing Through Repentance

Is there a path to healing the divisions within American Christianity and our society in general? We believe there is a way, but it is difficult because it starts by embracing humility as an ally of faith that keeps it open to fact-based data and helps avoid self-justification and confirmation bias. Faith becomes more flexible to changing situations when documented information is used to prevent manipulation of our beliefs by politicians, religious leaders, advertisers, and trolls on social media.

Perhaps Christians could "come to ourselves" as the prodigal son did when he recognized the disaster of the life that resulted from setting his own rules. According to Luke 15:17–20, he remembered life at home with his family and decided to return in humility. This is a story of repentance and a desire to return to wholeness—and of the promise of acceptance when one returns to more authentic values.

What are the values of Christianity to which we must return? Standing up for truth, defending the weak, and fighting injustice are rules Jesus described as essential to God's rule. The ultimate test for all forms of

11. Bill Leonard, "The *Christianity Today* editorial: exposing the American evangelical dilemma," *Baptist News*, December 27, 2019, https://baptistnews.com/article/the-christianity-today-editorial-exposing-the-american-evangelical-dilemma/#.XgeR__x7lyQ.

Christianity is the parable of the Sheep and Goats in Matthew 25:31–46. Amy-Jill Levine said the story tells us that "people are judged . . . on whether they cared for the poor, fed the hungry, or visited people in prison. Otherwise put, Jesus asks, 'Did you go the extra mile?'"[12]

The point Jesus made was that God cares about how people treat one another. Those who were judged harshly saw ordinary circumstances of people in need and habitually failed to respond. Those who were favored saw Jesus himself in need when they encountered ordinary situations. The story implies a question for today. What actions did we take when we should have seen Jesus himself in those being abused by a president who callously set his own rules?

The evangelical message features the "plan of salvation" heard in the churches each of the authors attended in his youth. Emphasis is usually on accepting Jesus as one's personal savior, but the same procedure can be used to promote social healing. The process begins when we admit our failures, repent and ask forgiveness, then trust in God to forgive and heal as we take corrective actions showing a new course. A change of direction—a conversion experience—then happens that sets us on a path to recovery. This is the process illustrated in the parable of the prodigal son.

Who should repent and what is it that calls for repentance? Bill Leonard reminds us that conservative evangelicals are not the only Americans who need to change direction if national healing is to begin. There are large numbers of Americans in the Trump base who gladly attend his rallies, cheer at his lies, and join in shameful chants. All varieties of Christians can point the way for every American, no matter their political or religious views, by heeding the words of Mark Galli in his editorial in *Christianity Today*: "Remember who you are and whom you serve."[13]

Americans witnessed an example of a courageous response to Mark Galli's challenge when Senator Mitt Romney explained his vote to convict President Trump on the first article of impeachment. The simple and moving justification for his vote was that religious beliefs required him to take seriously his oath to God taken at the beginning of the Senate trial.[14]

President Trump could have viewed the statements of Nancy Pelosi and Mitt Romney, at the beginning and end of impeachment, as the

12. Amy-Jill Levine, *Short Stories by Jesus* (New York: HarperOne, 2014), 304.

13. Mark Galli, "Trump Should Be Removed from Office," *Christianity Today*, December 19, 2019, https://www.christianitytoday.com/ct/2019/december-web-only/trump-should-be-removed-from-office.html.

14. See the interview given before his speech in the article by McKay Coppins, "How Mitt Romney Decided Trump Is Guilty," *The Atlantic*, February 5, 2020, https://www.theatlantic.com/politics/archive/2020/02/romney-impeach-trump/606127/.

equivalent of Nathan's denunciation of David, and he could have responded
with sorrow and repentance. But his behavior throughout the impeachment
process was more reminiscent of the bully Samson. Charles Sykes, known
for his conservative Republicanism, described the outbursts of the acquitted
president at a National Prayer Breakfast and a gathering of supporters in the
East Room of the White House this way:

> In the Gospel According to Donald, forgiveness is for suckers,
> losers, and cucks . . . If Trump prays at all, they are not prayers
> of forgiveness or humility. . . . How someone like this identifies
> as Christian, or is asked to address a prayer breakfast, is one of
> the deepest mysteries of American ecumenism.[15]

Thus far, evangelical leaders have not acknowledged the dangers of
blind faith in inflexible doctrines and immoral champions of their political
agenda. This is a problem of accelerating importance in a world in which
propaganda and slander are dominating social media and now have been
adopted by prominent news outlets as well as imitated by the Trump administration. Charles Sykes also described how the Republican base is living
"inside the Trump bubble," at home in a world that ignores information they
do not want to believe.[16]

Part of the remedy for all Americans is to start giving priority to verifiable truth. Recognizing the many forms of fact-resisting faith that are com-
manding our allegiance is an essential first step. The point is not to eliminate
faith but to ground it in evidence when possible and, when not possible, to
be flexible and open to verifiable truth that may require adjustments. One
reward for this change in attitude is increasing freedom from the cognitive
dissonance that comes with trying to live in conflicting realities. Healing is
possible, but Jesus reminds us it is not found on the highway that is wide
and easy to travel (Matthew 7:14).

15. Charles Sykes, "The Gospel According to Mad King Donald," *The Bulwark*, February 7, 2020, https://thebulwark.com/the-gospel-according-to-mad-king-donald/.

16. Charles Sykes, "Inside the Trump Bubble," *The Bulwark*, February 11, 2020,
https://thebulwark.com/inside-the-trump-bubble/.

PART III

ON THEOLOGICAL, HISTORICAL,
AND CONSTITUTIONAL ISSUES
REGARDING TRUMP

Chapter 18

Christ the Center and Norm

Miroslav Volf & Ryan McAnnally-Linz

Christian faith has an inalienable public dimension. Christians aren't Christ's followers just in their private and communal lives; they are Christ's followers in their public and political lives as well. Christ must be the center and norm for Christian public engagement because Christ and his Spirit are at work, not just in our hearts, families, and churches, but also in our nations and the entire world. We don't need to waste words defending this commitment; most Christians today embrace it. But it is important to be clear about what the commitment means, for it both sets the course of Christian public engagement and places limits on it.

At first glance Jesus Christ seems a remarkably odd choice for the role of determining the shape of our political lives. He calls "blessed" those who are meek, the pure of heart, and the persecuted (Matthew 5:5, 8, 10). He stoops down to wash his disciples' feet (John 13:1–17), he often shies away from public attention (e.g., Matthew 8:4; Mark 1:43–45), and he rebukes his followers for trying to use the sword (the classic symbol of political power) to rescue him from an unjust arrest (Matthew 26:52; Luke 22:51; John 18:11). His whole way of speaking, his bearing, and his mannerisms often seem unworldly, more saintly than kingly. And his message seems, frankly, too radical to apply to political life. "Turn to them the other cheek," he says (Matthew 5:39 NIV). "Do not judge" (Matthew 7:1). "Love your enemies" (Matthew 5:44). How could any of that possibly have something relevant to say to the rough-and-tumble, publicity-seeking, deal-making world of public life and engagement?

On closer examination, however, Jesus' life and message are unmistakably public, even political, though not in the usual sense of the term. After all, the core of Jesus' preaching is that "the kingdom of God has come near" (Matthew 4:17; Mark 1:15). Whatever else it might be, *kingdom* is surely a political term. In line with the political character of the kingdom, the book of Revelation portrays the final advent of God's reign as the "holy city, the new Jerusalem, coming down out of heaven from God" to be established on earth (Revelation 21:2). We get our word *political* from the Greek word for "city" in that verse (*polis*).

Christ, the Spirit, and the Kingdom

On its own, Jesus delivering the message of the kingdom wouldn't justify our making *Jesus himself* the norm for Christian public engagement. Couldn't Jesus have been just a prophet of the kingdom, merely sketching a vision of it, or a philosopher of the kingdom, merely explaining and justifying its constitution? Or might he be an example for us to follow? In fact, he is more than that. The kingdom Christ proclaimed is inseparable from who he was during his ministry and crucifixion and who he continues to be after his resurrection. Jesus insisted on a close tie between himself and the kingdom. Rejecting the charge that he cast out demons by Satan's power, he said, "If it is by the finger of God that I cast out the demons, then the kingdom of God has come to you" (Luke 11:20). The kingdom has come in Jesus' own activity. You cannot have the kingdom without having Jesus Christ; you cannot have Jesus Christ without having the kingdom. Consequently, his entire life is of public import.

As Jürgen Moltmann has argued in *The Crucified God*, Jesus' "way to the cross" was a path of conflict with the religious and political rulers of his day, who saw his teaching, his ministry, and his very life as a threat.[1]

From Herod's desperate attempt to kill the infant Christ to the Romans who crucified him for insurrection under the mocking sign, "This is Jesus, the King of the Jews" (Matthew 27:37), the powers that be considered him a problem to be dealt with, violently if need be. Expanding on Moltmann's thesis, Michael Welker has shown that Christ was crucified under the

---

1. Jürgen Moltmann, *The Crucified God*, trans. R. A. Wilson and John Bowden (Minneapolis: Fortress, 1993), 126–45.

auspices of a broader set of public institutions and agents—not just religion and politics but also law and public opinion.[2]

Their role in the crucifixion reveals just how susceptible to corruption these structures of human life are. Christ's entering the conflict with them, making the conflict part of his mission, and engaging in it in his own way marked by nonviolence brings the corruption of the public structures of human life under God's judgment.

The way the conflict between Christ and the public institutions and agents of his day turned out might seem to leave little room for Christ to serve as the norm for our political engagements. After all, he seemed to have been defeated. But in fact, the conflict serves as a model for his followers in their own times and places. For Christ's death on the cross was a *central victory* in a series of victories over corrupted forms of human life. In the Acts of the Apostles, we read that "God raised him up" and that he now sits "at the right hand of God" and pours out the Spirit so that his mission can continue in the world (Acts 2:24, 33).

Christ, then, is alive and at work in the world through the Spirit. His death did not expose him as a false pretender to kingly rule, nor did it bring his rule to an end. To the contrary, Jesus' resurrection and ascension confirm and establish his rule in a new way. Christ is exalted into universal lordship, a lordship that is "far above all rule and authority and power and dominion" (Ephesians 1:21). In the image of 1 Corinthians 15, he governs the kingdom until its eschatological fulfillment, when he will hand it over to the Father. As the conflict-heavy language of this passage ("after he has destroyed every ruler and every authority and power" [v. 24]) and Colossians 2:15 suggests, Christ's mission remains one of resistance to sin, unmasking the corruptions and pretensions of earthly powers. But it is also one of bringing about foretastes of the kingdom in history. Christ works not only against but also within institutions and agents concerned with common life. Sin corrupts them, but Christ is at work redeeming them.

The kingdom that Jesus brought near is radically different from run-of-the-mill political regimes. It wasn't established as one more kingdom alongside others in the way that Rome was founded in 753 BC and then struggled for supremacy with Carthage and other political powers. Nor did it succeed other regimes in the way that one government administration follows another. Rather, the kingdom is the ultimate goal of all history and

2. See Michael Welker, *God the Revealed: Christology*, trans. Douglas W. Stott (Grand Rapids: Eerdmans, 2013), 192–97, 261.

all creation. It is the fulfillment to which everything is being drawn. It is the indescribable future when God will be all in all (1 Cor. 15:28).[3]

This kingdom is not only final (it can never be undone) and universal (it will extend across the whole creation), but it is also all-encompassing. It *includes* but also far *exceeds* all that we usually classify as "public," its reach extending from our most intimate desires to the fate of the entire cosmos.

Christ and Public Engagement

All this is not to say, however, that there is no difference between Christ's work in the church and his work in the wider world. Karl Barth (1886–1968) provides a helpful image for understanding what the universal work of Christ means for the relationship between Christians, the church, and political societies. Christ, he says, is like the center of two concentric circles. The smaller circle is the Christian community, which knows that Christ is the center and aims to live in light of that knowledge. The larger circle is the civil community, which has Christ as its center even though it may not know it. Christ's rule in the outer circle is neither identical with nor completely different from his rule in the inner circle, but it is analogous to it.[4]

As a *community*, the church is of major public significance, a point many theologians have made in recent decades. But the edges of the church are not the limits of Christian public engagement. As participants in the civil community, Christians strive to bring it into greater conformity to the character and rule of Christ.

Christians ought to be active in the "outer circle" because *Christ calls us to follow him in our whole lives and to work in the power of the Spirit wherever he is at work.* Throughout the Gospel stories of his life, Jesus calls people to follow him, to orient their lives around him, in ways that leave no part of their lives untouched. Discipleship affects family life (Matthew 10:37). It affects relationships with wealth and possessions (Matthew 6:24; Luke 16:13). It affects work (Mark 1:16–17). It affects social life (Matthew 5:42–48). And so on. The point is: if we are committed to following Jesus in the power of the Spirit, we are committed to letting him determine the character of our whole lives—no exceptions. We are his disciples in our judgments, words,

---

3. Our point that the hope for a kingdom in which God will be all in all ought to inform our public engagement stands independently of whether we think that this verse implies universal salvation or not.

4. Karl Barth, "The Christian Community and the Civil Community," in *Community, Church, and State: Three Essays* (Eugene, OR: Wipf & Stock, 2004), 149–89.

and deeds that affect the common good, just as we are his disciples in every other aspect of our lives.

Commitment to public engagement as Christ's disciples draws us to the Scriptures as the touchstone for discerning Christ at work. Christ in the world cannot be different than Christ in the Scriptures. For *Christ always remains true to himself:* "Jesus Christ is the same yesterday and today and forever" (Hebrews 13:8). His character as we see it in Scripture is consistent with his character always and everywhere. Granted, we should expect Christ to surprise us not just because we can never fully comprehend him but also because the situations in which he is at work are changing. To give the same talk to two different audiences is to give two different talks; to act in the same way in two different situations is to act in two different ways. Nevertheless, we can be confident that Christ will never turn on a dime and become someone antithetical to the Christ we see in Scripture. For example, in market economies he won't command acquisitiveness instead of generosity; in bureaucratized social-service systems he won't say that compassion is obsolete; and to citizens under threat from terrorists he won't claim that it's just fine to hate those enemies instead of loving them.

Putting all these observations together results in the following line of thought: Because (a) Christ is working everywhere bringing about anticipations of the kingdom of God, (b) we are called to follow wherever Christ is working, and (c) the character of Christ as testified to in Scriptures faithfully expresses his character as it is always and everywhere, we can conclude that (d) *the person of Jesus as we encounter him in Scripture and discern him at work today through the Spirit is the norm for our public engagement.*

Although Jesus brought the kingdom of God in his life, death, and resurrection, the kingdom will be fully actualized only at the end of history. We live, therefore, within a field of tension: the kingdom is in some sense actual "now," but in another sense it is still "not yet." The transition to the full actuality of the kingdom of God is not a matter of gradual progress within history as we know it. Rather, the change is so stark that Scripture talks about it as a "new creation" that God makes out of the "old" one (2 Corinthians 5:17; Isaiah 65:17). Consequently, we shouldn't think of any human community, whether the church or a civic community, as progressively "expanding" the kingdom of God on earth, as some conquering force might. For the most part, Christians have rightly abandoned the false dream, associated with progressivist accounts of history, that if we just keep working at it, eventually, one stone at a time, we will build the New Jerusalem. According to the book of Revelation, the holy city must *come down from God* (Revelation 21:2).

Our primary stance toward the kingdom, therefore, ought to be one of hope, an eager expectation that God will bring to completion the kingdom work begun in Christ's incarnation and continued through the Spirit. To hope isn't merely to dream, of course. To hope is to live into the reality of the kingdom that we hope for. That kingdom is the fundamental aim of human existence and the deepest longing of human hearts. Those who follow Christ in the power of the Spirit should let it determine the character of their lives and their projects. Even though we cannot make the kingdom arrive, our lives and our world, including our political societies and global realities, can reflect some of its character.

Authors' Note: This chapter was originally published as the first chapter of our book *Public Faith in Action: How to Engage with Commitment, Conviction, and Courage*, which came out several months before the 2016 election. We believed then, and we are only more firmly convinced after more than three years of the Trump presidency, that electoral support for Donald Trump does not fit with faithful Christian public engagement. Making Jesus Christ the center and norm of our public engagement ought to lead us to oppose a president whose character, actions, and policies are in such large measure un-Christlike.

Chapter 19

Evangelical Double-Mindedness
in Support Of Donald Trump

JAMES W. SKILLEN & JAMES R. SKILLEN

DONALD TRUMP IS NOT THE SOURCE OF THE CURRENT DYSFUNCTION OF American politics. He is, however, the most prominent and outlandish expression of the crisis in his actions, language, exercise of presidential responsibilities, and the degree to which he holds captive Republicans in Congress. He is one of the least spiritual persons ever to hold that office. So how is it that so many evangelicals are dedicated to him and, in some cases, even honor him as God's appointed servant?

The crisis we want to describe is not political in the narrow sense but a religiously deep tumult of ideological, institutional, and personal dimensions that is polarizing politics and crippling government. Our particular aim is to try to account for the seemingly inexplicable support evangelical Christians are giving the president whose conduct in office violates many of the very norms and standards that evangelicals have traditionally insisted upon.

It is not for us to judge the heart or the spiritual condition of anyone, including Donald Trump. Nor are we called to judge the hearts of evangelicals who support him. Yet the fact that most evangelicals confess faith in Jesus Christ and put trust in the Bible provides a firm basis for assessing the relationship between what they confess and how they speak and act. The same holds for Donald Trump, who makes no profession of faith in Christ or of trust in the Bible as the guide to his life. In order to understand Trump and evangelical support for him we first need to consider briefly the civil-religious history of America. In the context of that history, today's evangelical double-mindedness becomes clear: on the one hand, commitment to Christ through faith for eternal salvation, and on the other hand, commitment to America—god's chosen nation—to lead the world to its earthly destiny of ever greater freedom, democracy, and prosperity.

Early American Developments

The Constitution of the United States of America, which established a weak federal government, protected slavery, and articulated certain civil rights for those who were not enslaved, was drafted with a religiously deep belief in the new nation's identity and mission. Leaders and people came to believe that America was divinely blessed, chosen by god to be a new Israel to serve as a light on a hill to all nations.

The divinity that was invoked was, in the eyes of most Christians, the God of the Bible, but non-Christians had few objections to invoking a national deity. This was America's god, the god with whom Americans, as a new Israel, were covenanting for divine authorization and blessings. "God bless America!" Sacvan Bercovitch points out that both literally and spiritually it was misleading to draw a parallel between Israel and America. Yet the New England Puritans constructed just such a myth for their colony that soon enough was adopted by the new nation as a whole. "Looking to past and future," writes Bercovitch, "the orthodoxy [of the Puritans] posited a dual identification between Old Israel and New. One was retrospective: the progress from Canaan to America, according to biblical prophecy. The other was proleptic, as Israel would in time receive the blessing of National conversion, so the New England Way would one day extend into the Theopolis Americana."[1]

Despite the Puritan failure to maintain their New England theocracy, their legacy proved durable for generations to come. The nation's founders, writes Bercovitch, took from the Puritan experiment "the larger, vaguer, and more flexible forms of symbol and metaphor (*new chosen people, city on a hill, promised land, destined progress, New Eden, American Jerusalem*) and so facilitated the movement from visible saint to American patriot, sacred errand to manifest destiny, colony to republic to imperial power."[2]

---

1. Sacvan Bercovitch, *The American Jeremiad* (Madison, WI: University of Wisconsin Press, 1978) 78.

2. Bercovitch, *American Jeremiad*, 92.

The development of thought and imagination was from the sacred to the profane by the incorporation of "Bible history into the American experience."[3]

Prior to the Revolutionary War, famed theologian Jonathan Edwards had already enlarged the constituency of God's new Israel "from saintly New England theocrats to newborn American saints."[4]

"Edwards sanctified a worldliness he would have despised, and lent support to new ideologies that linked American striving with Scripture prophesy, economic reform with the work of the spirit, and libertarian ideals with the approach of New Jerusalem."[5]

As historian Mark Noll writes, "In the thirteen colonies that became the United States, republican and Protestant convictions merged as they did nowhere else in the world."[6]

"What the Puritan canopy had once supplied as a boundary for theology, America's republican Christian convictions would provide for later generations."[7]

Tom Paine and "leaders of the Continental Congress deployed a vocabulary of traditional religion in support of the war [for independence] as an intensely religious cause. Religious use of the republican vocabulary may, in fact, have been more important than any other factor in drawing believers from throughout the new nation's various regions in to support of the war effort."[8]

For educational and religious leader Timothy Dwight, according to Noll, "a second conversion (to the patriot cause) followed naturally from his first conversion (to Christ)."[9]

James Byrd shows how the biblical picture of the Lord as a "man of war" was also pulled from the Bible and put to use to inspire colonists to see their war for independence as divinely blessed and guided. The colonists were the chosen nation fighting against enemies of freedom.[10]

By the end of the war and the adoption of the Constitution, Americans began to sing the praise of General George Washington as America's

3. Bercovitch, *American Jeremiad*, 93.

4. Bercovitch, *American Jeremiad*, 105.

5. Bercovitch, *American Jeremiad*, 109.

6. Mark A. Noll, *America's God* (New York: Oxford University Press, 2002), 73.

7. Noll, *America's God*, 54.

8. Noll, *America's God*, 85.

9. Noll, *America's God*, 89.

10. James P. Byrd, *Sacred Scripture, Sacred War* (New York: Oxford University Press, 2013) 51–54.

Moses. An early Yale president, Ezra Stiles, praised Washington to the heavens: "O Washington! . . . how do I love thy name! how have I often adored and blessed thy God for creating and forming thee the great ornament of humankind!"[11]

Although Washington was no evangelical, writes Byrd, he was highly supportive of religion and morality. His "favorable comments about God's providence and religion's benefit to society made up for his few displays of piety and his reluctance to mention Christ."[12] The revolution for *freedom* from British oppression was not without a longing for a strong, even monarchical leader who would lead them to defeat their enemies.

Where do we find Jesus in all of this? Orthodox Protestants certainly continued to worship Jesus Christ but in a way that understood him primarily as the savior of sinners for eternal life. America's god, however, was like the one who led Israel out of bondage in Egypt for an earthly purpose and an earthly promised land. For most white Anglo-Saxon Protestants (WASPs)[13] those two "salvation histories"—one for the church through Christ for eternal life, and the other for the world through America for earthly fulfillment—seemed to fit together hand in glove. That bond is what leads Bercovitch to conclude that America achieved something unique: "[O]nly the American Way, of all modern ideologies, has managed to circumvent the paradoxes inherent in [other] approaches. Of all symbols of identity, only *America* has united nationality and universality, civic and spiritual selfhood, secular and redemptive history, the country's past and paradise to be, in a single synthetic ideal."[14]

We are not convinced, however, that Bercovitch's "single synthetic ideal" has overcome the tensions of an unstable, combustible myth that hid for a time the explosions that would follow. *That unstable synthetic ideal is, we believe, the fount of today's evangelical doublemindedness that includes the belief that Donald Trump is God's appointed leader of America for such a time as this.*

---

11. Byrd, *Sacred Scripture*, 64.

12. Byrd, *Sacred Scripture*, 69.

13. The phrase, white Anglo-Saxon Protestant and its acronym WASP have a social and historical meaning that was coined in the first half of the twentieth century. For background see E. Digby Baltzell, *The Protestant Establishment* (New Haven, CT: Yale University Press, 1987).

14. Bercovitch, *American Jeremiad*, 176.

Two American Exodus Stories

In the American civil religion we've introduced above, Israel's exodus story was adapted as the figural analogue of god's liberation of Americans from British oppression under King George. That is the story familiar to most Americans. Courageous Puritans, making covenant with God, took leave by God's grace from British Egypt, crossed the Red Sea of the Atlantic, and entered a new promised land where they built a City on a Hill to serve as the light of liberty and a sign of promise to all nations. That story, as a national origin myth, became so powerful and widespread that John Adams, Benjamin Franklin, and Thomas Jefferson all wanted to feature Israel's exodus in the design of a Great Seal for the confederated states.[15]

It would be difficult to overstate the degree to which this story, like the biblical exodus story, has a spatial character. Great Britain was Egypt, and North America was the "new world" where God's people could start anew. Church historian Sydney Mead once wrote, "He who would understand America must understand that through all the formative years, space has overshadowed time—has taken precedence over time in the formation of all the ideals most cherished by the American spirit."[16]

And German theologian Jürgen Moltmann, after a visiting lectureship in the United States, commented how struck he was by the profound contrast between Americans' spatial eschatology and Europeans' temporal eschatology. In Europe, where space was limited, any exodus had to be temporal and come through revolution. In the United States, however, Moltmann observed a tendency to hope for a new society in spatial terms, which fed into Westward Ho and Manifest Destiny. It was a frontier eschatology.[17]

The WASP exodus story is not the end of America's adaptation of the biblical story, however. A second American exodus story was taking shape at the same time, composed from early slave songs and eventually by the powerful sermons and speeches of Frederick Douglass for the slaves, the original promise of America was written right in the Declaration of Independence—that all humans have been created equal. The pharaoh who oppressed the slaves and thwarted the Declaration's promise was not, however, a foreign monarch but the white slaveholder. And unlike the Americans in the WASP story, there was no new land to which the slave could escape. An

15. Byrd, *Sacred Scripture*, 45–47.

16. Sidney E. Mead, *The Lively Experiment* (New York: Harper and Row, 1963), 15. See also Mead's "The 'Nation with the Soul of a Church,'" *Church History* (September, 1967), 262–83.

17. Jürgen Moltmann, *Religion, Revolution, and the Future*, trans. M. Douglas Meeks (New York: Charles Scribner's Sons, 1969).

exodus from slavery would have to take place right here, within the Egypt of America. For slaves, time rather than space offered hope of a new society, and the federal government would need to act more like a Moses than a pharaoh. Indeed, the first stages of their exodus to freedom were driven by a strong federal government, which overthrew slavery in the Civil War and, after a hundred more years of black oppression, established equal civil rights for everyone in the *national* polity. From the viewpoint of former slaves, a strong central (federal) government proved to be a positive force for freedom and equal treatment, not a threat to those in bondage.

Byrd explains it this way: "African Americans reversed Revolutionary America's reading of the Exodus story: The United States was not the new Israel; it was the new Egypt. 'Slavery' in the Exodus was not a mere metaphor for political oppression; it was a literal counterpart to slavery in America. This interpretation of the Exodus," Byrd continues, "was widespread among slaves and abolitionists in the nineteenth century. Historian Albert J. Raboteau argued persuasively that 'no single symbol captures more clearly the distinctiveness of Afro-American Christianity than the symbol of Exodus.'"[18]

The hypocrisy of slaveholders who revolted against Britain's oppression of them but kept slaves in America was condemned in both England and America. John Wesley, the founder of Methodism, "ridiculed American patriots' complaints that the British had 'enslaved' them with taxes even as these same patriots held Africans in chains."[19]

And American theologian Samuel Hopkins argued that defenders of slavery "were like 'Pharaoh and the Egyptians' who likely 'had as many weighty' arguments against freeing the Hebrews as Revolutionary-era slaveholders had 'against freeing the slaves among us.' Eventually, however, God drowned all Pharaoh's arguments for slavery in the Red Sea."[20]

One hundred years after the Civil War and the end of slavery, African Americans were still awaiting their exodus into the promised land of a liberated America and their freedom to celebrate the full rights and equal treatment promised in the Declaration. From his cell in a Birmingham jail in 1963, Martin Luther King, Jr. wrote his famous letter to church leaders who had been urging him not to rock the boat over "social issues with which the gospel has no real concern . . . ."[21]

18. Byrd, *Sacred Scripture*, 56.

19. Byrd, *Sacred Scripture*, 56.

20. Byrd, *Sacred Scripture*, 61.

21. Martin Luther King, Jr., *I Have a Dream* (San Francisco: HarperSanFrancisco, 1986), 96.

King wrote, "Yes, I see the church as the body of Christ. But, oh! How we have blemished and scarred that body through social neglect and fear of being nonconformists. There was a time when the church was very powerful. It was during that period when the early Christians rejoiced when they were deemed worthy to suffer for what they believed. . . . [Christians] went on with the conviction that they were 'a colony of heaven,' and had to obey God rather than man."[22]

Both directly and indirectly King was calling into question the hand-in-glove fit of the church and the American nation as portrayed in the WASP Exodus story.

Nevertheless, African Americans recognized that their future was tied up with the oppression and the promise of this country.

> Abused and scorned though we may be, our destiny is tied up with the destiny of America. Before the Pilgrims landed at Plymouth we were here. Before the pen of Jefferson etched across the pages of history the majestic words of the Declaration of Independence, we were here. For more than two centuries our foreparents labored in this country without wages, they made cotton king; and they built the homes of their masters in the midst of brutal injustice and shameful humiliation—and yet out of a bottomless vitality they continued to thrive and develop. If the inexpressible cruelties of slavery could not stop us, the opposition we now face will surely fail. We will win our freedom because the sacred heritage of our nation and the eternal will of God are embodied in our echoing demands.[23]

In King's letter we hear the ring of faith in God, and the patience, hope, and dedication of those who sang their exodus story from the earliest days of slavery on up to the civil rights movement and continuing today. What also comes through is King's own blending of Christian hope in God for eternal salvation with the hope of fulfillment of the American dream of freedom and equality for all of God's children in this age. That synthesis represents a counter, civil-religious narrative. While many Americans today, including white evangelicals, are looking back with distress to the nation they believe they have lost or are in danger of losing, King and those who marched with him are looking forward to the America that has not yet been set free.

> I have a dream that one day every valley shall be exalted, every hill and mountain shall be made low, the rough places shall be made plain, and the crooked places shall be made straight and

22. King, *I Have a Dream*, 97.
23. King, *I Have a Dream*, 98.

the glory of the Lord will be revealed and all flesh shall see it together. . . . With this faith we will be able to work together, to pray together, to struggle together, to go to jail together, to stand up for freedom together, knowing that we will be free one day . . . when all of God's children—black men and white men, Jews and Gentiles, Catholics and Protestants—will be able to join hands and to sing in the words of the old Negro spiritual, "Free at last, free at last; thank God Almighty, we are free at last."[24]

The tension between the two civil-religious exodus stories outlined above is, we believe, the primary driving motor of the culture wars now being played out in American politics and other areas of life. These are deeply religious stories that portend little possibility of compromise unless a significant number of the protagonists undergoes conversion. Both exodus stories cannot be true at the same time. Radically different views of how America's god is related to America cannot both be correct. Which story tells the truth of what America should be? Who is America's god, or are there two of them, or none?

Many white evangelical Christians continue to embrace the civil-religious narrative of the founders, drawing on a host of revisionist histories. According to these histories, Americans had lived faithfully as god's chosen people in the beginning, but they strayed from god over time. The nation can only be restored by going back to the garden of its founding. By contrast, the heirs of those who were murdered, enslaved, and marginalized throughout much of American history see things quite differently. The founders interpreted principles of justice and equality so selectively that they applied primarily to white, land-owning men. The founders did not overcome oppression; they simply changed places with their own former oppressors. Those whose roots are in the second American exodus story do not want to go back to the founding; they want to go forward to the full realization of the promises of equal treatment and opportunity, and they continue to see the federal government as essential in their struggle.

Trump and the Evangelicals

After the 1960s, white evangelicals gradually became more uniformly supporters of conservative (mostly Republican) pro-life, pro-family political candidates of good character who promised to lower taxes, balance the budget, reduce the size of government, promote free trade, and defend the nation from foreign (especially Russian) aggression. But from 2016 till

24. King, *I Have a Dream*, 105–6.

today, these same evangelicals (and many other conservatives as well) have become unflappable supporters of Donald Trump, a law-defying, government-demeaning, perpetually prevaricating, would-be strongman. In three short years, with dedicated backing from Republicans in Congress, Trump has sent the annual budget deficit and the national debt skyrocketing; decimated the Department of State; gutted the Environmental Protection Agency; taken defense funds to try to build a wall to ward off immigrants from the south; taken no action against Russian aggression in Ukraine or its interference in our 2016 and 2020 election campaigns; taken the side of Putin against our own intelligence community and many of our allies; and applauded authoritarian figures in Turkey, Saudi Arabia, North Korea, the Philippines, and beyond. How in the world has this upside-down reversal taken place?

With Ronald Reagan's election to the presidency in 1980, most evangelicals were recharged in the hope that the nation could be cleansed down to its moral roots and would once again foster the right kind of religious freedom, family values, prosperity, and democracy. The two "salvation histories" that they held together in their hearts (one for eternal life through Christ and the other for earthly freedom, democracy, and prosperity through America) had become so closely bound together they were like a team of horses pulling a single wagon. That is why Jerry Falwell started the Moral Majority, not as a narrowly "Christian" organization but as a mobilizing force for Reagan's reestablishment of a true America. And his primary target for recruits was fundamentalist and evangelical Christians. Many other Religious-Right organizations were also taking shape at the same time to help the silent majority of true Americans regain its voice and engage in the great battle for the nation. Few of those leaders had any extensive political agenda or idea of what the federal government should do to uphold justice for the common good. They did not think in those terms. Their primary aim was to revive some version of the nation's WASP identity and moral character in the battle against illegitimate usurpers.

In their personal and church lives, most evangelicals have continued to believe and preach the gospel of God's grace, love, and forgiveness in Christ. But by the time of Barack Obama's election to the presidency they had grown more discouraged and angrier by the successes of the domestic, liberalizing, secularizing enemies of true America. Desperation about the plight of the nation seems to be more urgent for them than the plight of the worldwide church of Christ. Where is the King David or General Washington needed now to lead them to victory? Franklin Graham (Billy Graham's son), Jerry Falwell, Jr., and hundreds of evangelical pastors, teachers, bloggers, and authors have sounded the civil-religious alarm bells. They are admonishing their followers to place their trust in Donald Trump to take the fight to America's enemies and restore it to greatness.

Perceptive op-ed commentator for the *Financial Times* Janan Ganesh contends that the push for a commander in chief in the White House, who in times of crisis should be unrestrained by congressional and judicial checks and balances, has been building for fifty years. "Lots of Republicans," Ganesh writes, "sincerely believe in an all-powerful presidency, at least when one of their own occupies it. Their vote to acquit [the president in his Senate impeachment trial] is the culmination of half a century of conservative thought in that direction. And for all the uniqueness of Mr. Trump, his special knack for reducing once-serious conservatives to jelly, this deference to executive power will not vanish when he goes."[25]

Most congressional Republicans, including evangelicals, seem to accept that any necessary means can be justified if the end is to save the nation from the further advance of evil.

As president, Trump has been adept at affirming what evangelicals want, sensing especially their grievances over the success of enemies at home, and he is delivering on many of his promises. He has gone a long way already to reshaping the federal judiciary at the direction of the Federalist Society; he has gone further than all recent presidents in supporting Israel's territorial claims in disregard of international law and the interests of Palestinians; he pledged his support for prayer in public schools; he has decried abortion and was the first president to attend the annual Right-to-Life March (January, 2020); he has banned transgender military service members; and he has worked to ban or limit the immigration of Muslims to the United States while imposing some of the most restrictive policies at the border with Mexico.

Yes, many evangelicals admit, Trump has sinned like King David did, but we can accept him as God's appointed leader to cleanse the land of devastating threats to its existence as God's new Israel. Other evangelicals have identified Trump as a new Cyrus, the Persian king who opened the way for exiled Jews in Babylon to return to the promised land and rebuild the temple. Trump may not be an insider to evangelical faith in Christ for eternal life, they acknowledge, but like Cyrus, he is being used to do God's will.

Southern Baptist pastor Robert Jeffress famously said, "I don't want some meek and mild leader or somebody who's going to turn the other

---

25. Janan Ganesh, "How US Republicans came to deify the presidency," *Financial Times*, January 29, 2020, https://www.ft.com/content/8bac9b2c-41f0-11ea-bdb5-169ba7be433d.

cheek [as president]. I've said I want the meanest, toughest SOB I can find to protect this nation."[26]

According to Jeffress, "while Scripture commands individual Christians and churches to show mercy to those in need, the Bible never calls on government to act as a Good Samaritan."[27]

Jeffress interprets Romans 13 to say that God "gives the government the authority to do whatever, whether it's assassination, capital punishment or [other] punishments of evil. . . . God has endowed rulers [with] full power to use whatever means necessary—including war—to stop evil."[28]

The clear implication is that while the followers of Christ should, in their private roles, live according to Christ's standards of love for neighbors, American citizens, including Christians, should live as followers of the god of war who has chosen now-threatened America to lead in the history of god's purposes on earth. Jeffress is an enthusiastic backer of Trump who, he believes, is doing what a president should do, and therefore "his moral failings are irrelevant."[29]

The problem here with Trump, Jeffress, and their evangelical followers is that most of Trump's moral failings that should be of concern to us are not narrowly personal or private, though even those give abundant evidence of his character. The misdeeds on which we should focus are Trump's behavior in the high office of a public official. If the goal of restoring the America that evangelicals want and that Trump champions can justify any and all means of trying to reach it, then the American god who endorses that end and those means cannot, in our view, be the biblical God. To the contrary, the teaching of Jeffress and of many others who speak in a similar vein depends on belief in a double-faced god or on two gods locked in battle. Their teaching certainly demeans the identity and authority of Jesus Christ through whom all things are created and who, as the resurrected Lord, claims all authority in heaven and on earth.

Former editor of *Christianity Today* Mark Galli called for Trump's removal from office "out of loyalty to the Creator of the Ten Commandments."

26. Quoted in Michael J. Mooney, "Trump's Apostle," *Texas Monthly,* August 19, 2019, https://www.texasmonthly.com/articles/donald-trump-defender-dallas-pastor-robert-jeffress/.

27. Quoted in David R. Brockman, "The Little-Known Theology Behind White Evangelical Support of Donald Trump," https://www.texasobserver.org/the-little-known-theology-behind-white-evangelical-support-of-donald-trump/.

28. Quoted in Sarah Pulliam Bailey, "'God has given Trump authority to take out Kim Jung Un,' evangelical adviser says," *The Washington Post,* August 9, 2017.

29. Brockman, https://www.texasobserver.org/the-little-known-theology-behind-white-evangelical-support-of-donald-trump/.

In doing so he addressed "evangelicals who continue to support Mr. Trump in spite of his blackened moral record" with the following admonition: "Remember who you are and whom you serve. Consider how your justification of Mr. Trump influences your witness to your Lord and Savior."[30]

Evangelicals, it seems to us, should open their ears to the biblical commandment that we are to have no other gods before the Lord God. All of us should listen again and again to Christ's warning that we cannot serve two masters. We should examine critically, in biblical light, every sign of double-minded dependence on America's god, rejecting the idea that there is a place for it anywhere near the lordship of Jesus Christ in the kingdom of God.

---

30. Mark Galli, "Trump Should Be Removed from Office," *Christianity Today*, December 19, 2019, https://www.christianitytoday.com/ct/2019/december-web-only/trump-should-be-removed-from-office.html.

Chapter 20

What White Evangelicals Can Learn about Politics from the Civil Rights Movement

JOHN FEA

IN JUNE 2017, I SPENT TEN DAYS WITH MY FAMILY TRAVELING THROUGH the American South on a civil rights movement bus tour. Our trip took us to some of the most important sites and cities of the movement. We made stops in Greensboro, Atlanta, Albany, Montgomery, Selma, Birmingham, Memphis, and Nashville.

Along the way we spent time with some of the veterans of the movement. In Atlanta we heard from Juanita Jones Abernathy, the wife and co-laborer of Ralph Abernathy, one of Martin Luther King, Jr.'s closest associates. In Albany we sang civil rights songs with Rutha Mae Harris, one of the original Freedom Singers. In Selma we met Joanne Bland, a local activist who, at the age of eleven, participated in all three Edmund Pettus Bridge marches. In Birmingham, we talked with Carolyn Maul McKinstry and Denise McNair. McKinstry was fifteen years old when she survived the Ku Klux Klan bombing of the Sixteenth Street Baptist Church on September 15, 1963. That explosion took the life of McNair's older sister, whom she never had a chance to meet. In Nashville, we listened to the inspirational stories of Ernest "Rip" Patton, one of the early freedom riders, and Kwame Leonard, one of the movement's behind-the-scenes organizers.

As I processed everything that I learned on the "Returning to the Roots of Civil Rights" bus tour, I kept returning to thoughts about the relationship between religion and politics. Donald Trump had been in office for under five months, but my anger and frustration upon learning that 81 percent of my fellow evangelicals had voted for him were still fresh. As I listened to the voices of the movement veterans, walked the ground that they had walked, and saw the photographs, studied the exhibits, and watched the footage, it was clear that I was witnessing a Christian approach to politics that was very different from the one that catapulted Trump into the White House and continues to garner white evangelical support for his presidency.

Hope and humility defined the political engagement and social activism of the civil rights movement. The movement served, and continues to serve, as an antidote to a politics of fear and power.

*****

Those who participated in the civil rights movement had much to fear: bombs, burning crosses, billy clubs, death threats, water hoses, police dogs, and lynch mobs—to name a few. They feared for the lives of their families and spent every day wondering whether they would still be around to continue the fight the next day. For these reasons, many African Americans, understandably, did not participate in the movement and prevented their children from getting involved. The danger was very real.

Martin Luther King, Jr. knew this. When we visited the old Ebenezer Baptist Church in Atlanta, the church where King was baptized and where he (and his father) served as pastor, his final sermon, the one he delivered in Memphis on April 3, 1968, was playing over the speakers. King was then in Memphis to encourage sanitation workers fighting for better pay and improved working conditions. I sat in the back pew and listened:

> Well, I don't know what will happen now. We've got some difficult days ahead. But it really doesn't matter with me now. Because I've been to the mountaintop. And I don't mind. Like anybody, I would like to live a long life. Longevity has its place. But I'm not concerned about that now. I just want to do God's will. And He has allowed me to go up to the mountain. And I've looked over, and I've seen the Promised Land. I may not get there with you, but I want you to know tonight, that we as a people will get to the Promised Land. So, I'm happy tonight. I'm not worried about anything. I'm not fearing anything. Mine eyes have seen the glory of the coming of the Lord.

It was a message of hope. Because of his faith, God had given him—and the women and men of the movement he led—all the strength they would need to continue the struggle. King made himself available to do the Lord's will. Now he was looking forward. Was he talking about his eternal life in what now seems like prophetic fashion, or was he talking about God working out his purposes on earth? No matter: King was confident in God's power to work out his will: "Mine eyes have seen the glory of the coming of the Lord." An assassin's bullet took King's life the next day, April 4, 1968, but the movement went on.

Can evangelicals recover this confidence in God's power—not just in his wrath against their enemies but in his ability to work out his purposes for good? Can they recover hope?

The historian Christopher Lasch once wrote this: "Hope does not demand a belief in progress. It demands a belief in justice: a conviction that the wicked will suffer, that wrongs will be made right, that the underlying order of things is not flouted with impunity. Hope implies a deep-seated trust in life that appears absurd to most who lack it."[1]

I saw this kind of hope in every place we visited on our trip. It was not mere optimism that things would get better if only we could elect the right candidates. Rather, it was a view of this world, together with an understanding of the world to come, forged amid suffering and pain. Not everyone would make it to the mountaintop on this side of eternity, but God's purposes would be worked out, and eventually they would be able to understand those purposes—if not in this life, surely in the world to come. The people in the movement understood that laws, social programs, even local and voluntary action, would only get them so far. Something deeper was needed.

There was something kingdom-oriented going on in these Southern cities. I thought of the words of the Lord's Prayer: "Thy Kingdom come, they will be done, on earth as it is in heaven." I saw this kind of hope in the eyes of Rip Patton as he sat with us in the Nashville Public Library and explained why (and how) he had such a "good time" singing while incarcerated with other freedom riders in Parchman Prison in Jackson, Mississippi. I heard this kind of hope in the voice of Rutha Mae Harris as she led us in "This Little Light of Mine" and "Ain't Gonna Turn Me 'Round" from the front of the sanctuary of the Old Mount Zion Baptist Church in Albany. As I walked across the Edmund Pettus Bridge in Selma, Alabama, I wondered if I could

---

1. Christopher Lasch, *The True and Only Heaven* (New York: W. W. Norton, 1991), 80–81.

ever muster the courage of John Lewis and Joanne Bland as they marched into the face of terror on Bloody Sunday. Such audacity requires hope.

But too often fear leads to hopelessness, a state of mind that political scientist Glenn Tinder has described as a "kind of death." Hopelessness causes us to direct our gaze backward toward worlds we can never recover. It causes us to imagine a future filled with horror. Tyrants focus our attention on the desperate nature of our circumstances and the carnage of the social and cultural landscape that they claim to have the power to heal. A kernel of truth, however, always informs such a dark view of life. Poverty is a problem. Rusted-out factories often do appear, as Trump once described them, like "tombstones across the landscape of our nation." Crime is real. But demagogues want us to dwell on the carnage and, to quote Bruce Springsteen, "waste our summer praying in vain for a savior to rise from these streets." Hope, on the other hand, draws us into the future, and in this way it engages us in life.[2]

*****

It is nonsensical to talk about the civil rights movement in terms of political power, because even at the height of the movement's influence, African Americans did not possess much political power. Yes, the movement had its leaders, and they did have time in the national spotlight. But when the movement leaders entered the halls of power, they were usually there to speak truth with a prophetic voice. King, for example, was willing to break with Lyndon Johnson when he disagreed with him on the Vietnam War, even if it meant losing access to the most powerful man on earth.

Most of all, though, the civil rights movement was shaped by people of humble means who lived ordinary lives in ordinary neighborhoods. Many of them never expected to step onto a national stage or receive credit for leading the great social movement in American history. These ordinary men and women fought injustice wherever God had placed them. They offer us a beautiful illustration of what scholar James Davison Hunter has called "faithful presence."

For Hunter, a theology of faithful presence calls Christians to serve the people and places where they live. "The call of faithful presence," Hunter writes in his book *To Change the World*, "gives priority to what is right in front of us—community, the neighborhood, and the city, and the people in which these are constituted." It is in these places, through "the joys, sufferings, hopes, disappointments, concerns, desires, and worries of people with

2. Glenn Tinder, *The Fabric of Hope* (Atlanta: Scholars, 1999), 13.

whom we are in long-term and close relation—family, neighbors, co-work-ers, and community—where we find authenticity as a body of believers." It is here, Hunter adds, "where we learn forgiveness and humility, practice kind-ness, hospitality, and charity, grow in patience and wisdom, and become clothed in compassion, gentleness, and joy. This is the crucible with which Christian holiness is forged. This is the context in which shalom is enacted."[3]

I thought about Hunter's words as I stood in the hot Selma sun and listened to Joanne Bland explain to us the significance of a small and crum-bling patch of pavement in a playground behind Brown Chapel AME church. This was the exact spot, she told us, where the 1965 Selma-to-Montgomery marches began. For Bland, who was raised in a housing complex across the street from the church, this was a sacred space.

The humility on display during the civil rights movement was just as countercultural then as it is now. This is usually the case with nonviolent protests. Those who participated thought of themselves not as individuals but as part of a movement larger than themselves. Rip Patton was a twenty-one-year old music major at Tennessee State University when he met Jim Lawson in 1959. Lawson trained Patton (and others) in nonviolent protest. Soon Patton found himself seated at a lunch counter in downtown Nash-ville, where he would be spit on, punched, covered with ketchup, mustard, salt, and water.

Patton did not retaliate because he had been educated in the spiritual discipline necessary for a situation like this. Martin Luther King, Jr. was leading a political and social movement, but he was also the high priest of a spiritual movement, something akin to a religious revival.

The civil rights movement never spoke the language of hate or resent-ment. In fact, its Christian leaders saw that all human beings were made in the image of God and sinners in need of God's redemptive love. Many in the movement practiced what theologian Reinhold Niebuhr described as "the spiritual discipline against resentment." They saw that those who retaliated violently or with anger against injustice were only propagating injustices of their own. Instead, the spiritual discipline against resentment unleashed a different kind of power—the power of the cross and the resurrection. This kind of power could provide comfort amid suffering and a faithful gospel witness to the world. The Mississippi voting rights activist Fannie Lou Ham-er said it best: "The white man's afraid he'll be treated like he's been treating the Negroes, but I couldn't carry that much hate. It wouldn't have solved any

---

3. James Davison Hunter, *To Change the World* (New York: Oxford University Press, 2010), 253.

problems for me to hate whites because they hate me. Oh, there's so much hate! Only God has kept the Negro sane."[4]

*****

Where does all this reflection leave us? Where did it leave me as I got off the bus and headed back to my working-class, central Pennsylvania neighborhood? How might hope and humility inform the way we white American evangelicals think about politics and other forms of public engagement? It is time to take a long hard look at what we have become in this so-called "age of Trump." We have a lot of work to do in order to replace fear with hope and power with humility. What we decide to do at the ballot box in November 2020 is only the tip of the iceberg.

4. On the civil rights movement as a religious revival, see David Chappel, *A Stone of Hope* (Chapel Hill, NC: University of North Carolina Press, 2004), 74, 87–104.

Chapter 21

At Odds

The Collision of Scripture and Current Immigration Policy

REID RIBBLE

Jesus loves the little children,
All the children of the world,
Red and yellow, black and white,
All are precious in His sight.

IF THEOLOGY IS THE STUDY OF THE NATURE OF GOD AND RELIGIOUS BELIEF, then the words of the children's song by George Frederick Root might be a good place to start. As a lifelong evangelical Christian, I was taught this simple song at a very young age. About the same time, I was also taught the childhood song "Jesus Loves me" in Sunday school. My father, an ordained Baptist minister, reinforced this teaching in our home. In many ways, this very simple understanding of God's love for all persons and God's desire for them to come to him was central to the Judeo-Christian system of belief. Scripture is replete with this message of God's love.

Like many of my evangelical brothers and sisters, I consider myself a Republican in my political thought. Although Republicanism is an imperfect representation of our founder's vision, it most accurately reflected my own understanding of our republic and its constitutional principles. While I do have many evangelical friends, who are either Democrats or Independents, most of my friends were certainly more like me. As such we were surprised (I was shocked) by the words of candidate Trump at his announcement of his presidential campaign in Trump Tower. His negative and critical view of the United States alone would normally end a presidential campaign. We came later to understand that he would frequently use language that others would never consider using. Shortly into the speech he said this:

> When do we beat Mexico at the border? They're laughing at us, at our stupidity. And now they are beating us economically. They are not our friend, believe me. But they're killing us economically. The U.S. has become a dumping ground for everybody else's problems.

He went on . . .

> *Thank you. It's true, and these are the best and the finest. When Mexico sends its people, they're not sending their best. They're not sending you. They're not sending you. They're sending people that have lots of problems, and they're bringing those problems with us. They're bringing drugs. They're bringing crime. They're rapists. And some, I assume, are good people.*

And so, it began. A campaign and then an administration filled with vitriolic language to anyone other than us. Let's look more closely at some of those words.

"*A dumping ground* . . ." No candidate in history has essentially called the United States a landfill. Now stop and consider the implication and the meaning in the words about who was being "sent" to the dumping ground. The Mexican government was actually sending, in his way of thinking, trash to the landfill.

"*They're bringing drugs. They're bringing crime. They're rapists.*" The purpose here is to create fear. To make the listener feel like a victim, and the immigrant to be a villain. Of course, there is a criminal element with any population of people, including immigrants. But that certainly was not the point. The point was that this was an example of the United States losing and he would fix it. But what is the reality?

The reality is the great majority of immigrants from Mexico and other Central American countries come to the United States to flee poverty and crime and to work and be productive. Many are people of faith, conservative, industrious, family oriented—the very type of people Mexico needs for its own economy.

Months later, in December of 2015, the presidential campaign of candidate Trump said this: "Donald J. Trump is calling for a total and complete shutdown of Muslims entering the United States until our country's representatives can figure out what is going on." The idea that the United States would bar entry of any people group based on religious affiliation or belief stunned many of us. The First Amendment to the Constitution protected religious expression of all forms. Not just to citizens but to all persons. Freedom of religious expression is foundational to the American experience.

Once candidate Trump became president, he moved quickly to address issues of asylum, refugees, and immigration. On January 27, 2017, just days after the inauguration, President Trump signed Executive Order 13769, titled "Protecting the Nation from Foreign Terrorist entry into the United States." Political opponents quickly rebranded the order as a Muslim Ban. Although it was blocked by a number of court decisions, the president continued to work to restrict not just the flow of immigrants from places like Iraq, Iran, and Syria but famously he also attempted to reduce immigration, asylum and refugees from other countries he labeled as "shit-hole" nations.

He cancelled President Obama's executive order on DACA, Deferred Action on Childhood Arrivals. While he tried to negotiate a solution with congress to the DACA issue, he was unable to come to an agreement that would pass, having opponents in both political parties. DACA's intent was to provide some protection to more than one million people who were brought here as young children by parents from Central America. These children, through no fault of their own, now find themselves threatened by the only government that they know. If the protection of these people ends, what are we to do with them? Without a permanent solution, they cannot get a driver's license. They cannot get a college education. Nor do they have a permanent opportunity to work legally in the United States. Their lives are suspended, in limbo.

Trump also announced the end to Temporary Protected Status (TPS) for people from the Sudan, Haiti, El Salvador, Nicaragua, and six other countries. TPS is a designation providing protected status to people affected by war, famine, and extreme weather and earthquakes. Hundreds of thousands of these people have worked legally in the United States for decades. They have married American spouses and have American children. How do we benefit from their removal? At a time when unemployment is the lowest in fifty years, certainly we have work for them to do. Fortunately, the courts have temporarily stopped this termination of TPS but the uncertainty remains.

So, what is a Christian to do? President Trump could not have won election without evangelical support. Were evangelicals even listening to his anti-immigrant rhetoric during his campaign or even more problematically do they agree with him now that he is making policy? Has the evangelical church moved so far from the teachings of my youth that they no longer believe that God loves these people? Or am I simply missing something?

What I most often hear from my evangelical friends who are supporters of the president is that Trump just wants people to follow the law and they immediately direct the conversation to those that have entered the country illegally. It's fair to have this discussion. It's also very narrow. Depending on whose numbers you use, approximately 8–12 million people are in the United States who have entered the country without legal status to do so or had temporary legal status and simply decided to stay here.

The vast majority of immigrants historically have come to the country with legal status—either as legal migrants, refugees, those granted asylum, and those given temporary protected status. How we talk about these people, and more importantly those still seeking to come to the US, is in my opinion important. Even more important is what we believe about these people.

So, what guidance do we find in Scripture? Beyond what we already know on how we should treat others, there are some very specific things that Scripture teaches us about treatment of those less fortunate and aliens living among us.

Let's start where God started. In the beginning, "God created man in his own image. In the image of God he created him; Male and female He created them" (Gen 1:27). Verse 28 goes on to say that "God blessed" them. Until we are ready to accept that all humanity has been created in God's image and with that deserve a level of respect and dignity, it does not even pay to read on. All humanity, as sons and daughters of Adam and Eve, have intrinsic, God-breathed value. How we think about immigrants and how we speak about them should begin and end with an understanding of the human dignity God has given them.

James 3:9–10 says, "With the tongue we praise our Lord and Father, and with it we curse human beings, who have been made in God's likeness. Out of the same mouth come praise and cursing, My brothers and sisters, this should not be." Ask yourself, is the language spoken by the president and people in the administration consistent with these words of James?

Throughout the Old Testament God is particularly concerned with fairness. He reminds his people to remember when they themselves were aliens in a foreign land. In Exodus 22:21, Scripture says "Do not mistreat an alien or oppress him, for you were aliens in Egypt." And in Deuteronomy

27:19, we read, "Cursed is anyone who withholds justice from the foreigner, the fatherless or the widow."

Let's look at the words of Jesus in Matthew 25:35–40:

> For I was hungry and you gave me something to eat, I was thirsty and you gave me something to drink, I was a stranger and you invited me in, I needed clothes and you clothed me, I was sick and you looked after me, I was in prison and you came to visit me.

> Then the righteous will answer him, "Lord, when did we see you hungry and feed you, or thirsty and give you something to drink? When did we see you a stranger and invite you in, or needing clothes and clothe you? When did we see you sick or in prison and go to visit you?"

> The King will reply, "Truly I tell you, whatever you did for one of the least of these brothers and sisters of mine, you did for me."

This topic deserves an entire book. Our treatment of others, and our proper understanding of the role immigrants have played in the development of the United States, can reshape our opinions. It's clear that President Trump wants to minimize both legal and illegal migration to the country. His belief is that it is the best way to protect Americans from terrorism. He believes that this restriction will help grow wages. Both of these objectives, while admirable, are easily debunked by real data. What concerns me more, as a believer, is the continual demeaning language he uses to discuss immigrants, particularly those from non-white nations. The entire topic of diminishing people reminds me of the bracelet I used to wear with the letters WWJD printed on it. What do you suppose Jesus would do?

In the verses quoted above, I believe God demonstrates his heart. I can hear some of you right now wanting to argue the nuance of immigration reform. Others want to argue the theology. But to what end? I wrote this chapter in the hope that it would cause you to reconsider how you think about immigrants, how you speak about immigrants, and how you may treat immigrants. I wrote this to challenge you to ask if you believe that the current administration is using principles like the ones these Scriptures have called us to.

I remember clearly when I was serving in the House of Representatives, I made the case in a public forum of Republican members of congress, about the need for a compassionate and pragmatic reform to our nation's immigration policy. From the back of the room a member shouted out these words: "Come on Ribble! Get serious. We have an immigration crisis in this country!" I calmly turned around and looked at him and said "Let me tell you what an immigration crisis looks like. It's when no one wants to come here, not when too many do. It's not like people are rushing to immigrate to North Korea or the Sudan. When people stop wanting to come here is when we will have a real crisis."

Finally, I want you to consider Galatians 5:19–26:

> The acts of the flesh are obvious: sexual immorality, impurity and debauchery; idolatry and witchcraft; hatred, discord, jealousy, fits of rage, selfish ambition, dissensions, factions and envy; drunkenness, orgies, and the like. I warn you, as I did before, that those who live like this will not inherit the kingdom of God.

> But the fruit of the Spirit is love, joy, peace, forbearance, kindness, goodness, faithfulness, gentleness and self-control. Against such things there is no law. Those who belong to Christ Jesus have crucified the flesh with its passions and desires. Since we live by the Spirit, let us keep in step with the Spirit. Let us not become conceited, provoking and envying each other.

No matter what your personal feelings are on immigration policy, I hope we all can agree on how we should treat these children of God. In Galatians the author clearly describes what the life of a Christian should look like if the Spirit of God lives in him or her. As you read the verses from Galatians chapter 5 what words remind you the most of our president? Verses 19–21 or verses 22–26? I am not looking for the president of the United States to be my pastor. I am not. But is it too much to ask that he, as a self-proclaimed believer in Christ, live out the "fruit of the Spirit" in word and deed, and lead this nation in a manner consistent with it?

Chapter 22

Quo Vadis, America?

Steven E. Meyer

"An nescis, mi fili, quantilla prudentia mundus regatur?"
("Do you not know, my son, how poorly the world is governed?")

Axel Oxenstierna, 1583–1654,
Lord High Chancellor of Sweden

ARGUABLY, THE UNITED STATES IS AT A CROSSROADS. PERHAPS THE COUN-try is even at the cusp of one of those rare tectonic shifts in the structure and function of politics. But, unfortunately many, if not most, of our political leaders are in denial. Granted, it is emotionally, psychologically, and physi-cally very difficult to engage in the hard work of adapting to a fundamental change in the political landscape. The problem is as old as the human race. Plato explored the difficulty of accepting reality 2,400 years ago in his allegory of the cave in book seven of *The Republic*. The prisoners in the cave accepted the shadows on the wall as reality because that was the only perspective they had. In the twentieth century, Thomas Kuhn, in his remarkable book on *The Structure of Scientific Revolutions*, discusses the difficulty humans have in accepting the death of one paradigm and the birth of a new one. Although Kuhn was talking primarily about the world of so-called "hard" science, his argument also is applicable to the world of politics and society. Kuhn argues that humankind usually is willing to recognize change from a worn out, dying paradigm to the birthing of a new paradigm, only when forced to do so by some inertia-stopping event. One would have thought that the end of the Soviet era would be sufficient to end the inertia of that period and see the dawning of a new post-Soviet period. But, for many observers this was not to be and—much to the detriment of the country and the world—we have continued to act as if the old world is still with us.[1]

Although we need a national debate about what conditions are and how we should confront them, I think there are two larger interconnected political realities that will make that very difficult to happen with the present circumstances. First, the staggering political-cultural split in the country. Many, perhaps most, of the population of the US today does not view politics first from a national perspective, but rather first from a "tribal" perspective. Large numbers of US citizens seek out and find sources and methods that support and reinforce their already held positions. The explosion in technology has reinforced this propensity. It is easy—usually with the press of a button or the turn of a knob—for all of us to get exactly the perspective we want.

Second, we have two major political parties that seem to be stuck in the past, oblivious or willfully dismissive of the emerging international political reality. We have a Democratic party that is wedded to a model of politics and government that rests substantially on the heady days immediately after the collapse of the Soviet Union. This was a time of an American hegemony, a new world order, an emphasis on human rights, democratic nation-building (really, state-building), and security (military) architecture and policy that changed very little from the Soviet days. In effect, this means that the Cold War never really ended. For the Democratic Party not much has been learned by the failure of democratic nation-building, as witnessed by the disastrous course of events of the Arab Spring, and the obsolescence of NATO for the current era.

A Faustian Bargain

We have a Republican Party that is now almost completely captured by Donald Trump and his philosophy and power to bend the party to his will. In the process, the Republican Party, except for a few holdouts, has sold its soul in a Faustian bargain that is debilitating for the country. Essentially, it has sold its soul to an overweening dolt and bully. The Republican Party now looks

1. Thomas Kuhn, *The Structure of Scientific Revolution* (Chicago: University of Chicago Press, 2012).

back even further into history than do the Democrats. For the Republicans, success is found in a witch's brew of autarky, xenophobia, and aspects of rentier economy. Economically, their answer is to jettison multi-national organizations based mostly on the false charge that they are taking American jobs (when the culprit in the majority of cases is job-displacing technology). Unfortunately, an uncomfortable number of Trump's opponents have described him as a latter-day Hitler. While such historical comparisons often are tempting, they usually do not bear any resemblance to reality.

The comparison of Trump with Hitler would be risible if it were not such a historical inaccuracy. Trump is no Hitler and in the most profound ways the US is not the Germany of the 1920s and 1930s. Among other things, we do not have death camps and the economic situation (especially the hyperinflation that hit the early Weimar Republic) is far from the desperate conditions that plagued Germany (and Italy) at that time. However, there are some eerie and uneasy similarities to the "atmosphere" that pervaded Germany and Italy during the 1920s and 1930s: lying and misleading rhetoric; a burgeoning cult of personality; the mounting, staggering debt; a compliant political party; scapegoating and blaming classes of people for the country's ills; social divisions based on race and class; blackmailing other countries; the poor conditions in immigrant detention facilities—especially for children; and, an economic system based on a beggar-your-neighbor philosophy.[2]

Donald Trump has been astute enough to recognize the unrest in the country. He sees the anger, the yearning for a different path, the gridlock in Washington, and the glaring lack of effective and ethical leadership. The problem is that Trump is the wrong leader, at the wrong time, who capitalizes on the national discontent with his own brand of perverted leadership. For Christians—and, quite frankly, all people of good will—the administration and the president himself should be an anathema. It is beyond comprehension why many Christians, especially those who describe themselves as evangelicals, support Trump and his policies. This is as much a commentary on the sad state of evangelical Christianity as on Trump himself.

Not only should Trump and many of his policies be seen as violations of long-standing Christian ethical norms, but his spiritual depravity should be seen as melding with unwise, dangerous, and counter-productive policies. Paul Thomas notes in an article in *The Listener* (March 10, 2018) that

2. Donald D. Antonio, "Is Donald Trump a Racist? Here's What His Record Shows," *Fortune*, June 7, 2016, https:fortune.com/2016/06/07donald-trump-racism-quotes. Christopher Pieper and Matt Henderson, "10 Reasons you can't be a Christian and vote for Donald Trump," *The Dallas Morning News*, November 6, 2016.

Trump exhibits "authoritarian tendencies, boastfulness, capriciousness, disloyalty, irresponsibility, nepotism and unseemliness."[3]

Thomas's analysis is reflected in dozens of other studies. Kevin Williams describes Trump as an "ego maniac," a man of "moral ambiguity" who is "lazy and arrogant."[4]

We can add to this vindictiveness, pettiness, and childishness. Moreover, Trump—blissfully ignorant of Colossians 3:9–10 and other verses—has turned lying into a major art form; a way to present himself and his administration as something they are not. Certainly, other politicians lie, but no one does it nearly as often and with such devastating effects as Trump. According to the *Washington Post Fact Checker*, with 759 days into his presidency Trump had uttered 8,718 false or misleading statements. He is a blasphemer (Matthew 12:30–32); a sexual deviant (1 and 2 Corinthians); an enemy of the poor (Proverbs 28:27 and 31:9); an enemy of refugees and immigrants (Matthew 25:35 and Leviticus 19:34); and lacking in the essential elements of Christian character (Philippians 4:8).

Why Then?

If this analysis is accurate, why do so many Christians who describe themselves as evangelicals not only support Trump fervently, but condemn those Christians—and others—who oppose Trump? *Time* columnist, author, and analyst David French argues that the overriding factor in evangelical support for Trump is fear.[5]

Christianity, they believe, is under attack by dark, foreboding powers. It is a struggle between good and evil, a struggle that is as old as humanity. In the theme of Sophocles's *Oedipus Rex*, Heracles is defending the Olympian order against chthonic monsters and, of course, it is the struggle of Christians in a hostile world to be in that world, but not of it. This also is an easy formula because it provides a convenient enemy as well as psychological succor for the aggrieved parties. The boundaries are obvious, the enemy is easily identified, and the remedies are firmly and clearly established.

Of course, the world of the self-styled evangelical needs a hero—one of Olympian stature is best. That hero is Donald Trump. Note what Ralph

3. Paul Thomas, "President Donald Trump's Seven Fatal Flaws," *The Listener*, March 10, 2018, 3.

4. Kevin D. Williams, "The prince," *National Review* (The Morning Jolt), September 27, 2019.

5. David French, "Evangelicals Are Supporting Trump Out of Fear, Not Faith," *Time*, June 27, 2019, https://time.com5615617/why-evangelicals-support-trump.

Reed, founder and chairman of the Faith and Freedom Coalition, said about Trump: "There has never been anyone who has defended us and who has fought for us, who we have loved more than Donald J. Trump. No one!"[6]

This *weltanschauung* provides a way for Christians to avoid grappling with hard issues. It is easy—actually comfortable—from inside their cocoon to see the world in stark good and evil terms. It is the wicked world of the devil versus the righteous world of Christ—there is no middle ground. Note the following particularly egregious—and ridiculous—quote: "Last week (i.e., the last week in November 2019) on the Eric Metaxas Show, Franklin Graham said that the efforts to impeach Donald Trump were 'almost a demonic power.' Metaxas, the conservative pundit and court evangelical . . . responded with these words: 'I would disagree, it's not *almost* demonic. You know and I know that at the heart it's a spiritual battle.'"[7]

Moreover, the attack by this group of Christians on those who oppose Trump are heavily connected to the Republican Party. In fact, political party may be the independent variable that determines the political outlook and philosophy of this group of Christians. For them there is a positive correlation between religious belief and political party that is easily exploited by Trump and right-wing Republicans. This is made manifest in a comparison between how these self-identified evangelicals see Trump versus former President Clinton. They either ignore or explain away the most heinous behavior by Trump and condemn Clinton for behavior which, while unacceptable, was arguably not anywhere near the caliber of Trump's behavior. In effect, for these critics, character was an important determinant for Clinton, but not for Trump. Note the following resolution passed by the Southern Baptist Convention in 1998 with respect to Clinton's behavior. "Resolution on Moral Character: Tolerance of serious wrong by leaders sears the conscience of the culture, spawns unrestrained immorality and lawlessness in society, and surely God's judgement."[8]

No such resolution has been passed concerning Donald Trump.

This world of fear and darkness characterizes so many of the Christians who self-identify as evangelicals and many uninformed outside commentators also describe them as evangelicals. However, if we rely on the definition of the term *evangelical* as it was understood in the ancient church, the Christians who are often described as "evangelicals" really should be

6. Peter Wehner, "The Deepening Crisis in Evangelical Christianity," Ideas, July 5, 2019, https://eppc.org/publications/the-deepening-crisis-in-evangelical-christianity.

7. Jon Brown, "Demonic Power: Franklin Graham claims supernatural element behind attacks on Trump," *Washington Examiner*, February 4, 2020, https://www.Franklin-Graham-claims-demonic-power-behind-attacks-on-trump.

8. David French, "Evangelicals Are Supporting Trump Out of Fear, Not Faith."

identified as "fundamentalists." The term *evangelical* is the English deriva-
tion of the Greek term *euangelion*," meaning "gospel" or "good news." It refers to a "person, church, or organization that is committed to" the Christian
gospel. The meaning of the word *evangelical* has become corrupted as a result of movements that began in the United Kingdom and the United States
in the mid-nineteenth century. Evangelicalism began to move away from its
original meaning into the world of dispensationalism and millennialism.
Evangelicals who hold to these views are more rightly called "fundamentalists." The term "fundamentalism" was coined in 1920 as the result of a series
of twelve pamphlets called *The Fundamentals: A Testimony to the Truth* that
appeared between 1910 and 1915. It is essentially this group of Christians
who support Trump so fervently and vilify others who do not agree with
them.

L'etat, c'est moi!

Standing in front of parliament in 1655, Louis XIV reportedly uttered his
famous aphorism: "L'etat, c'est moi. Dieu a-t-il oublie tout ce que j'ai fait
pour lui? ("I am the state. Has God forgotten how much I have done for
Him?") There is no direct evidence that King Louis said this, but even if not
true it seems to sum up the character of Donald Trump perhaps as well as
the character of Louis XIV. It is a brief, yet powerful expression of Trump's
view of life and government. In short, the quote actually is saying that what
is good for Louis/Trump is good for France/the US. Trump is quoted as
saying that he is "The Chosen One, The King of the Jews." Even if he was half
joking, it reveals something about him that is highly arrogant, and deeply
disturbing and obviously offensive. It is the essence of blasphemy and ironically and sadly, there are Christian leaders who are equally blasphemous
by declaring him to be God's chosen man. If, as Heraclitus argued, a man's
character—that is, his values, ideas, beliefs—is his fate, Trump's character
bodes ill for the country and perhaps the world.

Trump's view of himself seems to personify what Friedrich Nietzsche
called *Der Wille zur Macht (The Will to Power)*, that is "the drive to perfect
and transcend the self through the possession and exercise of power; the
desire to exercise authority over others."[9]

Acting as a friend and champion of "evangelical" causes, then, becomes
a means to an end and that end is power; it is power for its own sake. For
Trump playing the "Christian card" gives him an electoral edge. It did so
in 2016 and may very well give him another four years in the White House

9. Wehner, "The Deepening Crisis in Evangelical Christianity."

after the 2020 election. As the 2020 campaign heats up, not only will he try to disparage whoever the Democratic candidate is as a stooge of the far left. But he presents himself as fervently opposed to abortion (except when he was for it), opposed to gay marriage and in favor of prayer in public schools. Interestingly, he made these same claims in 2016, but throughout his first term has done little to oppose gay marriage and the courts already have allowed prayer in public schools.

Trump certainly is cunning and determined. He knows how to promise things he likely will never be able to deliver. But, as Dan McAdams notes, in describing comparing Trump to Richard Nixon: Nixon was "callous, cynical and Machiavellian, even by the standards of American politicians. Empathy was not his strong suit. This sounds a lot like Donald Trump, too—except you have to add the ebullient extroversion, the relentless showmanship, and the larger-than-life celebrity. Nixon could never fill a room the way Trump can."[10]

The Policy Jumble

We are faced with a president who not only presents a deeply flawed character and personality, but also shows those same deep flaws developing and instituting policy. Let me briefly discuss five policy areas where Trump has violated Christian norms.

The Economy: Trump has lied or made misleading statements consistently about the economy, including as recently as his State of the Union address on February 4, 2020. Unfortunately, the lies have been meshed with and compounded by some very poor, detrimental policy decisions. During the 2016 Presidential campaign, Trump promised to grow the economy by 6 percent annually. This was either a gross misrepresentation of what would be possible or a knowing lie; in fact, during the three years Trump has been in office we have seen growth rates of just 2 to 3.1 percent. For three years he also has falsely argued that he rescued an economy that had been failing under President Obama and reiterated that claim during—and since—the State of the Union Address. In fact, the economy has been growing steadily since the end of the recession in 2008–2009. This eleven-year growth began with a $152 billion stimulus package initiated by President George W. Bush and a second stimulus of $831 billion by President Obama.

Trump is an advocate of supply side economics—or, "trickle-down economics"—and the Laffer Curve. The Laffer Curve works only when

10. Dan P. Adams, "The Mind of Donald Trump," *The Atlantic*, June 2016, https://theatlantic.com/magazine/archive/2016/06/the-mind-of-donald-trump/480771.

tax rates are above 50 percent and it was marginally successful during the Reagan administration because the top highest rate was 70 percent. Consequently, Trump's tax cut will not stimulate the economy enough to make up for lost tax revenue and it benefits primarily individuals earning more than $300,000 annually. Also, in spite of the tax cut, the Federal Open Market Committee predicts growth in GDP in 2020 to be only 2 percent, 1.9 percent in 2021, and 1.8 percent in 2022. Trump's proposed budget of $4.8 trillion for 2021 will increase the already mind-blowing deficit which is now at approximately $1 trillion. Moreover, with $23 trillion in current national debt, application of the Laffer Curve or "trickle-down" economics would be grossly insufficient to produce a substantial reduction in the national debt. The administration's proposed budget calls for an increase in the already bloated defense budget to $989 billion and an immoral decrease in foreign aid and domestic safety net programs. In each budget the Trump administration has put the lie to his promise during the 2016 campaign that he would eliminate the national debt in eight years. Instead his budgets will add an estimated $9.1 trillion to the debt during those eight years. In making the case for his economic policies, Trump points out that the stock market is booming. This is true, but most Americans do not own stock and, therefore, do not benefit from its meteoric rise.

From the perspective of Christians—and, hopefully people of other religions and, perhaps, no religion—the most devastating impact of Trump's economic policies have been on the poor. To put the issue into perspective, homosexuality is mentioned only seven times in the Bible, while Scripture mentions the poor and poverty 300 times and 250 times discusses how to use wealth wisely and properly. The administration's 2021 budget proposes massive cuts to domestic programs that help the poor: in the Department of Housing and Urban Development, the Labor Department, Health and Human Services Department, the Transportation Department, Education, and the Justice Departments. In the middle of proposing this draconian budget, Trump has argued that "inequality is down," but the US Census Department confirms that "income inequality has hit its highest level since the government started tracking it five decades ago."[11]

The richest 1 percent of Americans now rake in one-third of the country's net worth, while the bottom half of the population scrapes by with only 1.2 percent."[12]

---

11. Angela Albaladejo, "While Trump Boasts of economic growth, inequality deepens," *Capital and Main*, November 7, 2019, https//www.fastcompany.com/90427855/while-trump-boasts-of-economic growth-inequality-deepens.

12. Albaladejo, "While Trump Boasts."

The issue is compounded by the fact that Trump's budget cut two years ago has been most favorable to families and individuals who make more than $300,000 per year. Also, approximately 45 million Americans carry about $1.6 trillion in student debt, much of which they will carry well into middle age and beyond. Quite naturally, this impacts poor students most. At the same time, the rate of people who do not have health insurance is rising and as the administration continues to do what it can to undercut the Affordable Health Care Act (i.e., Obama Care), the number of uninsured will continue to rise. Finally, the Trump administration's Office of Management and Budget has made the rules much more difficult for determining when a family is in poverty and the Department of Labor and the National Labor Relations Board has instituted rules that are gradually stripping workers' rights and "prioritizes the interests of corporate executives and shareholders over those of workers."[13]

The Environment: Perhaps no issue demonstrates the perfidy and hostility to Christian values better than the Trump administration's views and policies concerning the environment. Trump's 2021 budget proposes slashing the Environmental Protection Agency by approximately $2.4 billion from last year's budget of about $6.4 billion. Generations of misuse and neglect had left the American environment in deplorable condition. The fact that the pollution on and in the Cuyahoga River literally resulted in the river catching on fire for the third time in 1969 remains a mind-numbing emblem of the neglect.

Then, everything changed beginning in the late 1960s, but mostly in the early 1970s, when much of the major environmental legislation was passed, Earth Day was introduced, and attitudes began to change for the better. Christians joined the cause because they saw that environmental responsibility was an essential stewardship issue. Christians began rejecting the thesis that the command in Genesis 1:28 to "Be fruitful and multiply and fill the earth and subdue it" was a license for mankind to do whatever it wanted to do to and with God's creation. Excuses to despoil the earth in the name of human domination and development no longer sufficed. Christians started arguing that the admonition in Genesis was a call to stewardship, to care for and be responsible for the creation. Christians began to reexamine the testimony of St. Francis of Assisi (1181–1226) and centuries later the writings of Pope John Paul II (in the papacy from 1978 to 2005). In 1986 a *Christian Declaration on Nature* (part of the "multi-denominational *Assisi Declaration)* notes that "Francis argues that we are sanctioned to take from the Earth what we need to subsist, but that this should be balanced with

13. Albaladejo, "While Trump Boasts."

preserving the Earth for future generations because: 'The earth is the Lord's (Ps 24:1); to him belongs 'the earth with all that is within it' (Dt 10:14)."[14]

Echoing his namesake, Pope Francis has written that "Climate change is a problem which no longer [may] be left to a future generation" and the papacy has been pushing this theme hard since the 2018 UN Climate Change Conference of the Parties. In similar manner, in 2015 the National Association of Evangelicals (NAE) endorsed the Lausanne Cape Town Commitment, which built on the NAE's 1970 Ecology Resolution. The NAE does not specifically embrace the reality of climate change, but it comes very close in calling for care, love, and human responsibility for God's creation.

Much of the progress that had begun fifty years ago has come to a screeching halt with the Trump administration. Very early in the administration's tenure, Scott Pruitt, the discredited Director of the Environmental Protection Agency, proposed revoking the Clean Power Plan and replacing it with the Affordable Clean Energy rule, which would allow more carbon pollution into the atmosphere, ignore climate change, and boost dirty energy.[15]

Also early on, the Trump administration decided to withdraw from the Paris Agreement of the United Nations Framework and to disavow the Fourth National Climate Assessment, which detailed the impact of climate change on weather patterns, wildfires, drought, heatwaves, and floods.[16]

The next major UN-sponsored meeting will be held in Glasgow, Scotland in 2020. These major meetings have not produced perfect results, but they are steps in the right direction and withdrawing from them sidelines the US from a major leading role in a resolution of the climate issue. If the Trump administration sends anyone, it almost certainly will be someone of lower rank with instructions to make no commitments.

In February 2020, the Trump administration announced revision of the 1970 National Environmental Policy Act (NEPA), which established the President's Council on Environmental Quality and provided procedures for "cutting edge" environmental impact analysis. If the revisions survive the inevitable court challenges, NEPA will be severely limited in its capacity to guarantee that large-scale, government-sponsored infrastructure programs will not have a deleterious environmental impact. In addition to this most

14. Matthew Hall, "Do passages in the Bible justify cutting down forests?" *The Conversation*, May 4, 2017, theconversation.com/do-passages-in-the-bible-justify-cutting-down-forests-76448.

15. Martha Roberts, "Trump's EPA is making a reckless and dangerous decision," Environmental Defense Fund, October 10, 2017.

16. Dan Lashof, "Trump policies will lead to more emissions, costs and deaths," https:www.wri.org/blog-series/Trump-administration.

recent effort to undermine environmental quality and the ones we have mentioned in the discussion above, *Clearview Energy* has produced a compendium of efforts by the Trump administration so far to roll back years of environmental laws, statutes, and practices that make our country and world more livable and more in line with Christian stewardship practices.[17]

Although the publication cites ninety-five specific instances, here we will show a summary by categories. Some of these rescinded regulations have been reinstated and most of the rest are facing court challenges. Please see the box below.

	58 rollbacks completed	37 rollbacks in process	95 total rollbacks
Air pollution and emissions	16	9	25
Drilling and extraction	10	9	19
Infrastructure and planning	11	1	12
Animals	7	3	10
Toxic substances and safety	5	3	8
Water pollution	4	6	10
Other	5	6	11

Foreign Policy: Early on, the Trump administration identified its foreign policy as America First. In pursuing his America First philosophy, Trump not only has damaged US interests, prestige, and leadership in the world, he has violated a core principle of Christian behavior in the international arena. He has no conception of what it means to follow Matthew 5:9 to be a peacemaker or to understand the Christian commitment to refugees and strangers found for example in Leviticus 19:34 and Hebrews 13:2. As with his economic and environmental policies, Trump's foreign policy blends and melds actions that are both devoid of moral grounding as well as initiatives that harm US interests.

Actions such as withdrawing from the Trans-Pacific Partnership and the deleterious trade war with China, demonstrate a misunderstanding of what it means to be an active trading nation in the age of globalization. The more a country can navigate the complexities of an expanding globalized world, the more the country—and the world—will prosper. Technology has ensured that the world of autarky is finished. In addition, Trump's trade and

17. Nadja Popovich, Livia-Albeck-Ripka, and Kendra Pierre-Louis, "Environmental Rules Being Rolled Back Under Trump," *Clearview Energy*, December 21, 2019.

tariff war have hurt several sectors of the economy, such as agriculture, steel, aluminum, and several other blue-collar intensive industries.

Four additional Trump foreign policies strike close to the heart of Christian ethics: Iran; North Korea; Israel; and refugees and immigrants. The Joint Comprehensive Plan of Action (JCOPA—the Iran nuclear deal), which was signed in 2013, established a *modus vivendi* between Iran and the P5+1 countries (the five permanent members of the Security Council—the US, Russia, the UK, France, and China—plus Germany). The JCOPA needed constant monitoring because it was not perfect, but it was working. Iran's compliance was being verified by the International Atomic Energy Agency and Teheran was beginning a new phase of cooperation on nuclear issues. Mr. Trump has said repeatedly that he wants to disengage the US from unending war in the Middle East, but his withdrawal from the JCOPA, coupled with new sanctions, actually brings the US and Iran closer to war. Trump has no knowledge of or interest in the concept of Just War Doctrine or in being a "peacemaker." Combat with Iran would be an "unnecessary war of convenience" and a severe violation of Just War Doctrine, which is a bedrock of the Christian justification for going to war.

Similarly, the effort to strike a deal with North Korea was dangerous folly. The Trump administration tried to play it as an effort to corral North Korea's nuclear ambitions and reduce or actually eliminate their nuclear arsenal. Rather, it was designed to feed Trump's voracious ego. Kim Jong-un actually emerged from his encounter with Trump in a stronger position and the effort by the US to play peacemaker came to nothing. North Korea already had attained the status of a major nuclear power—including Intercontinental Ballistic Missiles—and, once Kim met with Trump, North Korea had gained the legitimacy it did not have before. Trump went home with nothing but a bloated ego that was sustained by self-delusion.

Trump also has missed an opportunity to be a peacemaker in his long-awaited peace plan for the Palestinian-Israeli conflict, which was announced early in 2020. Unfortunately, but quite predictably, the plan was "dead on arrival." Even the most novice Middle Eastern observer could see that the peace plan worked out under the guidance of Jared Kushner, Trump's son-in-law, had no chance of success. Although the plan contained a provision for a two-state solution, the proposed Palestine was a geographically truncated, jagged, rump state controlled by Israel. Palestinians, who had been expelled or fled Israel during the 1948 and 1967 wars, were given no right of return under the terms of the Trump plan. Political naiveté combined with a heavily pro-Israel bias had doomed the plan. The outcome was predictable well in advance because Trump's decision to move the US Embassy from Tel Aviv to Jerusalem, his scuttling of the JCOPA—much to the delight of Israeli

Prime Minister Netanyahu—and his broadly lopsided support for Israel scuttled the peace plan before it was announced. Trump was not an honest broker, which undercut any role he might have claimed as a peacemaker.

Trump's deference to Israel also was a way to play to those in his base who take a millennialist/dispensationalist view of eschatology. Making a strong fundamentalist—but not, in my view, evangelical—statement can only reinforce his standing among the most right wing of his supporters. However, there is no evidence that Trump himself holds such eschatological views or that he even understands them.

Finally, Trump's handling of the refugee/immigrant issue should be seen as a particularly sad violation of Christian ethical norms in foreign policy. Of course, it would be best if every refugee and immigrant who wanted to come to the US did so in a lawful manner. But that is not the reality. We have in excess of 11 million undocumented aliens in the US and, despite the highs and lows of immigration over the past decade, we continue to see a flow of political and economic refugees, primarily coming from across our southern border. Many of them originate in the Northern Central American "triangle" (Guatemala, Honduras, and El Salvador). But they also come from other Central American countries, Mexico, and countries outside the Western Hemisphere. Interestingly, eight in ten immigrants from the Northern triangle have been in the US for more than ten years. Keeping out refugees and immigrants, especially from Central America and other "s---hole" countries has become an obsession for Trump. In the proposed 2021 budget, the Trump administration has moved a substantial amount of money from domestic safety net causes to help pay for the wall. Not only is the wall a violation of the Christian admonition to welcome strangers, it is very poor policy, and it harms the poorest and most vulnerable refugees. Refugees will find other—even more dangerous—ways to come to the US via longer routes to the east and by sea to California and the southeast of the US. The issue of illegal aliens will not be resolved until the questions of economic deprivation and deadly gang violence are addressed in the Northern Triangle. Instead, Trump threatens these countries with sanctions and political isolation, which not only will not solve the problem but will further endanger the lives and welfare of refugees.

Conclusion

Clearly, no politician is perfect and many of them lie and make promises they cannot fulfill. But, no politician within recent memory has reached the levels of perfidy that Donald Trump has reached. Not only is Trump devoid of many Christian values, he is ignorant of what those values are. He does not have a religious bone in his body. Moreover, he does not demonstrate a moral center of any kind. He uses gullible and shallow Christians to pursue cynical political ends. We can and must do better.

We conclude with a portion of the brave editorial in *Christianity Today* by Mark Galli:

> But the facts in this case are unambiguous: The president of the United States attempted to use his political power to coerce a foreign leader to harass and discredit one of the president's political opponents. This is not only a violation of the Constitution; more importantly, it is profoundly immoral. The reason many are not shocked about this is that this president has dumbed down the idea of morality in his administration. He has hired and fired a number of people who are now convicted criminals. He himself has admitted to immoral actions in business and his relationship with women, about which he remains proud. His Twitter feed alone—with its habitual string of mischaracterizations, lies and slanders—is a near perfect example of a human being who is morally lost and confused.[18]

---

18. Mark Galli, "Trump Should Be Removed from Office," *Christianity Today*, December 19, 2019, https://www.christianitytoday.com/ct/2019/december-web-only/trump-should-be-removed-from-office.html.

Chapter 23

Three Prophetic Voices against Silence

Edward G. Simmons

Silence and tacit consensus always, without fail, protect privilege. That is why
the privileged are characteristically silencers.

Walter Brueggemann, *Interrupting Silence*

In 2018, the Christian scholar Walter Brueggemann added his
voice to the prophetic literature opposing "our socio-political circumstance,"[1]
by which he meant Trumpism and the silence of its supporters about the
wrongness of the privilege and oppression making it possible. His examination of eight scriptural episodes, which is intended for discussion in adult
church classes, is most often poetic and allusive, like the biblical passages
themselves; but his message is clear. Scriptural traditions call for speaking
out against today's "establishment" and the many forms of privilege being enforced. Without directly naming the main political figure of 2018,
Brueggemann wrote a powerful assessment of Trumpism and the powers
supporting it that was aimed directly at evangelical study groups.

Brueggemann's defense of "God's command to speak out" was the third
notable warning against the dangers of Donald Trump to be published during Trump's second year in office. Presidential historian Jon Meacham used

---

1. Brueggemann, *Interrupting Silence* (Louisville: Westminster John Knox, 2018), 5.

the semi-religious terminology in Lincoln's First Inaugural Address as he examined the ongoing struggles since the Civil War between demonic forces in the American character and "our better angels." The role of presidents in guiding the nation to overcome its dark forces was a major emphasis as Meacham placed the dangers of Donald Trump in the context of American history. Former Secretary of State Madeleine Albright also used Lincoln as a comparison for Trump at the end of her account of fascism in the twentieth century and its re-emergence in recent decades with Donald Trump representing an effort to impose fascist principles in the United States. Albright also used Lincoln's term "our better angels," thereby bringing in her views on the role of religion in politics that were the subject of her earlier book *The Mighty and the Almighty*.[2]

This chapter will begin with the assessments of Trump in the Meacham and Albright historical accounts then show how Brueggemann's Bible studies are more direct in bringing out the religious dimensions of Trumpism. Although prominent evangelical leaders were praising the accomplishments of Donald Trump in 2018 while overlooking moral and legal transgressions, our three prophetic voices were pointing to a moral and religious basis for breaking the silence underpinning policies and oppressive privilege associated with Trumpism.

The very title of Meacham's book—*The Soul of America: The Battle for Our Better Angels*—reflects a semi-religious view of American character as expressed in Lincoln's two inaugural addresses. The term *soul*, for Meacham, means "the existence of an imminent collection of convictions, dispositions, and sensitivities that shape character and inform conduct." Since Lincoln, presidents have played a significant role in "the battle between the impulses of good and evil in the American soul" and victories of good impulses "have occurred just often enough to keep the national enterprise alive."[3] The purpose of his account is stated succinctly: "What follows is the story of how we have endured moments of madness and of injustice, giving the better angels of which Lincoln spoke on the eve of the Civil War a chance to prevail—and how we can again."[4]

Donald Trump is a mostly unnamed point of comparison as Meacham described presidential excellence and the forces of injustice they battled. His name is invoked only nine times, making clear in each instance that he represents a deficient example. The narrative of the personality and dangers

2. Madeleine Albright with Bill Woodward, *The Mighty and the Almighty: Reflections on America, God, and World Affairs* (New York: HarperCollins, 2006).

3. Jon Meacham, *The Soul of America: The Battle for Our Better Angels* (New York: Random House, 2018), 6.

4. Meacham, *The Soul of America*, 19.

of Senator Joseph McCarthy make it clear that McCarthyism has reappeared and occupied the Oval Office.

In an unusual ending for a work of history, Meacham's conclusion turns into a call for action:

> How, then, in an hour of anxiety about the future of the country, at a time when a president of the United States appears determined to undermine the rule of law, a free press, and the sense of hope essential to American life, can those with deep concerns about the nation's future enlist on the side of the angels?[5]

He answers with five recommendations: (1) become engaged; (2) avoid tribalism; (3) rely on reason and facts; (4) find a balance between being overly critical and overly loyal; and (5) recognize that history shows that time and facts help overcome mistakes. These recommendations amount to a description of the current failings of all those who support or oppose Trump—perhaps especially to evangelical Christian members of the Trump base.

Madeleine Albright also spoke out in *Fascism: A Warning*.[6] In a combination of memoir, history, and analysis, Albright exposed the ongoing threat of fascism. Her life has been spent fighting for democracy against the authoritarian tendencies that promote totalitarianism in all its forms. Telling her story in 2018 was partly motivated by the emergence of Trumpian support for fascism at home and abroad.

Albright begins by describing the positive experience of freedom she experienced at age eleven when her family escaped a war-torn Europe by immigrating to the United States. Then she asks what has dimmed that experience in contemporary America. The answers are that:

- democracy is under attack
- "people in positions of power" are actively undermining confidence "in elections, the courts, the media, and—on the fundamental question of earth's future—science"
- divisions exist "between rich and poor, urban and rural, those with a higher education and those without"
- the United States has lost its leading role in the world.

She asked why all of this is true and replied: "One reason, frankly, is Donald Trump. If we think of Fascism as a wound from the past that had

5. Meacham, *The Soul of America*, 266.

6. Madeleine Albright with Bill Woodward, *Fascism: A Warning* (New York: HarperCollins, 2018).

almost healed, putting Trump in the White House was like ripping off the bandage and picking at the scab."[7]

The foundation that makes fascism possible is fear that is stoked into grievances that undermine institutions and norms holding society together. Albright shows how democracies have elected leaders who promise solutions to the causes of resentment, thereby giving power to self-serving tyrants empowered to neutralize all democratic restraints on their actions. Like Hitler, Mussolini, and many others, they are called great leaders who know how to get things done as they claim they can do everything by themselves.

Albright concludes by comparing phony images of leadership with Lincoln and Nelson Mandela, who are generally recognized as among the most effective of modern leaders. "While the object of much ridicule himself, Lincoln never mocked the downtrodden, nor bragged of his own accomplishments, nor exhibited personal cruelty." In a country he could not save from civil war, he communicated positively, calling on the "better angels" at the start and encouraging charity and forswearing malice as the conflict wound down. Mandela faced worse than ridicule as he spent twenty-seven years in prison then became a reconciler when elected president. Albright observed: "Lincoln and Mandela each fought with monsters; neither became one."[8]

Finally, Albright concludes with ten sets of questions we should ask about our leaders if fascists are to be avoided. In short, do they bring out prejudices, emphasize grievances and anger, show contempt for institutions, undermine faith in information or justice, exploit national symbols, or refuse to acknowledge electoral losses?[9] All of these represent dark forces opposing our better angels.

The role of religion is not specifically mentioned in Albright's account, yet her earlier book *The Mighty and the Almighty* made clear her view that religion is always an inescapable factor in domestic and international relations. In that account, she acknowledged a Jewish heritage, even though she was raised a Roman Catholic, as well as her inclination to avoid discussing religion. "I did not consider spiritual faith a subject to talk about in public. For the generation that came of age when and where I did, this was typical."[10] When describing her personal outlook, she referred to the example of her hero Tomas Masaryk, the founder of Czechoslovakia:

7. Albright, *Fascism*, 4–5.

8. Albright, *Fascism*, 250–52.

9. Albright, *Fascism*, 253.

10. Albright, *The Mighty and the Almighty*, 6–7.

To him, religious faith meant showing respect for every person and being willing to help others. Masaryk did not think it was necessary to believe in God to be moral, but he did argue that religious faith, properly understood, did much to encourage and strengthen right behavior. I have similar views.[11]

The historical context provided by Meacham and Albright make clear the prophetic message in Walter Brueggemann's *Interrupting Silence: God's Command to Speak Out*. The studies move from Egyptian enslavement, to prophets defying exploitation, to penitential psalms that acknowledge sin, to encounters with Jesus illustrating multiple impacts of speaking out, and finally to Paul's call to the Corinthians to speak out.

Brueggemann begins with Israel groaning against slavery in Egypt. Symbolic interpretation of forced Egyptian brickmaking turns to contemporary application by looking at oppressive conditions of brickmaking in modern Pakistan. Although figurative language is the rule, direct comparisons are made that can't be ignored. "Indeed, when we consider permanent indebtedness of many people in our own predatory economic system, we can see how the drama of Egypt is endlessly reperformed."[12] The combination of figurative interpretation of Scripture and direct application to contemporary issues is repeated throughout these lessons intended for Christian study groups.

Prophets like Amos, Hosea, and Jeremiah are described as "uncredentialed poets without pedigree or authorization." They spoke against the "holy legitimacy" of the monarchy and temple because that alliance resulted in the "triad of *exploitative labor, unjust taxation,* and *exhibition of surplus wealth*."[13] Two pages later, the point of the italics is made clearer when Brueggemann says the rivalry of prophets versus the establishment "permits us to see that in our own time this same contestation is underway with the royal role performed by a wealthy, greedy oligarchy."[14] The criticisms of the temple for which Amos is famous were rejected by religious leaders, a phenomenon also seen today. "And of course, many churches in our own time are simply chapels for the establishment, in which those who speak in church are expected to support the establishment claims and so to 'show the flag.'"[15]

---

11. Albright, *The Mighty and the Almighty*, 13.

12. Brueggemann, *Interrupting Silence*, 13.

13. Brueggemann, *Interrupting Silence*, 25.

14. Brueggemann, *Interrupting Silence*, 27.

15. Brueggemann, *Interrupting Silence*, 32–33.

The theme of overcoming forces that tend to silence people is found in four passages involving Jesus and one from Paul. Jesus was interrupted by a Syro-Phoenician woman (Mark 7:24–30), dealt with a silencing demon his disciples could not handle (Mark 9:17–18), responded to the crowd trying to silence Bartimaeus (Mark 10:47–48), and told a story of a judge wanting to silence a widow (Luke 18:2–3). Paul's comments in 1 Corinthians 14:33–35 are discussed as an example of the church as a silencing institution.

Striking conclusions are drawn from these passages. First, Jesus listened and advocated listening rather than trying to impose silence. The overall impact of listening, rather than enforcing silence, was that people were "reeducated." "Reeducation comes from voices that dissent from the unexamined comfort zone, from those who abrasively shock our comfort zones with voices from outside that violate the consensus that has been silently accepted."[16] Second, Brueggemann's examples involve women speaking up in ways that gain approval from Jesus. In the case of Paul's statement, the church itself is challenged with the issue of silencing female members of a congregation.

The book is a consistent but indirect attack on the values of Trumpism and the silence of evangelicals and others who endorse them. Brueggemann does not mention how our current president uses messianic language to describe himself or how any criticism is seen as justification for torrents of abuse and bullying in return. How can any informed person today not be reminded of those daily messages in the media when reading how Jesus listened to women? And even learned from them? He did not ignore them and he never "counterpunched" in defense.

Brueggemann's book completes a historic 2018 anti-Trump trilogy by adding the voice of biblical prophecy against forces of oppression. The author's motives are expressed in the introduction:

> Since we now live in a society—and a world—that is fitfully drifting toward Fascism, the breaking of silence is altogether urgent. In the institutional life of the church, moreover, the breaking of silence by the testimony of the gospel often means breaking the silence among those who have a determined stake in maintaining the status quo.[17]

He is very specific as to the oppressive forces to be overcome:

- *White privilege* by multicultural possibilities
- *Western privilege* by the assertion of other cultural realities

16. Brueggemann, *Interrupting Silence*, 52.
17. Brueggemann, *Interrupting Silence*, 5.

- *Male privilege* by insistent feminine voices
- *Heterosexual privilege* by the legitimacy of LGBT voices and presence
- *American exceptionalism* by the rise of other political economies
- *Entitled Christendom* by the emergence of generous ecumenism.[18]

Speaking as a Christian who has felt increasingly alienated by sermons that refuse to speak about conscience-rending domestic and environmental policies and by Sunday school classes that avoid topics that threaten fellowship—I am especially grateful for Brueggemann's voice sounding so clearly messages from the Bible that challenge timidity.

When seen in broader historical contexts described by Meacham and Albright, the biblical message becomes increasingly imperative. Altogether, these works assess Donald Trump and Trumpism in rational, historical, and prophetic terms. They also prescribe similar paths for action. Thus, an important question is whether members of the Trump base—those who are evangelical especially—can open themselves to listen to views outside their comfort zone.

The same question applies to all those caught within hardened boundaries of tribal walls. Can we listen to experts on the presidency and diplomacy rather than demagogues? Can we take seriously the plight of refugees from failing states, wars, and climate disasters who are having children separated and incarcerated in cages? Can we listen to opponents and reject the glee of demonizing them on the Internet?

The forces of history and the requirement of fidelity to the gospel are calling on civic organizations, congregations, Sunday school classes, prayer groups, and every American to speak out then follow words with courageous action.

18. Brueggemann, *Interrupting Silence*, 57.

Chapter 24

An Anvil Which Wears Out Many Hammers

A Call for the Church to Remain Holy
in an Era of Bitter Partisanship

CHRISTOPHER HUTCHINSON

IN 1620, A BAND OF ENGLISH PURITAN SEPARATISTS LANDED IN "THE RE-
gions of Northern Virginia," which of course, would become Plymouth,
Massachusetts. Their governor, William Bradford, made plain their reasons
for establishing a colony in the New World: they wished to practice their
Christian faith according to their own conscience; they hoped to attract
more Englishmen to their cause; and they desired to evangelize the natives.
By 1628, however, their militia captain, Myles Standish, found it necessary
to protect their interests not against the natives, but against fellow Englishmen who had landed to their north on Cape Ann. These Englishmen,
under the leadership of Thomas Morton, had established a different sort of
settlement, one that sought to profit from the sale of whiskey and firearms.
And so, in one of the earliest military actions in American history, Captain
Standish made a raid upon this rival settlement and arrested Morton.[1]

While more complicated than the above telling, this small incident
serves as a simple metaphor for America's mixed beginnings. Some wished
to establish it as a "Bible Commonwealth," while others sought only selfish

---

1. George Willison, *Saints and Strangers* (New York: Reynal & Hitchcock, 1945),
279–81.

profit; and very often the two have intermixed with a mixture of motives. Thus, the same nation which built upon many biblical principles found in English common law was also the nation that permitted chattel slavery for more than a century, and in our day, many other injustices, notably the scourge of widespread abortion. But by and large, despite many imperfections, the United States has been a force for much good around the world. One only need consider the millions of lives that have been saved by the bipartisan PEPFAR program that successfully combatted AIDS in Africa.

I was born into this great nation in the middle of the Cold War era. My father is an Annapolis graduate and served in the US Navy for twenty-one years. As a teenager, I ate, drank, and breathed American patriotism. I attained an Army ROTC scholarship in college and afterwards served three years active duty, including a combat tour during Desert Storm. In addition, after professing personal faith in Jesus Christ in high school, I celebrated the many moral underpinnings of American society and its strong Christian-influenced heritage.

I was stunned, therefore, when the American electorate rejected a decent, honorable president in George H. W. Bush and chose an admitted adulterer in Bill Clinton, largely for economic reasons. I was awakened to the role that materialism and moral relativism plays in American society, and the way in which they are given power in our democratic system. Perhaps then I should not have been so surprised by the political rise of Donald Trump twenty-four years later. Moral relativism was no longer just a force on the left, as I thought, but had so infiltrated our culture that many on the right were subject to it as well. But at the time, as a conservative, I weathered the 1990s by listening to increasing amounts of Rush Limbaugh and celebrating the rise of Fox News. I voted straight GOP for twenty-eight years, largely in support of the pro-life cause.

And yet through all this, I knew that the kingdom of Christ and the cause of the United States were not synonymous. I knew that my patriotism should be separated from the work of the gospel itself, a message of mercy that knows no national boundaries. I knew that the work of the church must not be conflated with that of the United States, especially any use of force. When Jesus told Peter to put his sword away (John 18:11), he was announcing that the kingdom of God would be built by the preaching of the gospel and love, not by violence or political attainment. Even in Revelation, when Jesus returns in glory with a sword, we find that it is the sword of his mouth, of the proclamation of God's mercy and justice, not a sword of physical violence (Revelation 1:16; 2:16; 19:15, 21). I understood the difference between the cause of the gospel and the political causes that come and go, however just they may be.

In fact, as we look to the New Testament, we discover the gospel breaking forth into a world dominated by the pagan, violent, and despotic Roman Empire. And yet we never see the apostles advocating for one form of human government or another; their concern is for the church and her government with Christ as its head. The New Testament makes no claims about the proper size and scope of the civil magistrate, even though many Christians in our day make dubious claims to the contrary, assuming Christ would endorse their particular opinions about welfare, tax rates, or gun control. But Jesus came for something far different, far greater.

As if to highlight this point, Jesus himself chose two of his apostles from opposite sides of the political spectrum: Matthew the tax collector, a government bureaucrat, and Simon the Zealot, who believed in overthrowing the Roman oppressors. Both served together in the same church to highlight the grace of God to all manner of folk. As Paul puts it, "there is neither Jew nor Greek, there is neither slave nor free, there is no male and female, for you are all one in Christ Jesus" (Galatians 3:28, ESV). Indeed, this book of which this essay is a part is no doubt an illustration of that very principle, in terms of both theological and political diversity.

And thus, it should be possible in our day for Christians from a wide variety of political persuasions to worship together, as they each hold their own political cultures loosely in light of their common faith in Christ. If anything, the New Testament enjoins a conservative yet prophetic posture towards our surrounding culture, as we call out a society's sins, seeking change by persuasion and internal reform rather than by force or fiat. We see this attitude modeled in Scripture when Paul clearly rebukes Philemon for slaveholding, and yet desires for Philemon to free his slave, Onesimus, of his own accord out of love rather than by mere command (Philemon 14). This also means that Christians are free to disagree with one another about which government policies might best bring about a more just society, even if they agree on the ultimate goals. For instance, while we seek an end to abortion, the church itself must not take a position of how best to achieve that end, apart from eschewing all forms of violence.

And so as in all lands, the church in America is called to obey the same Scriptures that have guided Christians of every age and under a variety of governments. We are told to first fear God, but also to honor the emperor (1 Peter 2:17). In 1 Timothy, Paul commands us to pray for "kings and all who are in high positions," and the reason he annexes to that is significant—so that "we may lead a peaceful and quiet life, godly and dignified in every way" (1 Timothy 2:2 ESV). Paul never assumes that the government or culture will be Christianized, even as we seek to influence it for good, pursuing justice and equal treatment for all. Rather, we are to lead godly lives within a surrounding, unbelieving culture. If abortions continue around us, we do what we can to help those in need, pray for them to change their minds, but in the meantime, make sure that our own congregations are places of mercy and life and will not resort to such a sin ourselves.

We are also told to obey earthly authorities, knowing that, normatively, they are instruments of God's justice (Romans 13:1–7), even as Christians are called to love and forgive our enemies (Romans 12:9–21; 13:8–10). In the American context, we understand that this civil authority to be prayed for and obeyed is not only the executive branch, but the legislative and judicial branches as well. If American believers have an "emperor" to honor, it is the system of checks and balances codified in our Constitution. Moreover, it seems clear that Romans 13 requires respect for all levels of government bureaucracy that have been instituted by God. In this regard, Christians should take our marching orders from Scripture rather than the voices of talk radio who darkly speculate about a "deep state conspiracy," and whose profit depends upon their audience's anger towards civil servants and other so-called "elites." Of all people, Christians should be ones who lead lives of quiet contentment rather than give into the resentment that fuels this sort of anti-establishment suspicion (cf. 1 Thessalonians 4:11).

And through this all, the church must be prepared to suffer, losing many cultural battles outwardly, remembering that through many tribulations we must enter the kingdom of God (Acts 14:22). We recall how Theodore Beza responded to the King of Navarre when threatened with persecution during the Reformation: "Sire, it is truly the lot of the Church of God, for which I speak, to endure blows and not to strike them. But may it please you to remember that it is an anvil which has worn out many hammers."[2] More important to us than any temporal political victories is our spiritual witness to Christ's truth and grace to a needy world.

Perhaps most importantly, the American church must remember that we are to be holy. The New Testament teaches that the church is a "called out" society that stands as a distinct kingdom within the nations of this world. Jesus himself made this plain when he told Pilate that his "kingdom is not of this world" (John 18:36 ESV) as well as by the manner in which he prayed for his disciples, saying, "I do not ask that you take them out of the world, but that you keep them from the evil one. They are not of the world, just as I am not of the world" (John 17:15–16 ESV).

This distinction may be seen most clearly in Paul's instructions to the Corinthians as he directs them to discipline a man who was unrepentant of gross, sexual sin:

2. Owen Chadwick, *The Reformation* (London: Penguin, 1990), 159.

> I wrote to you in my letter not to associate with sexually im-
> moral people—not at all meaning the sexually immoral of this
> world, or the greedy and swindlers, or idolaters, since then you
> would need to go out of the world. But now I am writing to you
> not to associate with anyone who bears the name of brother if he
> is guilty of sexual immorality or greed, or is an idolater, reviler,
> drunkard, or swindler—not even to eat with such a one. For
> what have I to do with judging outsiders? Is it not those inside
> the church whom you are to judge? God judges those outside.
> "Purge the evil person from among you." (1 Corinthians 5:9–13
> ESV)

There are at least three principles in this text that the American church would do well to remember. The first is that we are not called to make all of society holy as we are. Christians are those who are first saved by God's grace in Jesus Christ, and then are to bear fruit as they follow him. We should not expect non-Christians to bear Christian fruit. Remembering this should take much of the heat out of the so-called "culture wars," which are so easily co-opted by one side of the political spectrum or the other. We can thus be in the world, interacting with all sorts of unbelievers in various civic and community activities, not offended by the various worldviews we will doubtless encounter as we attempt to be beacons of grace in their midst.

The second principle is that we are to hold all professing believers to the standards of basic Christian ethics, granting grace to the repentant, but giving warning to the unrepentant. And if a man or woman continues in unrepentant, blatant sin, at that point there must be a holy distancing of ourselves from such a person—not because they are sinful, but because they claim to bear the name of Christ and yet show no evidence that they take that claim seriously. In other words, the church's "culture war" should be foremost against our own sins and failures, offering forgiveness to all who seek it in Christ, but making plain that we will not have close fellowship with those who manifestly refuse to follow Christ. We are not to be of this world, and in part that means we must warn and, if necessary, clearly distance ourselves from professing believers who refuse to repent of blatant sin.

The third principle must also be remembered in our day, and that is that Paul does not just call out blatant sexual immorality, but sins of all kinds—greed, idolatry, reviling, and swindling. Worldliness takes many forms and few Christian movements have succeeded in fighting worldly influence from all sides. As a gross generalization, it can be said that in our day the Christian left has done well to call out sins of racism and materialism, while capitulating to culture on sexual ethics; while the opposite is true with the Christian right. When a believer is always facing just one direction in the "culture wars," they may be ill equipped to see other forms of worldliness creep in from behind. In my judgment, this is the case with many large evangelical ministries that have allowed greed, power, and nepotism to take root within their own ranks even as they fight against other cultural sins. And thus, it is not altogether surprising that when a strongman such as Donald Trump comes along and promises greater prosperity, this holds greater sway for these evangelicals than traditional forms of Christian morality such as marital fidelity and basic kindness. James reminds us that "religion that is pure and undefiled before God the Father is this: to visit orphans and widows in their affliction, and to keep oneself unstained from the world" (James 1:27). Worldliness takes many forms, and the church must be fair minded to call out sins of all kinds, including greed and swindling.

In light of these principles, we come to an application for our present day. Christians are free to make their best political judgments, but when a political party offers up a candidate who has trodden underfoot the very standards they profess, it would do well for Christians to clearly withhold their support until that party offers up a more suitable candidate. This is not a question of offering grace or church membership to a repentant sinner, but a question of what makes for a qualified leader of a large, pluralistic society. Christians are those who value moderation, kindness, and impartial governing, and Donald Trump has often represented the very opposite.

But what should be even more troublesome to conservative Christians is Mr. Trump's relentless assault upon the concept of truth itself. He lies blatantly, repeatedly, and without remorse. He has made clear that all that matters in the end is winning. In this manner, he has embraced a more vicious, divisive, mean-spirited partisanship than any president in our lifetimes. Added to this danger are his relentless attacks on many of the institutions that have held our society together peacefully for decades, such as federal law enforcement agencies and international agreements such as the Geneva Convention. While bombast alone cannot undo these institutions, it does have the effect of wearing down a populace so that when boundaries are actually crossed, it is barely noticed until it is too late. All of this is the practical result of embracing an explicitly amoral approach to governing, even if certain decisions are ones which Christians can support. We must remember the long game and that there are larger principles at stake. We are to be in this world, but never of it.

I will not attempt here to further specify the president's moral failings or document his many falsehoods. They are plain enough for anyone open to reason and exposed to mainstream fact-based sources of information. I have met some believers who are quick to dismiss basic investigative reporting or who only expose themselves to partisan media outlets, and have thus insulated themselves. The most I can do is to suggest to them that there are powerful corporate interests behind these outlets that do not care for Christian morality but are happy to appeal to the Christian market as part of their business model. And it is to their advantage for believers to remain their unwitting and uncritical participants.

If it helps, I can offer my own example of someone who was enmeshed in right wing media, but in time, began to see the gulf between the tone of such outlets and the scriptural admonition to love my neighbor as myself. It may be useful for believers to conduct a simple practical exercise. First, to read a passage of Scripture which describes Christian character: The Beatitudes (Matthew 5:1–8); the fruit of the Spirit (Galatians 5:22–23); wisdom from above (James 3:13–18); or Paul's definition of love (1 Corinthians 13:1–13). Second, to turn on a popular media personality who purports to defend Christian values such as Ann Coulter, Sean Hannity, Laura Ingraham, Rush Limbaugh, or Michelle Malkin. Third, regardless of the subject matter, compare the tones of these personalities to these passages found in Scripture, paying particular attention to how they treat their political opponents. Of course, there are personalities on the left who come to mind as well, but at least in my circles, conservative media has much more influence. By such an exercise, perhaps believers may allow our characters to be shaped by the Bible more than by the cultural influences around us.

Given this line of reasoning, we must address one final question. Why not leave all this alone? If indeed the church is to remain largely apolitical, why address the moral failings of our current president at all? Why not just pray for him, obey the government, and leave things be? There is some wisdom to this, especially in a church's formal deliberations. My own denomination forbids official church bodies from addressing political matters, "except by way of humble petition" and only then in extraordinary cases (Westminster Confession of Faith, 31.4).

The potential problem with this approach is that when Christians are so wholly aligned with one political party or personality, their ability to bring rebuke is compromised. Nor is it enough to quibble with a president's tone or a few tweets while remaining largely supportive and loyal. A real rebuke must come with a degree of holy distancing and therefore at likely political cost. The sins of corruption, infidelity, abuse, hatred, xenophobia, and dishonesty must all be called out clearly, or believers show themselves to be more beholden to political access than to the God of truth and grace.

Christians must always be the loyal opposition to any secular government, regardless of party. We are loyal, because we recognize that God in his sovereignty allows each government to rule as part of his overarching and inscrutable plan (cf. Genesis 50:20). We are the opposition because we know that "here we have no enduring city, but seek the city which is to come" (Hebrews 13:14 ESV). That means that even as we pursue just policies, we will not do so at the cost of failing to call sin, sin, even among our allies. We must not neglect the necessity of repentance as an essential part of the gospel (Mark 1:15).

We remember the courage of John the Baptist when he confronted King Herod for his adultery, even at the cost of his own head (Mark 6:14–29). We remember the wisdom of Ambrose, the bishop of Milan, who confronted Emperor Theodosius after he had ordered the massacre at Thessalonica, forbidding the emperor to take the Lord's Supper until he had repented. We recall what Andrew Melville proclaimed to King James:

> . . . there are two kings and two kingdoms in Scotland: there is king James, the head of the commonwealth; and there is Christ Jesus, the king of the Church, whose subject James the Sixth is, and of whose kingdom he is not a king, not a lord, not a head, but a member."[3]

We remember the courage of Dr. Martin Luther King, Jr. who called for nonviolent resistance to the racism of his day. And in recent years, we hail the pluck of Ben Carson at the 2013 National Prayer Breakfast, when he took President Obama to task on the subject of abortion. It is precisely because our citizenship is in heaven (Philippians 3:20) that we are able to issue such rebukes and thereby keep a holy distance from all political parties and movements, putting the cause of Christ first.

It is because we believe in grace for sinners that we call for repentance—private sins privately but public sins publicly. Otherwise, we trade political access for fidelity to the gospel itself and put in danger the souls of the very ones whom we seek to support. And when it comes to matters of investigations of alleged wrongdoings on the part of any politician, our loyalty to Christ first frees us from partisan commitments that distort the facts in order to seek a win for "our side." Our side must always be the side of truth, wherever that takes us. If the "other side" is correct about a matter, then we must agree with them, and leave the results to God. After all, the essence of Christian ethics is that the ends never justify the means.

So, in all this, our problem is not primarily with Mr. Trump himself. Worldlings come and worldlings go and are not, in the end, very interesting. Our problem is with a culture that is so materialistic and amoral that it elevated such a man to power in the first place. Our problem is also with a Republican Party that takes Christians for granted and has thrown its full

---

3. W. M. Hetherington, *History of the Church of Scotland* (New York: Robert Carter & Bros, 1856), 105.

support behind such an amoral leader. Opportunities abounded when the GOP could have offered the nation a more sound, moral, and reasonable leader, but they have refused to do so out of electoral fear. Therefore, biblical Christians should distance ourselves from such an unholy alliance however useful it may have been in the past. In my opinion, this most likely means withholding our votes not only from Mr. Trump, but from the GOP as a whole until they show themselves to be more principled. There is a middle ground between supporting this current president or the Democratic Party with its current pro-choice position. And that is to demand that the GOP do better, while at the same time pressuring the Democrats to return to more biblical positions on life and marriage; and until either party changes, to withhold our full support from either.

In our time, there is Christian freedom in how to respond to the political realities of our own day. But there is not freedom to become so aligned with the causes of this world that the cause of Christ becomes maligned and clouded to the very ones who most need to hear it. And even if Christians all around us give way to the prevailing winds of access to power, there must be a dissenting remnant of believers who refuse to bow the knee—both for the sake of our time and for the sake of history.

Chapter 25

The Constitution and Faith

Does It Matter?

Julia Stronks

I am profoundly religious. My faith is at the heart of who I am. I take an oath before God as enormously consequential . . . I believe that our Constitution was inspired by Providence.

Utah Senator Mitt Romney (R),
February 5, 2020 to his Senate colleagues explaining his vote to convict President Donald Trump of abuse of power.[1]

IN 2016 WHEN PRESIDENT TRUMP WAS ELECTED, I WAS ASKED TO SPEAK TO students, to alum of my institution, to church groups and to civic groups. Many of the people in these groups were in despair about our new president because of his offensive comments about women, Muslims, and Mexicans among others. My message was "be calm." The Constitution will hold; separation of powers will work. If you care about working toward justice, focus now on state and local measures. Four years will pass, and things will be okay.

1. Mitt Romney, "Impeachment Speech," *The New York Times*, https://www.nytimes.com/2020/02/05/us/politics/mitt-romney-impeachment-speech-transcript.html.

To some extent I still believe this. But though the Constitution held, today we are in a different place than I had anticipated. We have a president who has *disdain* for our Constitution. And, as a person of faith I think this is dangerous. I think it creates a situation in which we are less able to be responsive to the biblical norms of justice called for in the Old and New Testaments.

This chapter asks three questions. First, should people of faith care about the Constitution? Second, does President Trump care about the Constitution? Third, does any of this matter?

Faith and the Constitution

Scholars have written a great deal about whether the United States is or was intended to be a Christian nation. The answer depends on how one approaches the issue. No one would argue that the nation was supposed to be a theocracy, but scholars divide on who and what had the greatest impact on the Founders.

Some say rationalism and the Enlightenment were the strongest influence. But others argue that Christian belief, particularly Calvinism, influenced those who shaped the founding documents. Mark Hall writes that when our nation was founded, between 55 and 75 percent of white citizens were part of Calvinist churches.[2] He explains that the intellectual elites were significantly influenced by the Reformed tradition, pointing out that King George even referred to the War for Independence as a "Presbyterian Rebellion." Hall further argues that American founders believed John Locke's political philosophy was compatible with orthodox Christianity. So, what is it that constitutes that "compatibility"?

At the root of Christian belief is the understanding that humans were created in the image of God, but that when sin entered into the world, we all became "fallen." Jesus Christ has redeemed us, but we live in a world that though redeemed is nonetheless impacted by the fall in every way. Our identity as humans, our institutions, the creation itself—all fall short of what God intended in creation.

Though we fall short, however, we do have a job to do. With respect to government, the Christian's job is to seek justice as described by Old Testament prophets and to care for the sick, the weak, and the poor as described by Jesus throughout the early New Testament.

2. Mark David Hall, *Did America Have a Christian Founding?* (Nashville: Thomas Nelson, 2019).

The question is how do we do this? Do we trust elected representatives to achieve this for us or should we focus on the *structure* of government along with the character of those we elect? The founders of the US Constitution were clear in their perspective, and we can see in their justification for the Constitution a strong influence of Christian teaching. James Madison is largely credited with crafting the Constitution and he was also one of three men who wrote the *Federalist Papers*, an explanation for why the Constitution was shaped in a particular way.

In Federalist #10 and #51 he explains his belief about human nature. Along with the Calvinists of the day he believed all people would abuse power. If men were angels, he said, no government would be necessary. But because we are self-interested, we need a structure and process to limit our abuse of power. We can't just rely on voting in "Enlightened Statesmen" because enlightened statesmen will not always be "at the helm." And even if we vote for them, they themselves will eventually abuse power.[3]

Because of his dark view of human nature, Madison, along with the other founders, crafted a process by which power would be *dispersed*. Separation of powers, federalism, representation rather than direct democracy, and an emphasis on rights are all tools to divide power. If we have a system of divided power it should be very difficult for any one group to control and to get things done. Groups will be forced to compromise, and the public will learn to think about the whole rather than just their own self-interested parts.

As a Christian, I recognize this approach as reflecting concern about the sinfulness of humans, and I believe that the Constitutional division of powers is an important tool for pursuing justice. Separation of powers divides power between and among the different branches of government. Federalism ensures that states and even local governments play an important role in self-government. The emphasis on individual rights clarifies that there are some things, especially religious freedom and freedom of speech, that have to be protected even when majorities want to restrict them. Without the division of powers, a leader can destroy self-government. The *structure* of government is a necessary tool to provide room for us to constantly converse about what it means to do justice.

Of course, it doesn't always work correctly. There have been periods of history where despite divided power we have developed an unjust system, and the framers of the Constitution could not have anticipated the

---

3. James Madison, *Federalist Papers* 10, 51, *The Federalist Papers*, https://www.congress.gov/resources/display/content/The+Federalist+Papers.

tremendous impact that money and the technology of a twenty-four-hour news cycle would have on elections.

But the question still remains. Is the Constitutional framework that we have in the United States a *necessary* part of a biblical perspective on working toward a just government? I believe it is. It is not *sufficient*, but with Madison I agree that the structure of divided powers is a necessary precursor toward limiting the abuse of power that every human being will eventually fall prey to. History demonstrates that even the most committed Christians abuse power in churches, governments, families, and places of employment. Sin is so powerful that structure and process are necessary to help us in our pursuit of a government that provides justice.

President Trump and the Constitution

Does President Trump care about the Constitution? Let's put aside the issue of impeachment. For purposes of this discussion I do not think it is helpful to talk about whether high crimes and misdemeanors did or did not occur.

Instead, consider the last few years and ask whether this president values the Constitution. Does he believe that the rule of law embodied in the Constitution applies to him and his administration?

The president's tweets are aimed at his base and rarely lead to concrete policy, but they have an impact on the way that citizens understand what it means to self-govern. Both the National Constitution Center and the Libertarian Institute have traced the numerous ways that President Trump disparages the Constitution.[4]

For example, even before he became president, Trump said that people who burn the American flag should serve jail time or perhaps lose their citizenship. A comment like this flies in the face of the Constitution, particularly because the US Supreme Court has clearly said that flag burning is political speech protected by the First Amendment.

President Trump has also said that the National Football League should lose tax breaks because some of its players kneel during the national anthem, and he suggests that those who kneel should perhaps be deported. This violates the rights of citizens embedded in the Constitution and again the Supreme Court has been clear that leaders cannot strip citizenship away from us when they do not like what we do.

Trump says he'd like to take away press credentials of those who fail to cover him in a positive light. This would violate the First Amendment.

---

4. Rob Faust, "Donald Trump vs. the Constitution," The Libertarian Institute, May 16, 2018, https://libertarianinstitute.org/articles/donald-trump-vs-the-constitution/.

When Arizona Sheriff Joe Arpaio was convicted of unlawful search and seizure and racial profiling (Fourth Amendment), President Trump pardoned him.

The Fourteenth Amendment outlines the importance of protecting elections and the right to vote. The recent impeachment process focused on whether the president tied Ukraine's aid to an investigation into a political rival. But, even if we set aside this particular issue, it is clear that *other* nations have tried to influence our elections. Trump's own Defense secretary, two congressional committees, the director of national intelligence, national security advisors, and numerous cyber experts have all said that Russia, China, and Iran have devised a concerted effort to influence our election process. President Trump undermines elections, the significance of the vote, and his duty to care about elections every time he dismisses the importance of foreign influence.

Finally, Article 1, section 9 of the Constitution says that those in the federal government may not receive gifts or emoluments (remuneration) from foreign states without consent of Congress. The purpose of this clause was to prevent foreign governments from influencing our own government. Alexander Hamilton explained that though self-governing republics had many advantages, one of the concerns was that foreign governments could corrupt our processes.[5] President Trump called the Emoluments clause "phony" and then followed this with numerous references to the fact that Article II of the Constitution lets him do whatever he wants.

Does Any of This Matter?

In a self-governing republic the rule of law is critical. It might not always work the way we want it to and sometimes we might believe that certain people are treated as if they are above the law. But our leaders have to believe in the structure of our government or the people will not believe in the law.

The *Stanford Encyclopedia of Philosophy* puts it like this:

> The most important demand of the Rule of Law is that people in positions of authority should exercise their power within a constraining framework of well-established public norms rather than in an arbitrary, *ad hoc*, or purely discretionary manner on the basis of their own preferences or ideology. It insists that the government should operate within a framework of law in everything it does, and that it should be accountable through law

5. Alexander Hamilton, Federalist Paper 22, *The Federalist Papers*, https://www.congress.gov/resources/display/content/The+Federalist+Papers.

when there is a suggestion of unauthorized action by those in power.[6]

And, the Constitution is the *foundation* of our rule of law. So, disparaging the Constitution erodes the norms of self-government. When this happens, democracies can die.

In the important book *How Democracies Die,* Steven Levitsky and Daniel Ziblatt explain that the norms of democracy or self-government come down to two things. First, mutual toleration. This means that competing parties view one another as rivals rather than enemies, and they recognize the legitimacy of their rivals. Second, forbearance. This means that leaders exercise some element of restraint in trying to get their own way using the institutional means given them.

Levitsky and Ziblatt observe that President Trump's tweets and his rhetoric have shredded both mutual tolerance and forbearance. Furthermore, their book highlights what the nonpartisan Pew Research Center has found: our respect for the political legitimacy of the opposition is in significant decline. In the last three years, people on the right and the left are more likely to call into question the patriotism of anyone who disagrees with them.[7] They are more likely to say that people of the other party have no good ideas, and they are more likely to say those in the other party are immoral and close-minded.

This worries me. I believe that the consistent anti-constitutional messaging and the decline of mutual toleration create a situation in which we are less able to think about the biblical call to do justice in our communities.

6. Jeremy Waldron, "Rule of Law," *Stanford Encyclopedia of Philosophy,* June, 2016, https://plato.stanford.edu/entries/rule-of-law/.

7. Pew Research Center, "Partisan Antipathy: More Intense, More Personal," October 10, 2019, https://www.people-press.org/2019/10/10/partisan-antipathy-more-intense-more-personal/.

On Returning to Christ

RONALD J. SIDER

ALL OF THE AUTHORS IN THIS BOOK RECOGNIZE THAT THERE ARE MANY devout Christians who disagree fundamentally with the arguments and conclusions expressed here. To all such sisters and brothers in Christ, we say: "Let's ask our Lord and Savior to help us do a better job of listening to each other and praying together for the well-being of our beloved country and world."

We seek to keep at the center of our thoughts the biblical truth that all Christians are members of the one body of Christ. We believe that when we confess the risen Christ as our Lord, we affirm our commitment to welcome him as Lord of every room of our lives, including our politics. We know that our oneness in Christ is far more important than political disagreements, however large.

Tragically, those central biblical truths clash with the painful reality of huge—often harsh—political disagreements among Christians. Those dis-agreements and the seemingly impossible task of resolving them, lead some Christians to conclude: "Politics is too complex, too controversial, too nasty and corrupt. Good Christians should just forget politics and focus on their personal walk with Christ and their local congregation."

That is a mistake for two reasons: one theological, the other practical.

First, as we saw above, the central Christian confession is that Jesus is Lord—Lord of everything. He is even "ruler of the kings of the earth" (Revelation 1:5). That certainly means that Christ wants all Christians to seek with all their heart to let Christ be Lord of their political thinking and action.

Second, it is a simple historical fact that decisions by major political leaders influence the lives—for better or worse—of millions and millions of people. In the case of American presidents, their political decisions hurt or help literally billions of people. Think of the great benefit to millions of people because the British evangelical member of Parliament, William Wilberforce, succeeded in persuading his colleagues to vote to end slavery in the British Empire. Think of the devastating evil that flowed from the fact that millions of German Christians helped elect Adolph Hitler. Especially in a democracy where every person's vote helps determine what happens, politics is simply too important to neglect.

But how do we proceed at this point in American history when devout Christians sharply, too often harshly, disagree about the most faithful way to vote? If anyone had a perfect answer to that question, that person would probably be elected head of their denomination—or president of the United States of America!

But here are a few suggestions.

What would happen if all Christians would resolve to try to listen to and understand the reasons that other Christians give for their different political conclusions? What would happen if all or even some Christians decided to seek ways to pray together with other Christians with sharply different political conclusions? What would happen if we dared to come together across strong political differences to discuss major political issues and platforms on the basis of biblical standards?

Each of us personally could resolve to spend some time listening to political news and analysis from sources (newspapers, radio, TV, online) different from the sources to which we usually listen.

Each of us could pray daily that God would help us see what is right in the views of our political opponents. Each of us could pray daily that God show us how God wants us to vote this year.

Some of us could (as individuals or with the support of church leaders) explore ways to pray together with other Christians who disagree with us politically. We could establish weekly or monthly prayer meetings (that included Christians with very different political views) where we did nothing but pray that God would guide our nation to the right political outcomes this November. No discussion of political issues! Just prayer that God's will be done on earth as it is in heaven.

Some Christians could even develop groups composed of Republicans, Democrats, and Independents to meet regularly until November to openly, honestly, and respectfully evaluate the different political platforms on the basis of biblical values. If your congregation is entirely Republican or Democratic, then find a neighbor congregation whose members are largely from a different political party.

If that sounds totally utopian and impossible, ponder two things. First, our nation is in deep trouble because the political divisions are so deep and the politicians are so unsuccessful at listening to each other, that destructive gridlock permeates Washington. Many serious national problems are not being dealt with—with the result that our nation is in danger of paralysis and decay. Second, should not Christian people, who seek to make Christ the center of all their life, be the people most able to sit down with political opponents and model honest, careful listening? If we had enough politically diverse, weekly discussion groups, perhaps Christians could offer a model of honest listening that would eventually encourage our national political leaders to work together to end the national political deadlock that threatens our future.

We pray for ourselves and every Christian in this nation: "Please, Lord, show us how to pray and listen to each other so that you can use us to guide our nation to a better future. Even more important, please, Lord, help us Christians to act in our political engagement in such a way that non-Christians are attracted to our Lord."

Recommended Reading

Balmer, Randall. *The Making of Evangelicalism: From Revivalism to Politics and Beyond.* Waco, TX: Baylor University Press, 2017.

Carpenter, Amanda. *Gaslighting America: Why We Love It When Trump Lies to Us.* New York: Broadside, 2018.

Cho, Eugene. *Thou Shalt Not Be a Jerk: A Christians Guide to Engaging Politics.* Colorado Springs: David C. Cook, 2020.

Denker, Angela. *Red State Christians: Understanding the Voters Who Elected Donald Trump.* Minneapolis: Fortress, 2019.

Fea, John. *Believe Me: The Evangelical Road to Donald Trump.* Grand Rapids: Eerdmans, 2018.

———. "Does Robert Jeffress Think Morality Determined by Popularity?" *Christian Post*, July 11, 2017.

———. "'Evangelicals for Trump' Was an Awful Display by Supposed Citizens of the Kingdom of God." *USA Today*, January 11, 2020.

———. "Trump Threatens to Change the Course of American Christianity." *Washington Post*, July 17, 2017.

FitzGerald, Frances. *The Evangelicals: The Struggle to Shape America.* New York: Simon & Schuster, 2017.

French, David. "Evangelicals are Supporting Trump Out of Fear, Not Faith." *Time*, June 27, 2019. https://time.com/5615617/why-evangelicals-support-trump.

——— "Franklin Graham and the High Cost of the Lost Evangelical Witness." *National Review*, April 25, 2019. https://www.nationalreview.com/2019/04/franklin-graham-and-the-high-cost-of-the-lost-evangelical-witness/.

Galli, Mark. "Trump Should Be Removed from Office." *Christianity Today*, December 19, 2019. https://www.christianitytoday.com/ct/2019/december-web-only/trump-should-be-removed-from-office.html.

———. *When Did We Start Forgetting God?: The Root of the Evangelical Crisis and Hope for the Future.* Carol Stream, IL: Tyndale House, 2020.

Gartner, John, Steven Buser, and Leonard Cruz. *Rocket Man: Nuclear Madness and the Mind of Donald Trump.* Asheville, NC: Chiron, 2018.

Gerson, Michael. "Christians Are Suffering from Complete Spiritual Blindness." *Washington Post*, September 10, 2018.

———. "Evangelicals Are Naked Before the World." *Washington Post*, June 27, 2019.

———. "Franklin Graham Has Played His Ultimate Trump Card." *Washington Post*, June 3, 2019.

————. "The Trump Evangelicals Have Lost Their Gag Reflex." *Washington Post*, January 22, 2018.

————. "Trump Exposes the Hypocrisy of Christian Republicans." *Washington Post*, May 28, 2018.

————. "Trump's Politicization of the National Prayer Breakfast is Unholy and Immoral." *Washington Post*, February 6, 2020.

————. "White Evangelicals Are Fully Disrobed, and It Is an Embarrassing Sight." *Washington Post*, October 28, 2019.

Haynes, Stephen R. *The Battle for Bonhoeffer: Debating Discipleship in the Age of Trump* Grand Rapids: Eerdmans, 2018.

Howe, Ben. "Evangelicals Have Abandoned Their Mission in Favor of Trump." *Washington Post*, August 8, 2019.

————. "The Faith in Donald Trump." *Medium*, March 13, 2018. https://medium.com/s/story/the-faith-in-donald-j-trump-23878e5b8e66.

————. *The Immoral Majority: Why Evangelicals Chose Political Power Over Christian Values*. New York: Harper Collins, 2019.

Labberton, Mark, ed. *Still Evangelical?: Insiders Reconsider Political, Social, and Theological Meaning*. Downers Grove, IL: InterVarsity, 2018.

Lee, Bandy, ed. *The Dangerous Case of Donald Trump: 37 Psychiatrists and Mental Health Experts Assess a President*. New York: Thomas Dunne, 2019.

Lucado, Max. "Trump Doesn't Pass the Decency Test." *Washington Post*, February 26, 2016.

McRaven, William. "Our Republic is Under Attack from the President." *New York Times*, October 17, 2019.

Meacham, Jon. "Why Religion is the Best Hope Against Trump." *New York Times*, February 25, 2020.

Nazworth, Napp. "Evangelicals Trade Moral Authority for Political Gain in Defending Trump." *Christian Post*, February 6, 2019.

————. "Robert Jeffress a Big Fan of Straw Men After Defending 'S***hole Countries' Slur." *Christian Post*, January 26, 2018.

————. "Why Evangelical Leaders Opposed to Trump Speak for More Evangelicals Than You Think." *Christian Post*, April 19, 2018.

————. "Why Evangelicals Shouldn't Vote for Trump." *Christian Post*, August 23, 2016.

Rucker, Philip, and Carol Leonnig. *A Very Stable Genius: Donald J. Trump's Testing of America*. New York: Penguin Random House, 2020.

Sider, Ronald J. *Just Politics: A Guide for Christian Engagement*. Grand Rapids: Brazos, 2012.

Volf, Miroslav, and Matthew Croasmun. *For the Life of the World: Theology that Makes a Difference*. Grand Rapids: Brazos, 2019.

Wehner, Peter. *The Death of Politics: How to Heal Our Frayed Republic After Trump*. New York: HarperCollins, 2019.

————. "Trump Is Not Well." *The Atlantic*, September 9, 2019. https://www.theatlantic.com/idea/archive/2019/09/donald-trump-not-well/597640/.

————. "The Trump Presidency Is Over." *The Atlantic*, March 13, 2020. https://www.theatlantic.com/ideas/archive/2020/03/peter-wehner-trump-presidency-over/607969/.

————. "Why I Can No Longer Call Myself an Evangelical Republican." *New York Times*, December 9, 2017.

Wilson, Rick. *Everything Trump Touches Dies: A Republican Strategist Gets Real About the Worst President Ever.* New York: Free, 2018.

Wolff, Michael. *Fire and Fury: Inside the Trump White House.* New York: Henry Holt and Company, 2018.

————. *Siege: Trump Under Fire.* New York: Henry Holt and Company, 2019.

Woodward, Bob. *Fear: Trump in the White House.* New York: Simon & Schuster, 2018.

CPSIA information can be obtained
at www.ICGtesting.com
Printed in the USA
BVHW042130110723
667113BV00001B/41